IMAGES
of Modern America

CLARKSVILLE

On the Front Cover, Clockwise from the Top: Taken in 1985, William Bailey Allen observes his cattle on the Allendale Farm in Clarksville (page 20, photograph by Amelia Hartz); during Volunteer Day at the L&N Train Station, many visitors came to see the progress (page 11, photograph by Benita Martin, courtesy of Montgomery County Historical Society); while strolling through downtown Clarksville, one might hear Ron Michaels playing his trumpet (page 35, author's collection); the Stables on the bypass, pictured here in 1980, was a popular place to hang out with friend and have a few drinks (page 40, courtesy of Billyfrank Morrison); during a 1996 day-care tour at the L&N Train Station, students and teachers alike enjoy the tours and have stopped for a quick photograph on the front of the train (page 16, photograph by Benita Martin, courtesy of Montgomery County Historical Society).

On the Back Cover, from Left to Right: In 1996, the *Spirit of Tennessee* pays a visit to downtown Clarksville in celebration of the completed L&N Train Station (page 15, photograph by Benita Martin, courtesy of Montgomery County Historical Society); Ringgold Mill was visibly affected by the 2010 flood, as were many other areas (page 78, courtesy of Billyfrank Morrison); two students at Austin Peay State University come to a head while trying to park their cars on campus (page 45, courtesy of Austin Peay State University).

IMAGES
of Modern America

CLARKSVILLE

Angela Rodesky

ARCADIA
PUBLISHING

ISBN 978-1-4671-1306-9

Published by Arcadia Publishing
Charleston, South Carolina

Printed in the United States of America

Library of Congress Control Number: 2014940807

For all general information, please contact Arcadia Publishing:
Telephone 843-853-2070
Fax 843-853-0044
E-mail sales@arcadiapublishing.com
For customer service and orders:
Toll-Free 1-888-313-2665

Visit us on the Internet at www.arcadiapublishing.com

This book is dedicated to my family for all of their love and support.

Contents

ACKNOWLEDGMENTS

I want to thank and acknowledge many for their advice, dedication, and donation of photographs and time in helping to complete this colorful book. Without the support of our local Montgomery County Historical Society (MCHS), this project would not have been completed. The MCHS was formed in 1924 and for many years has been active in promoting local history and identifying and promoting the preservation of historical sites and structures in the community. The society can be found at the historic L&N Train Station on 189 Tenth Street, where monthly board meetings are held. Regular meetings for all members are held the third Monday of each month at the Civic Center located at Veterans Plaza. There is no charge to attending these fun, informative meetings about the history of businesses, organizations, and people of Clarksville and Montgomery County. The MCHS also hosts cemetery tours, historical reenactments, and tours of historical homes.

This book could not have happened if not for the work of all of those at Arcadia Publishing. I would like to especially think my editor, Julia Simpson, for all of her guidance and patience throughout this process. Through address changes and phone and computer difficulties, she constantly offered words of encouragement and understanding. Without her expert advice, I would have been lost.

There are several others who I would like to personally name and thank; without their additional research, this would not have been accomplished. Those people include Jill Hastings Johnson, Billyfrank Morrison, Amelia Allen Hartz, Molly Cook, Kurt Bryant, Gail Longton, Paige King, and local professional photographer David Smith. I must not forget Scott Schumate, who has a wealth of information on the history of Austin Peay State University at his hands.

Finally, I would like to thank my husband, Terry, my daughter, Ashley, and my sons, Jeremy, Brett, and Cody. Thank-you for all of your love and support during this process, along with another military move.

INTRODUCTION

In 1785, the fifth-largest city in the state of Tennessee, Clarksville, was founded. It was named after Gen. George Rogers Clark, a frontier fighter, Revolutionary War hero, and brother of William Clark of Lewis and Clark fame. Clarksville is located in Montgomery County and was incorporated in 1808. Situated near the confluence of the Cumberland River and the Red River, it was the perfect location to become a major tobacco port. European tobacco buyers helped to put Clarksville on the map in the tobacco-trade industry with dark-fired tobacco. It was easy for anyone to see the growth that was taking place in Clarksville. Around 1819, the town's commercial growth amounted to more than 22 stores, including a bakery and silversmith. The Cumberland River played a large role in this development by providing a way for supplies to be brought into and out of the town. Steamboats carried cotton, corn, coffee, sugar, fabric, flour, and tobacco, among other items, up and down the Cumberland.

Fort Defiance, Fort Donelson, and Fort Henry were established in preparation for the advance of Union soldiers, but they fell in 1862 to Federal troops. In 1872, the city began its rebuild, and the Louisville & Nashville Railroad purchased the existing railroad. However, a disaster that no one saw coming—still known as the Great Fire of 1878—struck. The flames whipped through the downtown business district of Clarksville, destroying 15 acres of land, the courthouse, and many historic buildings.

Clarksville has held many distinct honors, including being the home of the oldest newspaper in the state, the *Leaf Chronicle*, as well as the oldest bank in the state, Northern Bank (established in 1854, later First American). It is also still the fifth-largest city in the state of Tennessee and one of the fastest-growing cities in the South. It is said that Clarksville is the city of many firsts, and that is true on many accounts. During the women's suffrage movement, many women felt the need for separate banking from their husbands and fathers. It was during this time that the first and only bank established and operated by women open its doors in Clarksville. The First Woman's Bank of Tennessee that opened in 1919 and was founded and directed by Brenda Vineyard Runyon, the wife of Dr. Frank Runyon. Another first would come with current mayor Kim McMillan, who in January 2011 became the first female mayor in the state of Tennessee to hold her position with a population of over 100,000.

While touring through Clarksville, there are many historical sites that one might visit, including three Confederate States of America Army camps: Camp Boone, Camp Burnett, and Camp Defiance. Camp Boone, located at Guthrie Road and Wilma Rudolph Boulevard along the Kentucky-Tennessee border, was the training area for the Confederate States of America Army of Tennessee. Camp Burnett was named after Henry Cornelius Burnett, a US representative of the state of Kentucky; it was a Confederate recruiting post and an organization point of the 4th Kentucky Infantry. Fort Defiance is one of the three of the Confederate army camps located here in Clarksville. A Civil War outpost that was occupied by both Confederate and Union soldiers, it overlooks the Cumberland River and the Red River with a completed museum chronicling the local chapter of Civil War history.

The city of Clarksville is also the home of 22 different parks that have playgrounds, picnic areas with shelters and pavilions, and walking, hiking, and biking trails. There are also five public swimming pools and three community centers that offer year-round activities to young and old alike—that is over 700 acres of parks and facilities for all members of the community to enjoy every day.

In 2013, Clarksville's Greenway opened to the public, giving easy access to McGregor Park, Trice Landing, Liberty Park, and Billy Dunlop Park. While in the area, visitors will see kayakers and people on paddleboards or even in canoes enjoying the water and fresh air. Staying on dry land, one can always enjoy the Clarksville Greenway, which provides trails for walking, biking, and hiking along the banks of the Red River and West Fork Creek. To walk and view the historical homes and buildings in Clarksville and stroll through the heart of the downtown community, one must find the Uplands Trail. McGregor Park and the Riverwalk connect with the Upland Trail, connecting to the Commerce Street pedestrian bridge and ending just shy of Valleybrook Park. The Riverwalk is also the place to be for some of Clarksville's most popular outdoor events, such as the Independence Day Celebration, Riverfest, and of course Christmas on the Cumberland. If the weather is questionable, there may be an alternative at one of the three community centers: Burt-Cobb on Franklin Street, Crow on Richview Road, or Kleeman on Cunningham Lane.

Clarksville remains the site of Fort Campbell, home of the 101st Airborne Division and Austin Peay State University. The city's population continues to grow; it was 77,785 in 1990 and 142,519 in 2013.

Obviously, Clarksville, Tennessee, has come a long way. With the pending arrival of Hankook Tire Company, which is building its plant and bringing in 1,800 jobs, there is sure to be a surge in population. The tight-knit Clarksville community continues to grow and prosper even after facing the wrath of Mother Nature—including the F3 tornado of 1999 and the flood of 2010—and an economic roller coaster. These pages of color photographs depict the ever-changing history made here in Clarksville, Tennessee.

One

Fun in Clarksville

One thing is for sure, there is always something fun to do in Clarksville. Some things from years past do not change. The Roxy Theatre, for example, continues to pack them in with enjoyable plays and musicals while offering camps and classes to both adults and youth alike. There is also fun to be had strolling through shops downtown. It would be wrong not to mention the modern way of shopping that showed up in the form of Governs Square Mall, with all its stores and a movie theater. For fresh air, Clarksville boasts 32 parks, each including numerous playgrounds, pavilions for parties and cookouts, and dog parks where four-legged friends can also enjoy those nice days outdoors. Some of these parks even have public pools to splash around in during the warm summer months. At one time, roller-skating rinks and drive-in movie theaters were the places to gather with friends. Some are still around, but as times change, so do some of the extracurricular activates community members enjoy. Paintball is one of those growing outdoor activities that friends and families enjoy doing. Red Leg Action Sports along the Red River happens to be the center of all the paintball fun in Clarksville; the field was even rebuilt after the flood of 2012. There are also a number of wonderful parades that take place throughout the year. The pages of this first chapter provide a glimpse of some of the fun to be had in Clarksville.

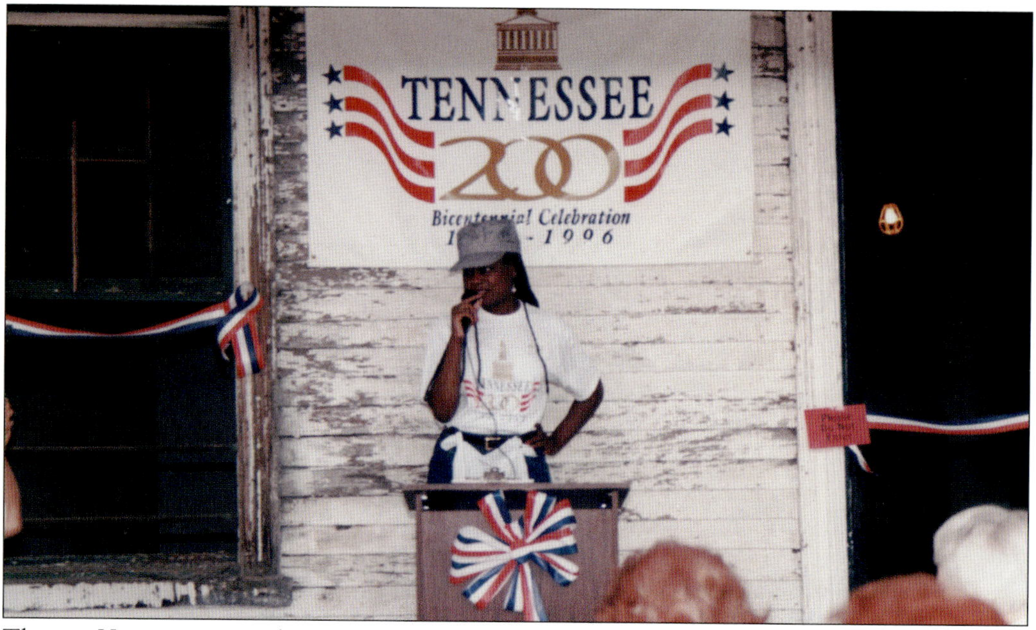

Theresa Harrington speaks to a crowd during Volunteer Day in June 1995. Many Clarksville residents and some members of the surrounding communities came out for this day's event. There is always some kind of activity taking place in Clarksville that acknowledges those who contribute or pave the way for families and the community to flourish. (Photograph by Benita Martin, courtesy of MCHS.)

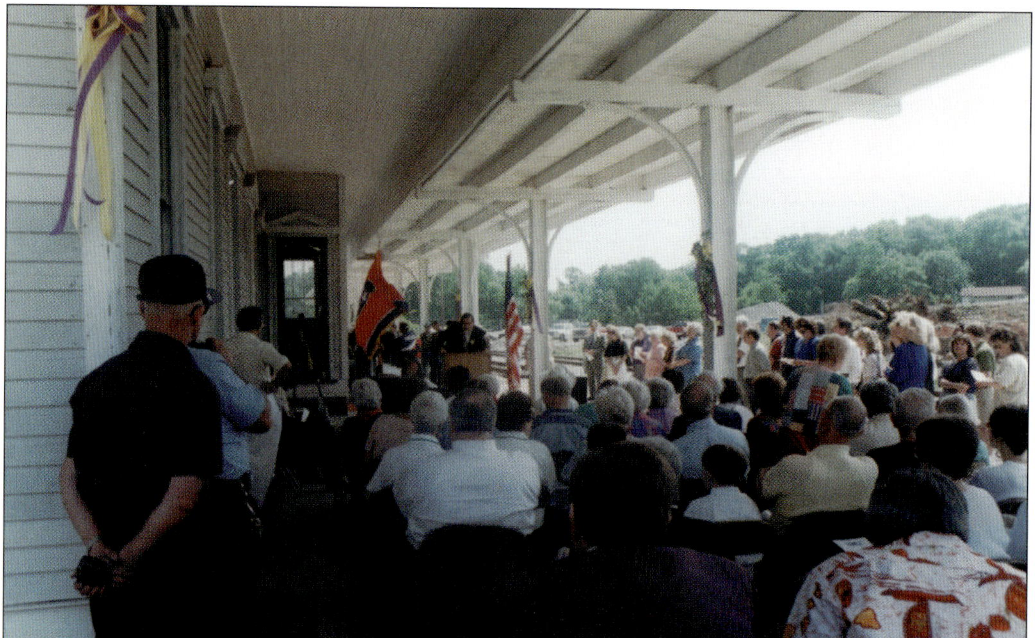

The *Spirit of Tennessee* paid a visit to Clarksville in August 1996. It was an added attraction to the celebration of the completed restoration of the L&N Train Station. The crowd sits quietly, facing the podium, and listens to a speech given by Mayor Don Trotter. (Photograph by Benita Martin, courtesy of MCHS.)

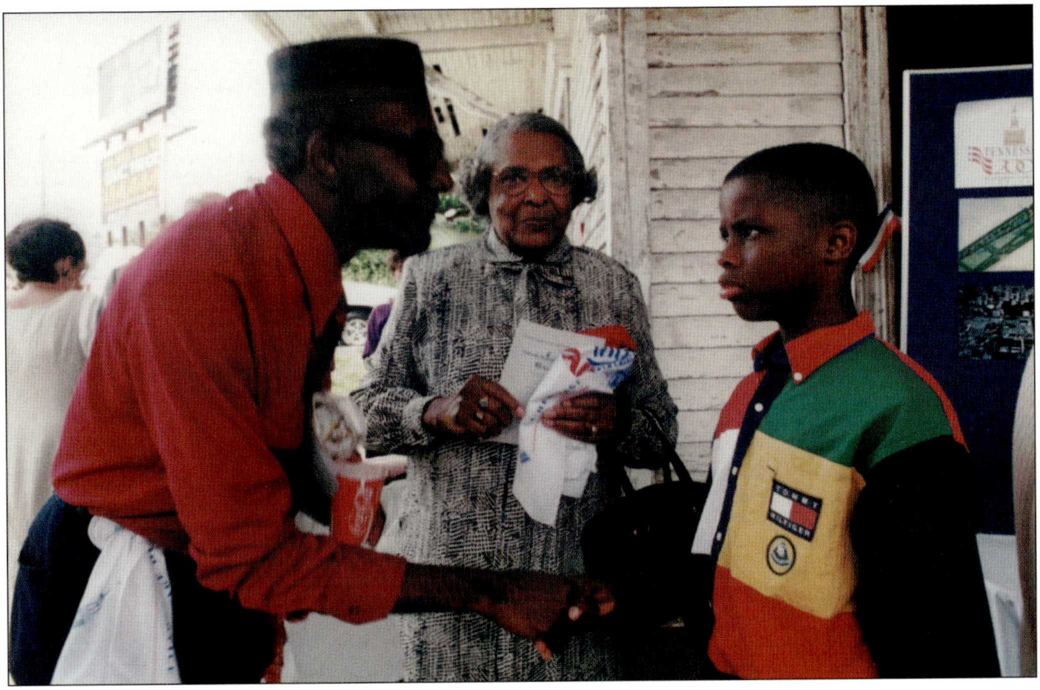

Pictured above is Volunteer Day on June 1, 1995, which brought out community members of all ages. Lewis Jones is seen shaking the hand of a young Robert Sanders, while Lorenza R. Collier observes. Below, Nat Allen (right) shakes the hand of Bill Harpel during a celebration at the L&N Train Station during the same event. (Both photographs by Benita Martin, courtesy of MCHS.)

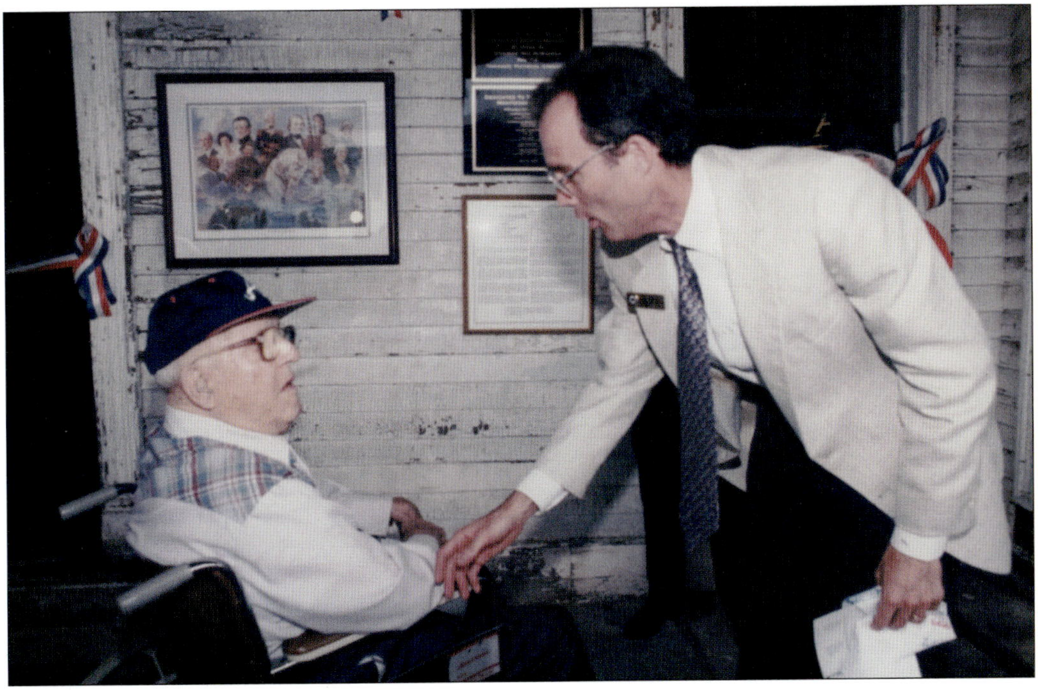

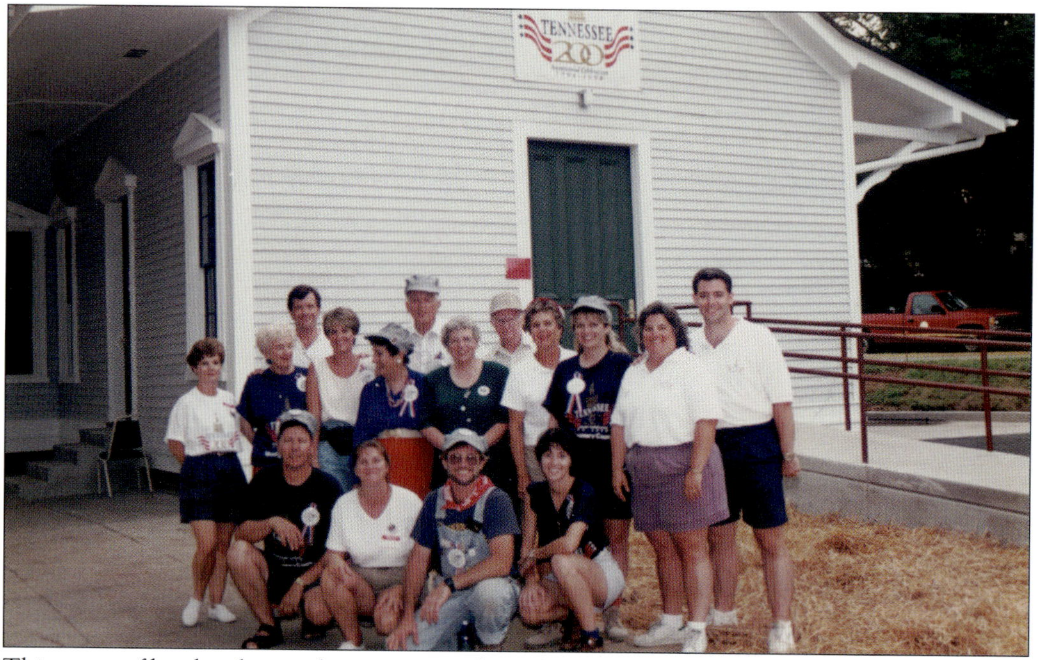

This group of hardworking volunteers poses for a photograph in front of the L&N Train Station. Some of those pictured include Bill Ogles, Norman Young, county commissioner Jay Albertia, Mrs. Rubel, Teresa Harrington, and Eleanor Williams (Photograph by Benita Martin, courtesy of MCHS.)

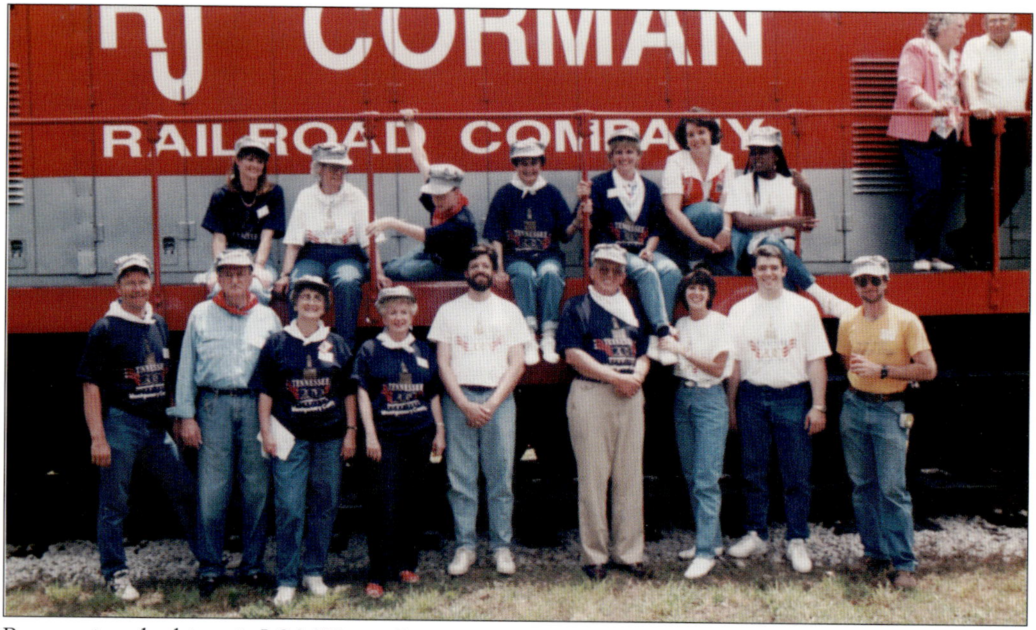

Renovating the historic L&N Train Station was a process that continued into 1996. During the *Spirit of Tennessee* event at the station that year, residents and members of the MCHS take a moment to pose on the *RJ Corman*. Dr. Martin, Mrs. Martin, Eleanor Williams, Alan Henderson, Benita Martin, Jay Albertia, and Mrs. Rubel are just a few of the people in this photograph. (Photograph by Benita Martin, courtesy of MCHS.)

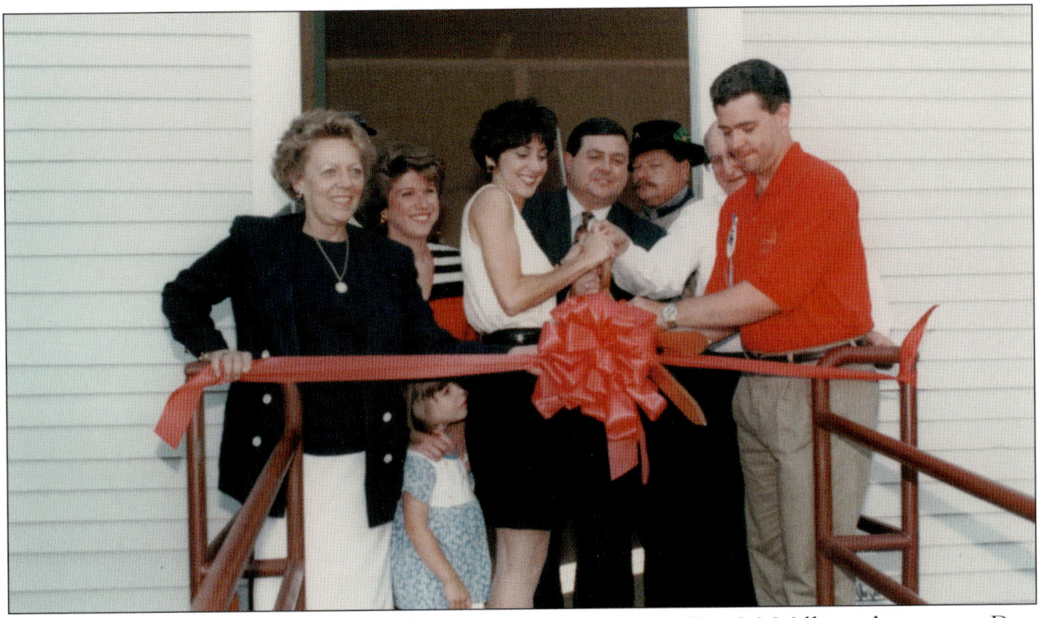

Pictured here are state representative Carol Rice, current mayor Kim McMillian, then-mayor Don Trotter, Benita Martin, county executive Robert Thompson, and chair of the restoration team Jay Albertia as they take part in the 1996 ribbon-cutting ceremony at the main entrance of the L&N Train Station. Many attended this long-awaited event, including some from the Clarksville community. Among those in attendance were all of the volunteers who put in so many hours of their time to help make the transformation possible. (Photograph by Benita Martin, courtesy of MCHS.)

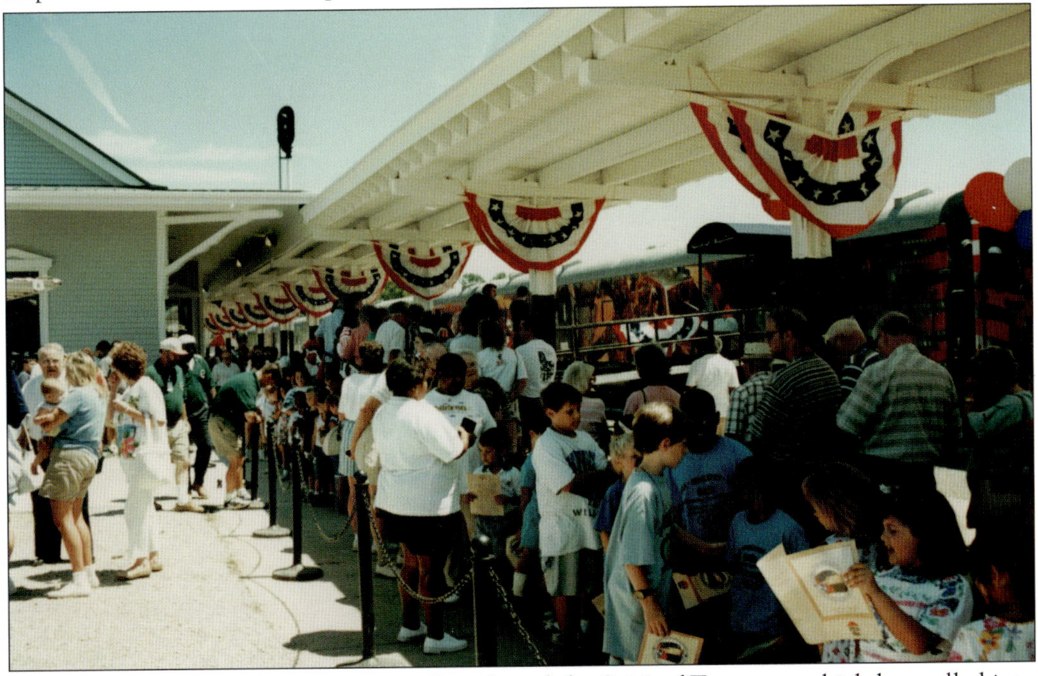

Lines have formed, and everyone is ready to board the *Spirit of Tennessee*, which has pulled into the station. The brightly painted cars kept everyone's attention while they waited to embark. (Photographs by Benita Martin, courtesy of MCHS.)

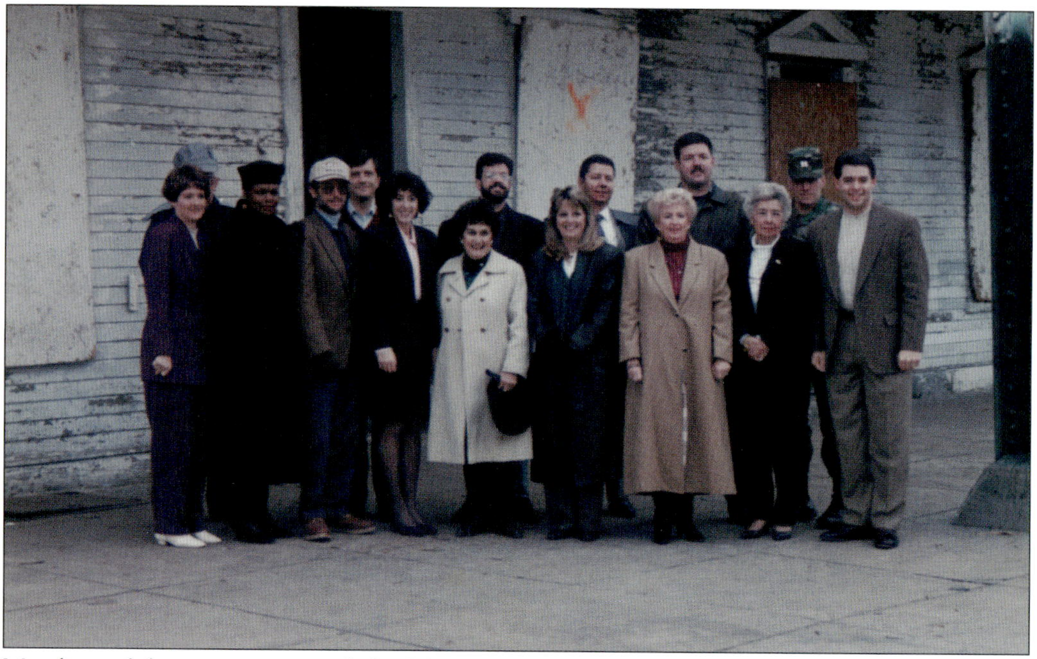

Members of the community and the Montgomery County Historical Society pose for a group photograph in 1995 at the beginning stages of the restoration project. Bonita Martin, Mrs. Rubel, Jay Albertia, Alan Henderson, Bill Ogles, and Eleanor Williams are some of those pictured. (Photograph by Benita Martin, courtesy of MCHS.)

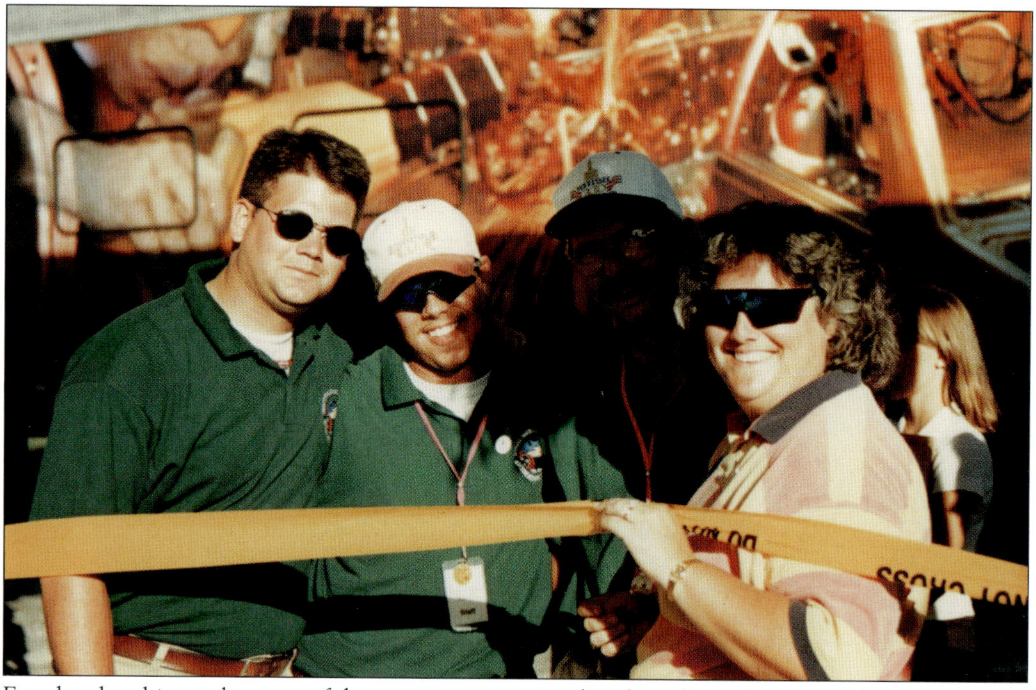

Four hardworking volunteers of the community are smiling broadly as they enjoy the nice weather and the *Spirit of Tennessee* visit. A lot of work went into the renovation process, so many residents came out to lend their support. (Photograph by Benita Martin, courtesy of MCHS.)

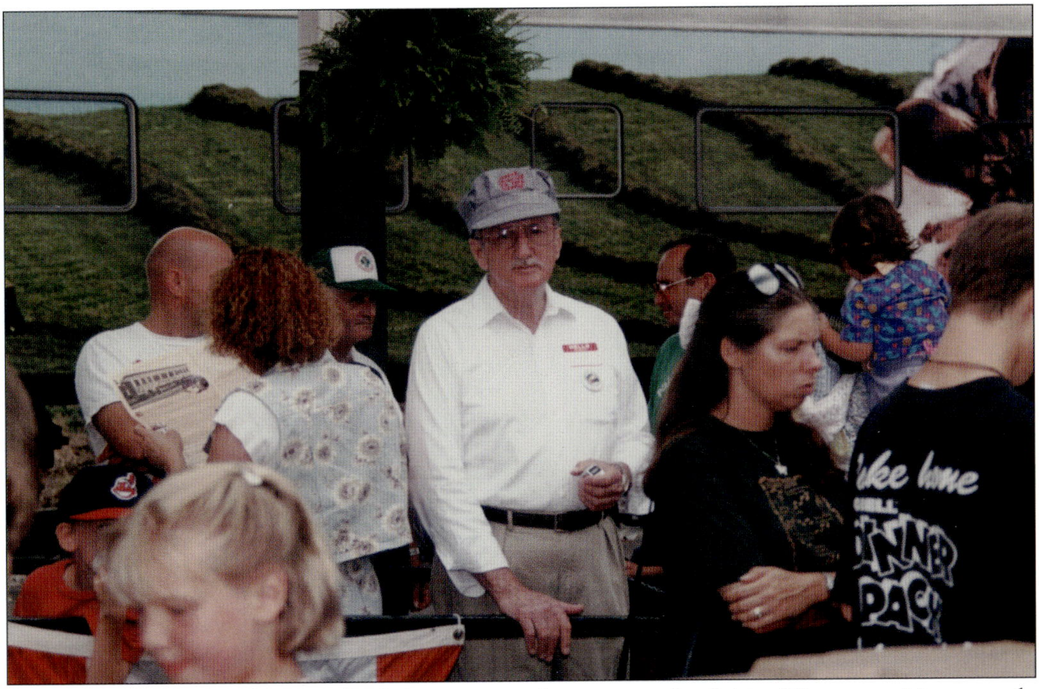

Dr. Martin stops for a photograph while waiting in line to tour the *Spirit of Tennessee*. Many people came to visit with their friends and family while touring through the train station and walking aboard the *Spirit of Tennessee*. (Photograph by Benita Martin, courtesy of MCHS.)

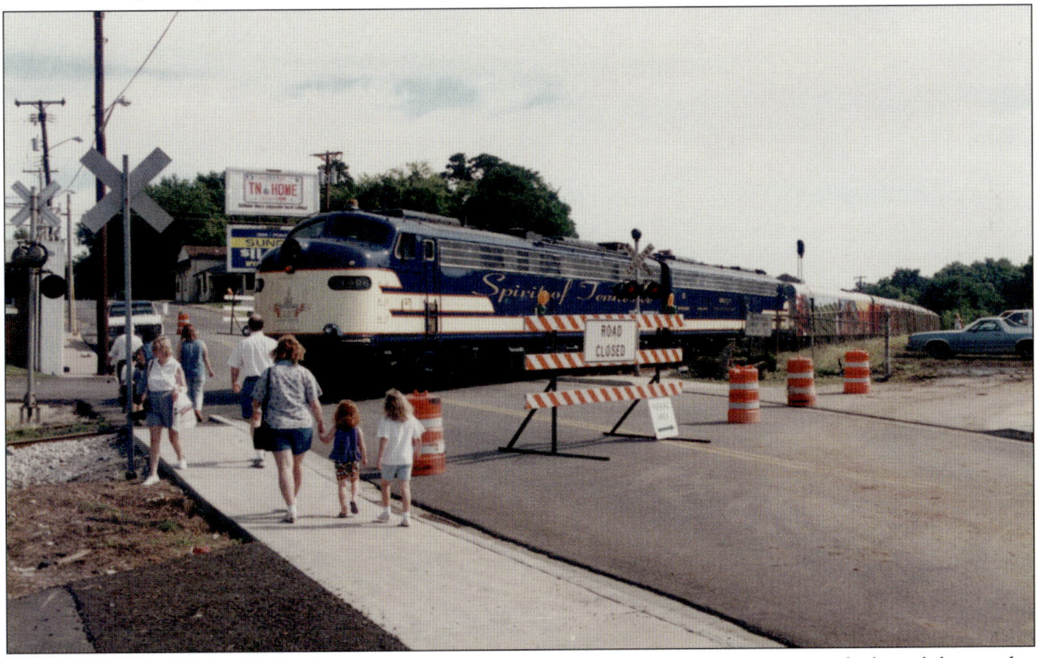

The *Spirit of Tennessee* pulled into the L&N Train Station on Tenth Street to help celebrate the historic renovation of the structure and the Clarksville centennial. The train arrived in town on the August 11, 1996, helping to draw a large crowd to all of the downtown area. (Photograph by Benita Martin, courtesy of MCHS.)

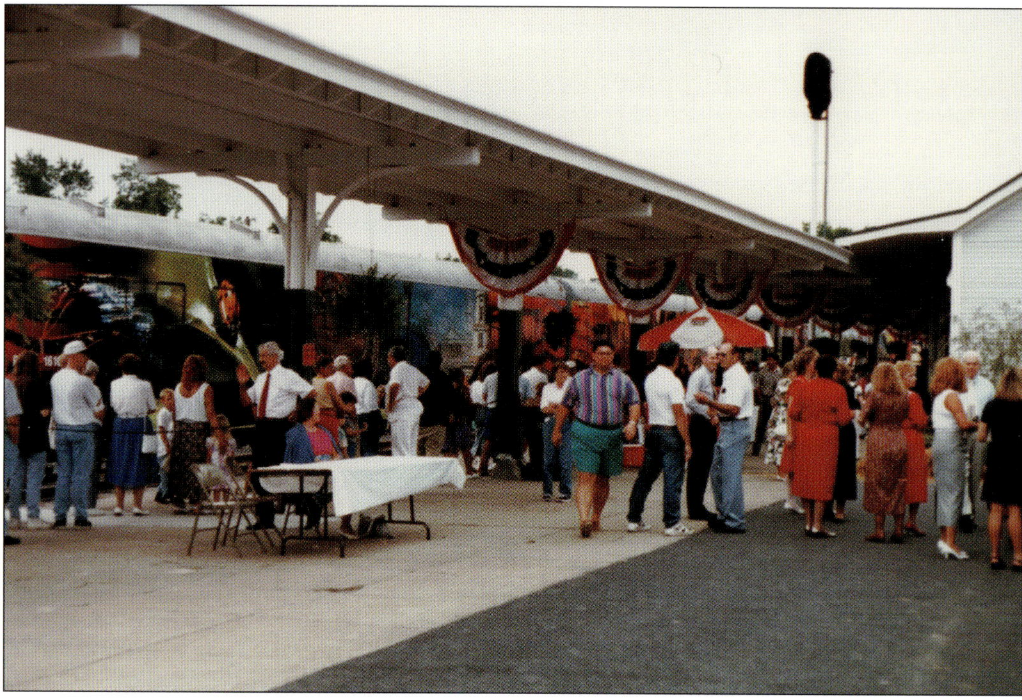

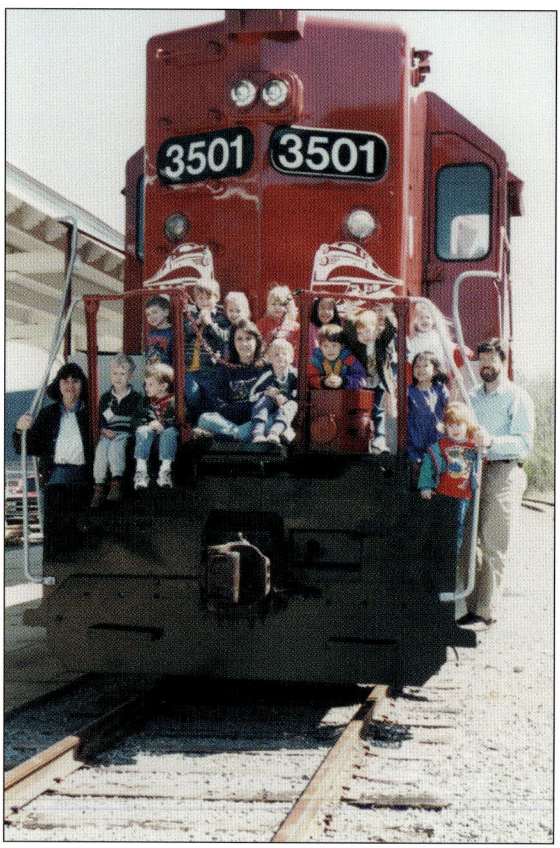

The *Spirit of Tennessee* drew a large crowd from Clarksville and some of the surrounding communities. After taking a tour through the train, visitors then focused on the memories found inside the station. Long-time residents enjoyed reminiscing with others about the station's earlier years, while younger visitors were able to learn more about this form of transportation no longer utilized as in years past. (Photograph by Benita Martin, courtesy of MCHS.)

During a 1996 day-care tour of the L&N Train Station, students and teachers stop for a quick photograph on the front of the train. They were also able to tour the inside of the station itself. Many people pose at this spot, whether it is for a wedding, family, prom, or senior-year photograph. (Photograph by Benita Martin, courtesy of MCHS.)

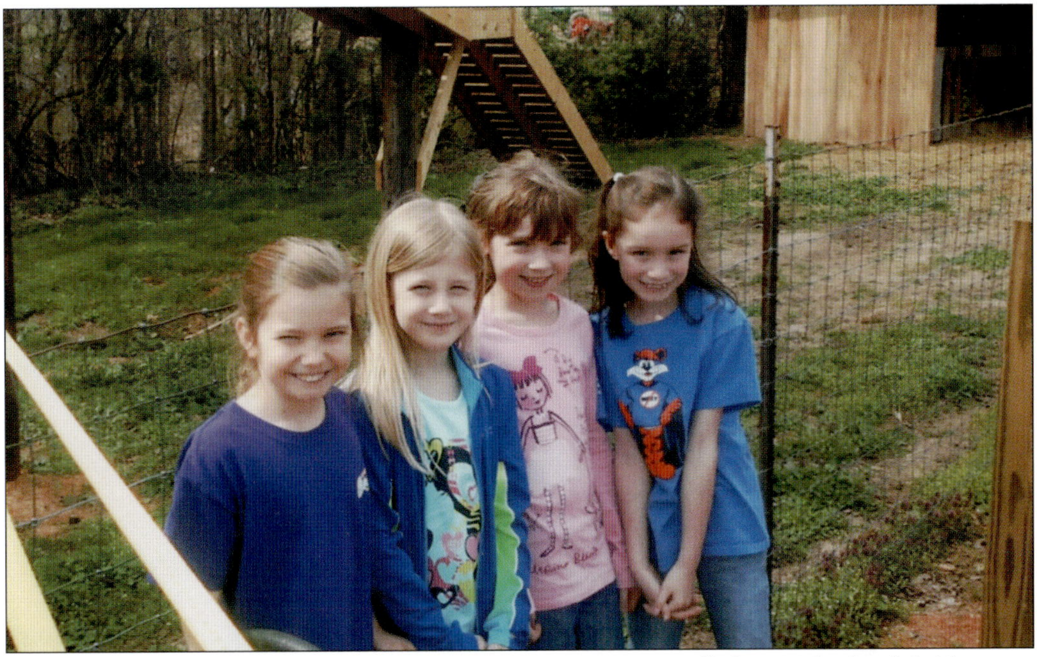

These Barksdale Elementary second-graders are enjoying a well-deserved school field trip to Honeysuckle Hill Farm, a favorite destination among youth and adults in Montgomery County. Pictured from left to right are Kyleigh Koyarma, Bonny Powell, Meghan Routzakn, and Annlee Head. (Photograph by Billyfrank Morrison.)

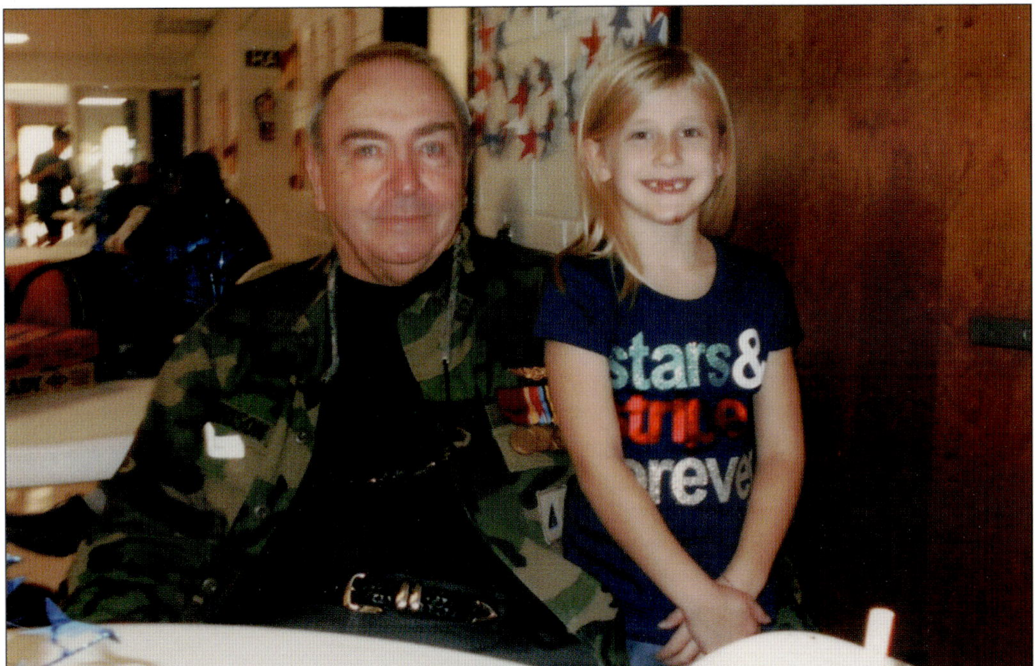

Many local schools take the time to celebrate Veterans Day, and Barksdale Elementary is no exception. Here, at the 2014 Veterans Day celebration, Bonny Powell proudly sits upon the knee of her grandfather, Billyfrank Morrison. (Courtesy of Billyfrank Morrison.)

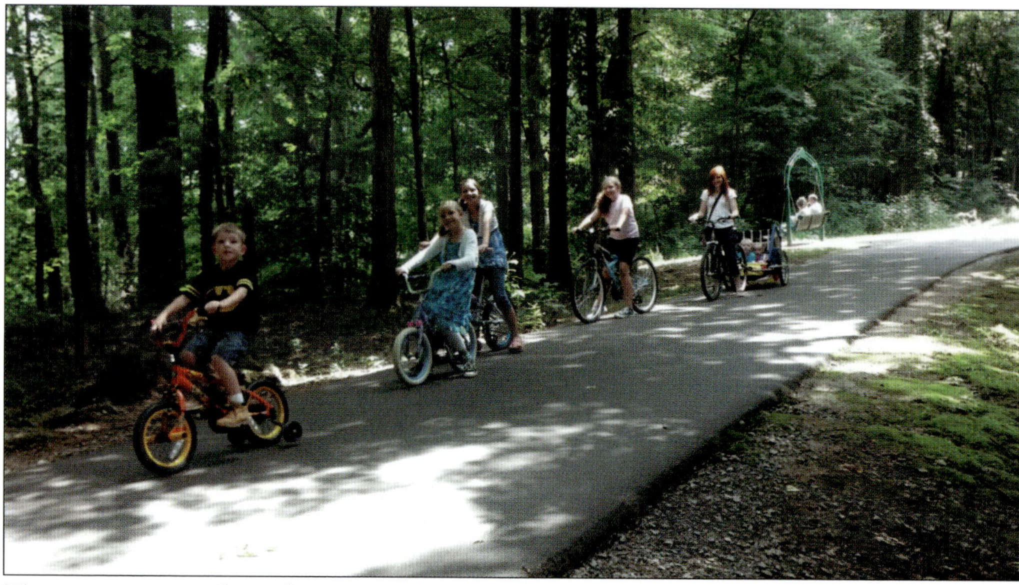

There are many parks with running and riding trails that residents can access. The Spillane family spends a lot of quality time together enjoying the outdoors. As a military family, they enjoy getting out and experiencing all that Mother Nature has to offer. The lead bicyclist is Thomas, followed by Sydney, Karley, Shelby, and Makayla, who is pulling Benjamin and Kensley in a bike cart. (Photograph by Kristy Spillane.)

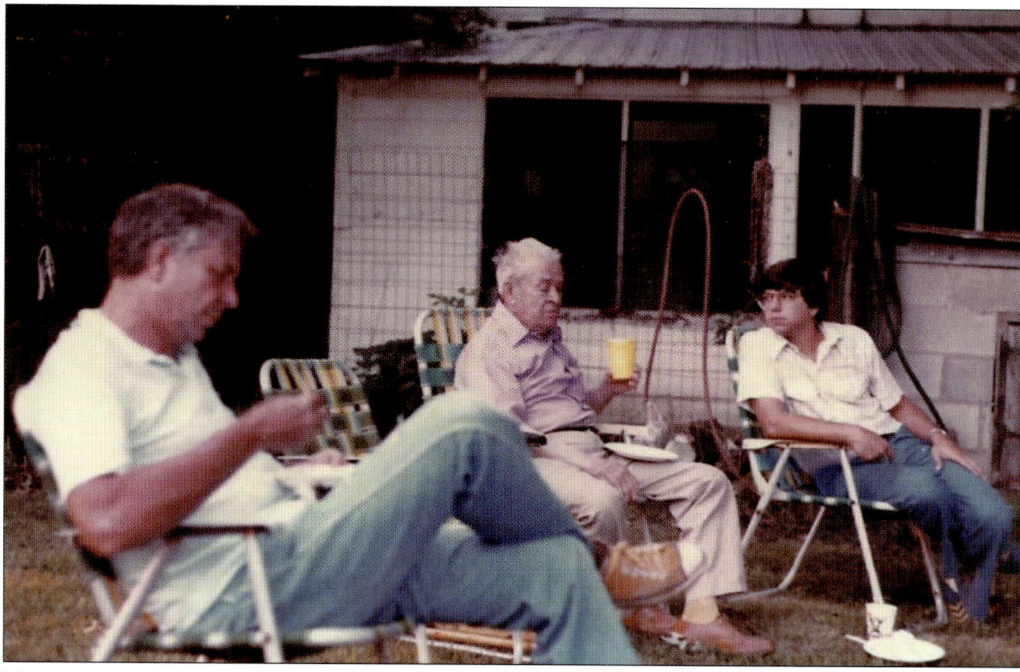

Horace M. Lisenbee (center), who was a professional baseball pitcher for the Washington Senators and Cincinnati Reds, is enjoying some well-spent family time. To the left of Horace is his son Charles E. Bryant Sr., a World War II veteran who worked for the US Postal Service Student Post Office in Clarksville. To the right of Horace is his grandson Kurt Bryant, the local MCHS president. This photograph was taken in the summer of 1970. (Courtesy of Kurt Bryant.)

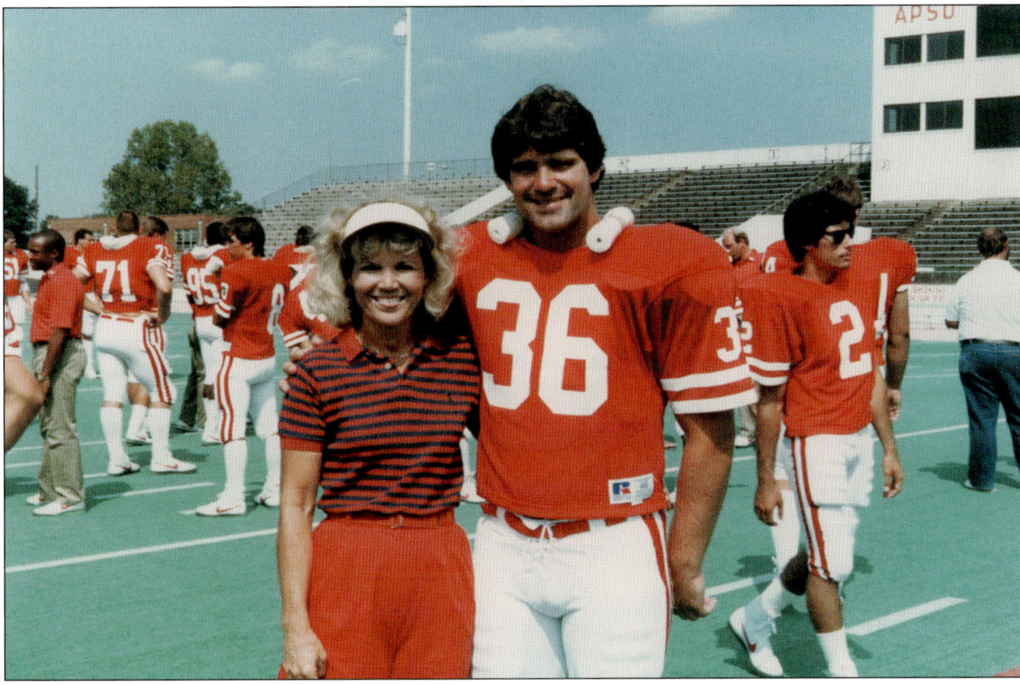

Pictured here during an Austin Peay State University campus event is Evelyn Morrison, who is married to local author Billyfrank Morrison. Evelyn is a proud supporter of both Austin Peay State University (APSU) and the MCHS. Posing with her is Brad Minear, from Orlando, Florida, who played tight end at APSU from 1983 to 1986. He previously played tight end and fullback for Bob Williams at Colonial High School. During his sophomore year at APSU, he played in all 11 games and caught one touchdown pass. (Courtesy of Billyfrank Morrison.)

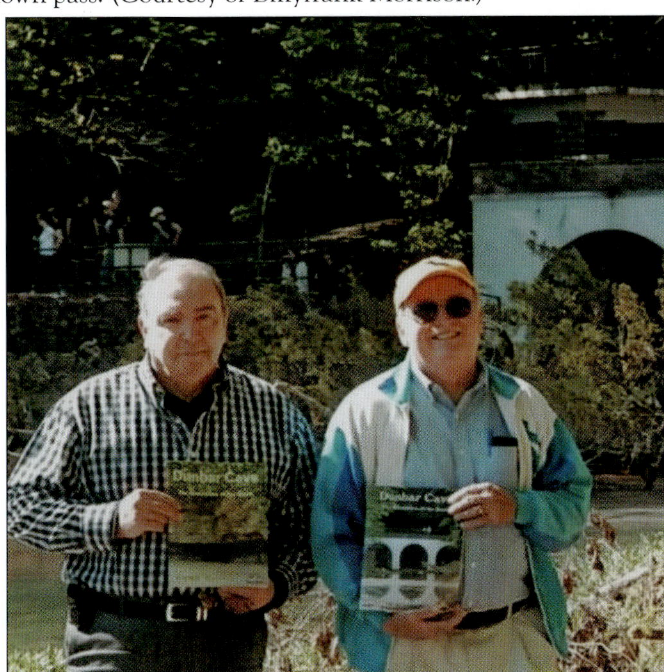

Local Tennessee authors Billyfrank Morrison (left) and Larry Mathew, author of *Dunbar Cave: The Showplace of the South*, pose holding both the first and second editions of Mathew's book. Morrison assisted in the research of postcards about Dunbar Cave for the first edition and has himself written *Fort Campbell in Vintage Postcards*, *Clarksville in Vintage Postcards*, and *Marion County in Vintage Postcards*. Morrison is from Clarksville, and Mathews is from Nashville. (Courtesy of Billyfrank Morrison.)

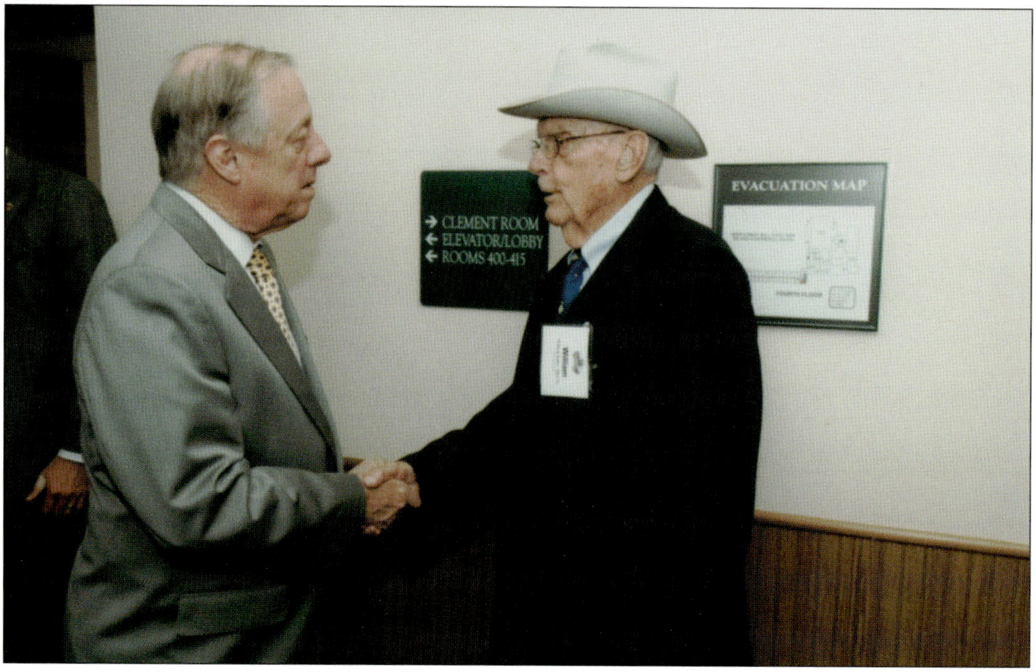

Above, Gov. Phil Bredesen (left) shakes the hand of William Bailey Allen during a Tennessee Farmland Legacy Conference recognizing pioneer Century Farms, held at the Montgomery Bell State Park. Allendale Farm was recognized for having remained in constant agricultural production by the same family since it was founded in 1796. Below, Allen is watching over his cattle on the Allendale Farm, which is entirely devoted to pasture to support his operation. As a member of the Grassland Reserve Program, the farm no longer grows crops. (Both courtesy of Amelia Allen Hartz.)

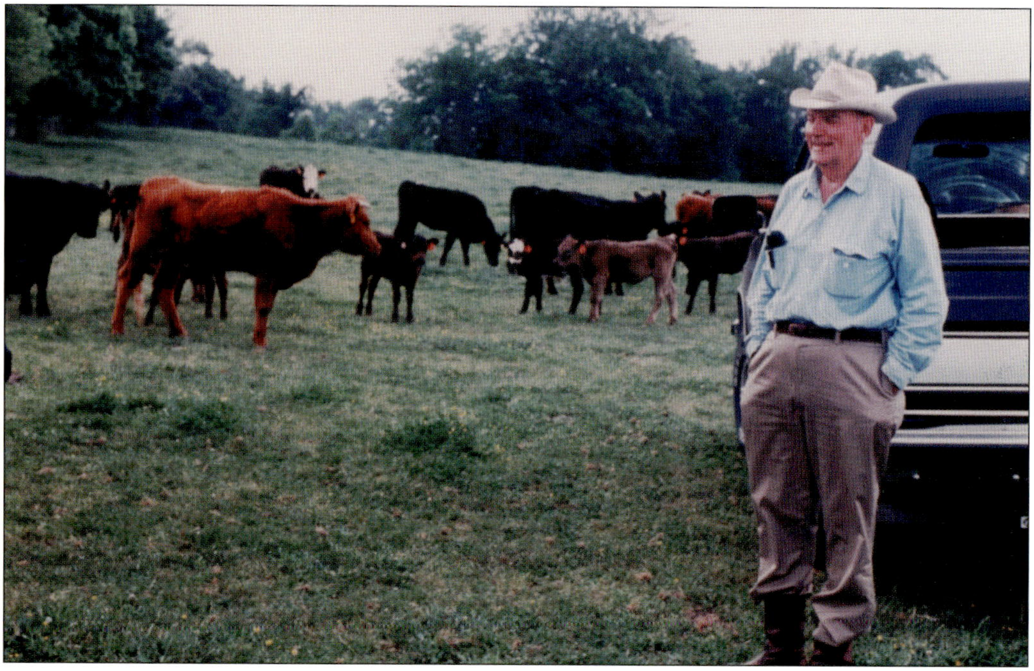

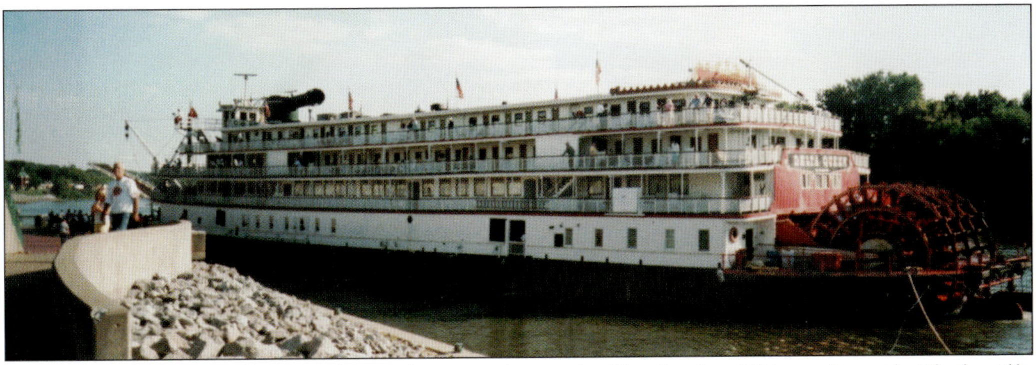

The *Delta Queen* riverboat makes its last trip down the Cumberland River through Clarksville in 2008. Those who were fortunate enough to voyage on this authentic wooden-strutted steamboat, measuring 285 feet in length, felt as if they were losing a family member. (Photograph by Molly Cook.)

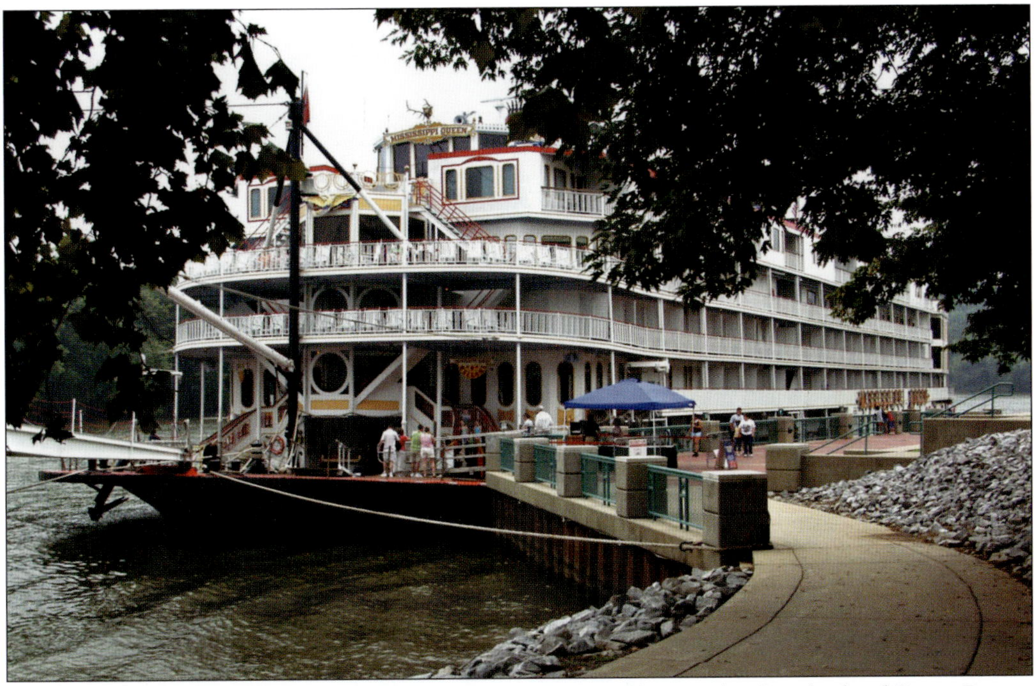

An amazing and fun sight to see, the *Mississippi Queen* pulls into the Cumberland River Center in 2006. No matter how long the lines were, people could feel the excitement and anticipation while waiting to board the vessel. (Photograph by Clifton Whittaker, courtesy of Paige King.)

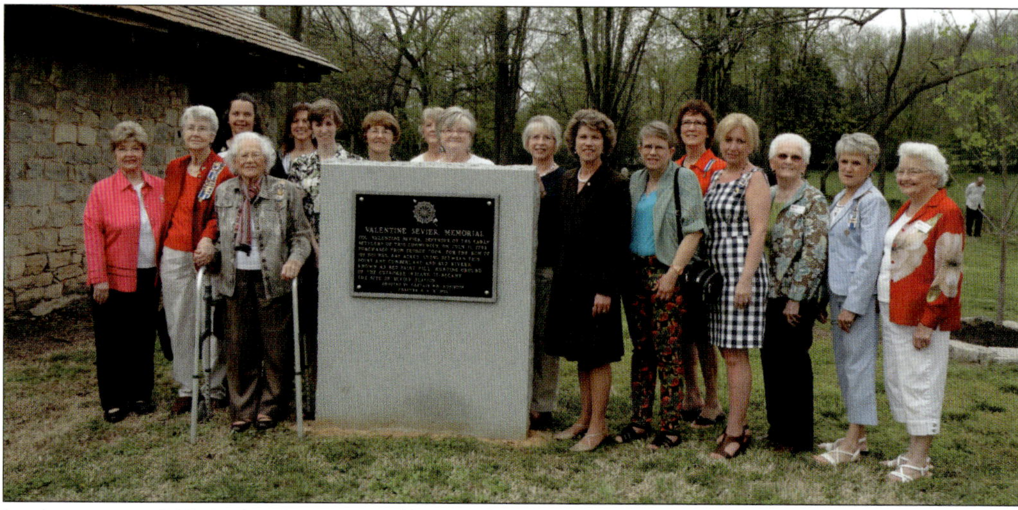

In the spring of 2012, the Captain William Edmiston Chapter of the Daughters of the American Revelation dedicated a new monument to the Sevier Station. Pictured here among the group are Joan Harris, Elsie Smith, Ruby Jean McLeod, Alicia Clark, Michelle Newell, Kristen Bollmeier, Jan Bollmeier, Wanda Ferell, Jenny McCarty, Marla Grinstead, Mayor Kim McMillan, Sheri Ripple, Gail Longton, Cynthia Gray, Margaret Bowman, and Ella Hay. The photograph below was taken at an event in November 2013 honoring Vietnam veterans and an active-duty solider. The veterans posing here include SGM Billie Hedrick, USA Retired; Maj. Bennie Parks; LTC Tracy Jackson, USA Retired; CW3 J.C. Whitney, USA Retired; and Sgt. Paul Buske and LTC Greg Lane, USA Reserves. (Both courtesy of Gail Longton.)

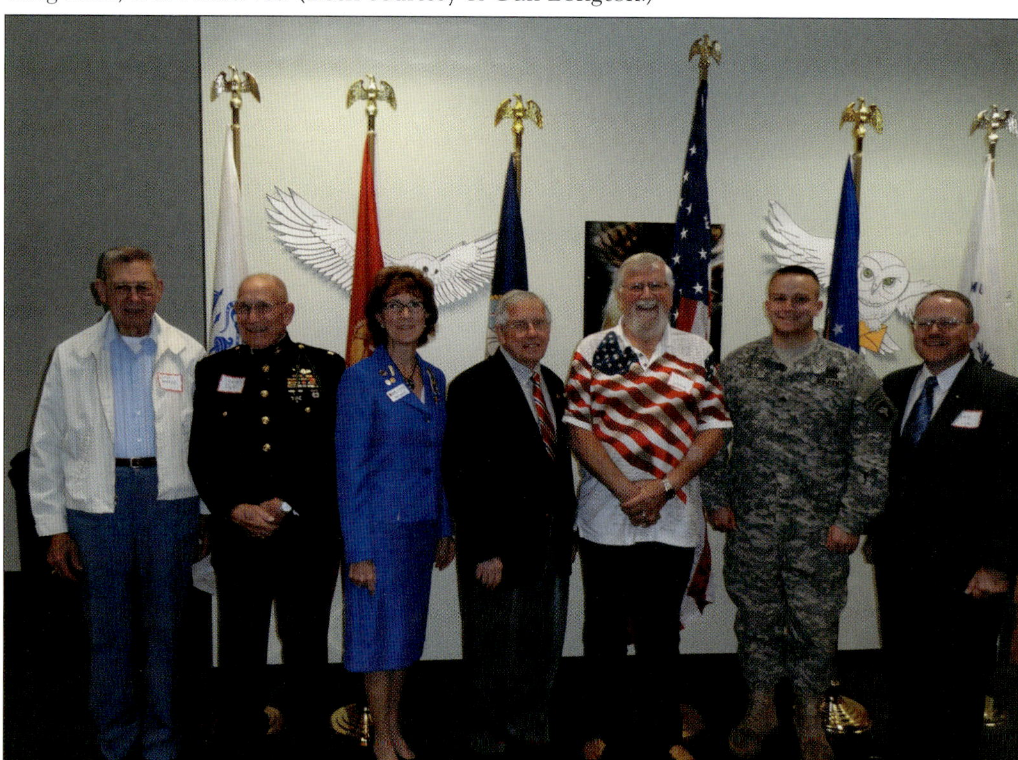

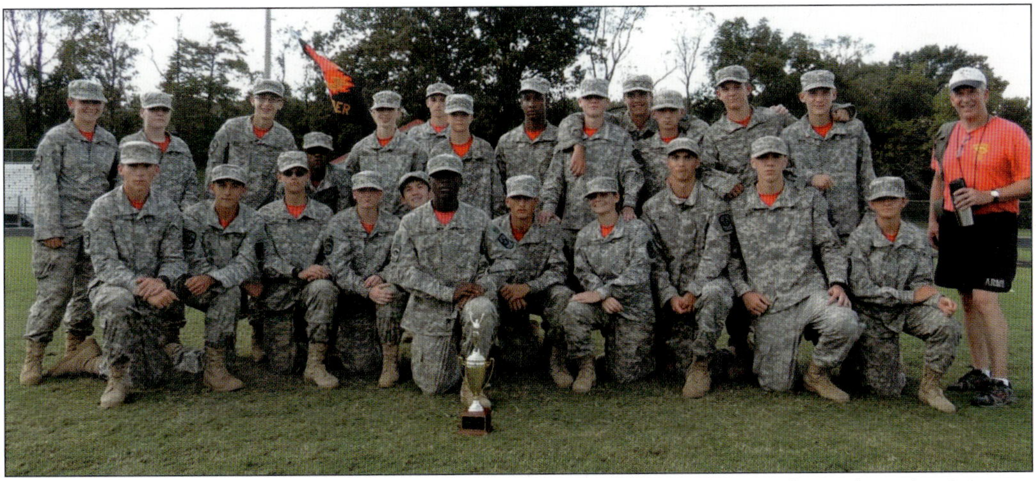

The 2014 JROTC Raiders team from Rossview High competed in the Creekwood Raiders Meet in October 2013, placing third overall. Pictured in the front center is Cadet Goulsby, and behind him are, from left to right, (first row) Cadet Baird, Cadet Valencia, Cadet Newman, Cadet Bradshaw, Cadet Hunt, Cadet Kfouf, Cadet King, Cadet Utt, Cadet Levy, Cadet Bostwick, and Ret. Col. Miller; (second row) Cadet Baird, Cadet Walker, Cadet Major, Cadet Springfield, Cadet Ligo, Cadet Knight, Cadet McDonald, Cadet Fox, Cadet Rodesky, Cadet Colby, Cadet Hoffman, and Cadet Byers. (Courtesy of JROTC Booster Club.)

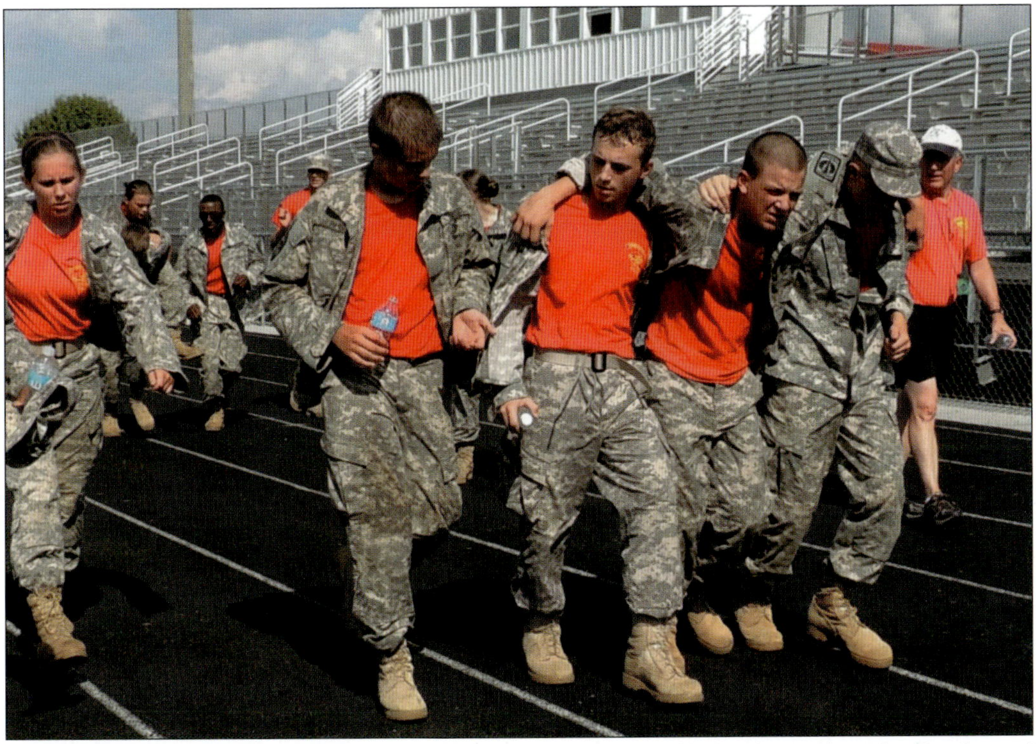

This group of the Rossview JROTC Raiders team is coming to the final stretch at the Creekwood Raiders Meet in October 2013. No matter how sore and exhausted they felt, they were determined to complete the event. From left to right are Cadet Baird, Cadet Rodesky, Cadet Colby, Cadet Huffman, Cadet Byers, and Ret. LTC Miller. (Courtesy of JROTC Booster Club.)

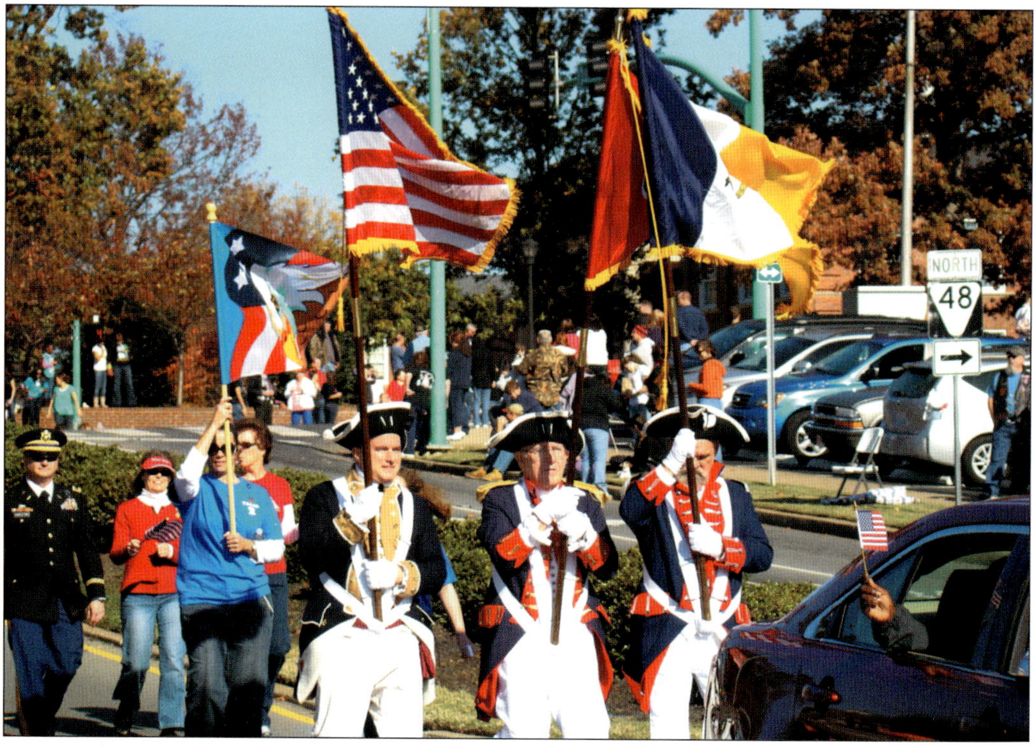

During the 2014 Veterans Day parade, these three reenactment Colonial soldiers march in formation while dressed in full uniform and carrying flags. (Author's collection.)

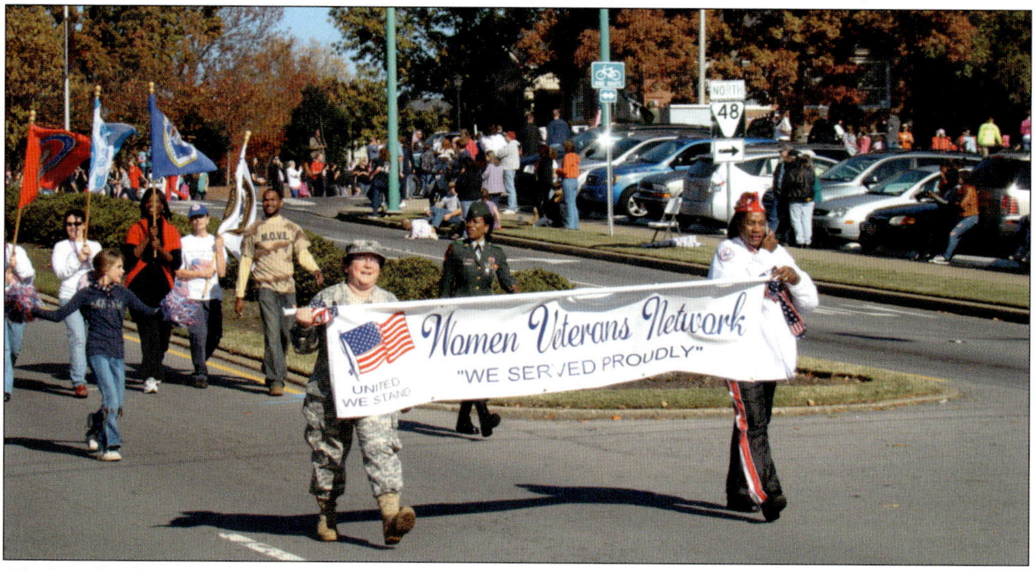

Clarksville shows its support for service members in many ways, one of them being the Veterans Day parade. This parade brings out members of the community and surrounding communities. Attendees can see and feel the support both along the parade route and among those participating in the parade. Two women proudly carry the banner for the Women Veterans Network during the 2013 parade. Walking with the young and old alike, they show their support for each other and for those women who continue to serve. (Author's collection.)

This float in the 2013 Veterans Day parade reads, "VFW Post 11160 Proudly Supports All Those Who Served." The men aboard the float wear uniforms representing different branches of the armed services. From left to right are Dale Johnson (kneeling), Robin Castello, Tommy Dennis, Lupe Jacques, and James McKinstry. (Author's collection.)

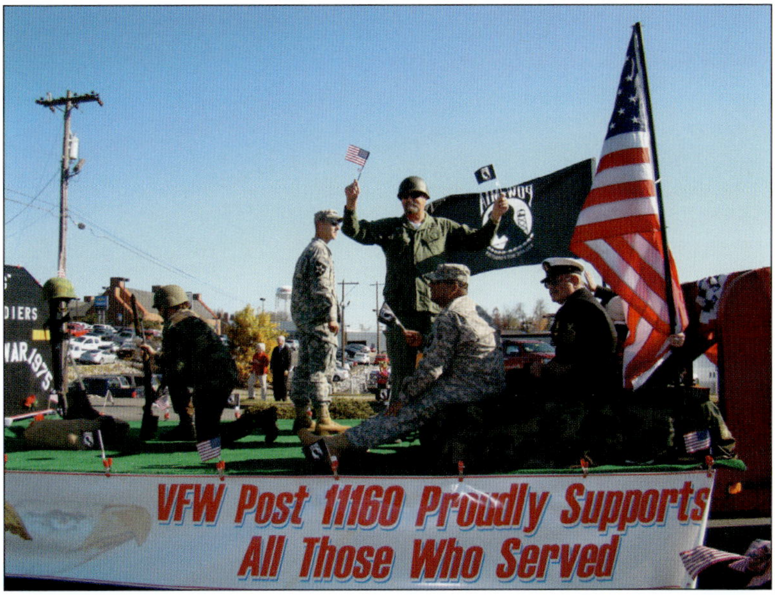

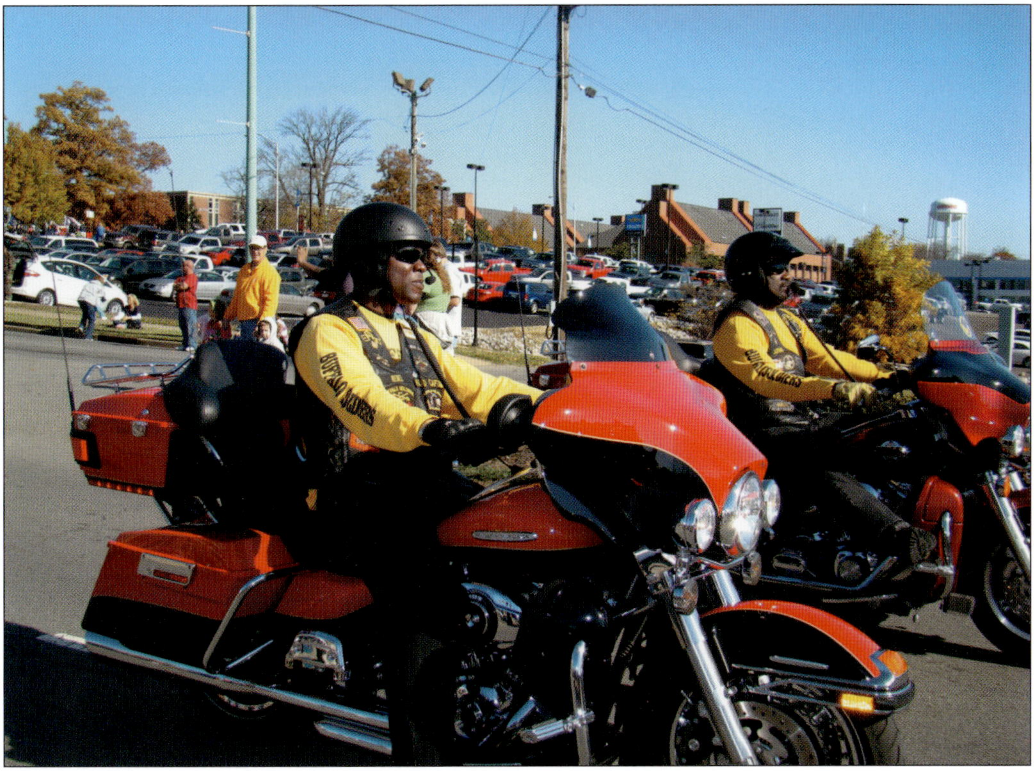

Veterans Day in 2013 would not have been complete without the Buffalo Soldiers' local chapter. The group makes regular appearances during all Veterans Day parades, riding on their motorcycles. Dressed in bright yellow with black lettering, they too show their support and receive the respect of the community. This local chapter became active in 2008. As a nonprofit club, it continues to support the community through various events and even made a generous donation for the victims of the 2010 flood. (Author's collection.)

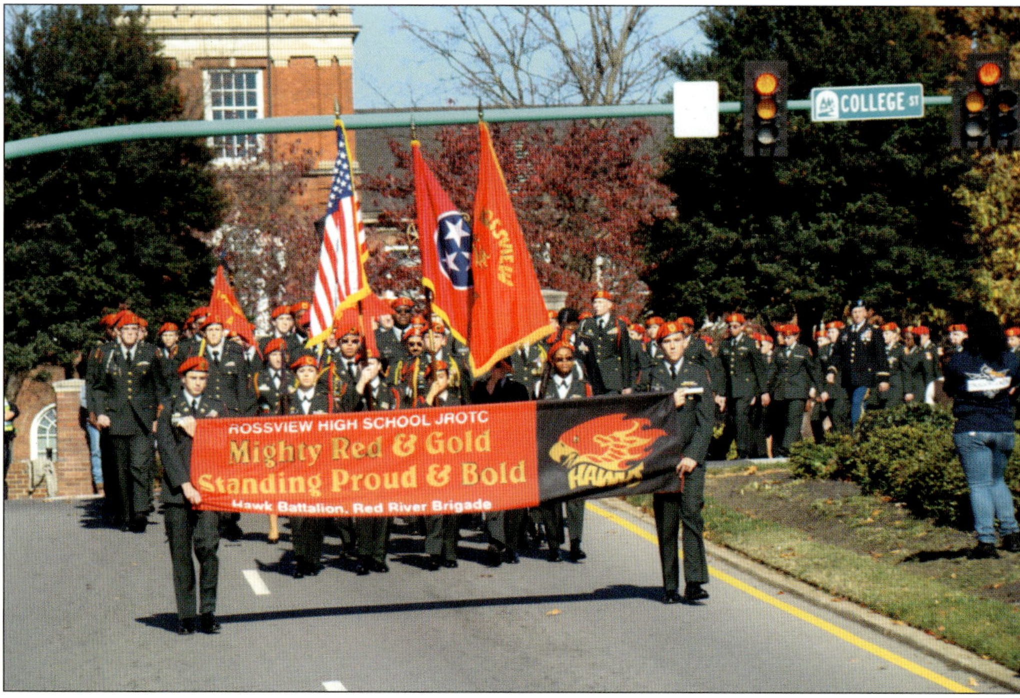

Above is the Rossview High School JROTC at the 2013 Veterans Day parade. Many students who join JROTC programs have family members who served or are currently serving in the military. Some of these young men and women will continue on to a branch in the armed forces once they graduate. Pictured below among the soldiers marching are J.R. Brown, Brandon Coleman, Jeremy Rodesky, Garrett Eberly, and Matt Burton. (Both author's collection.)

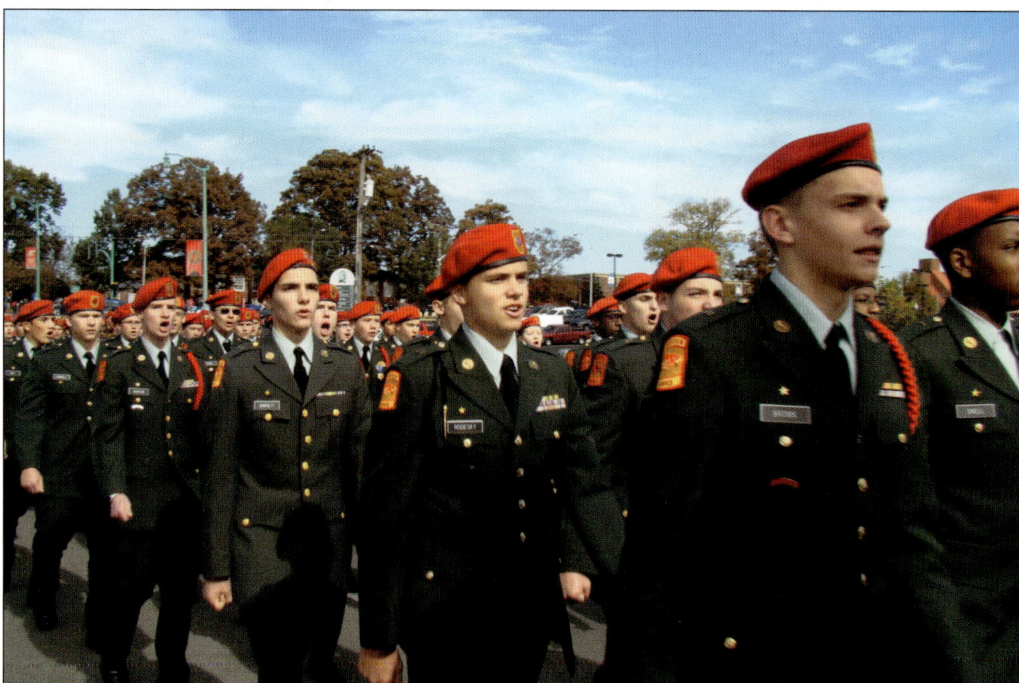

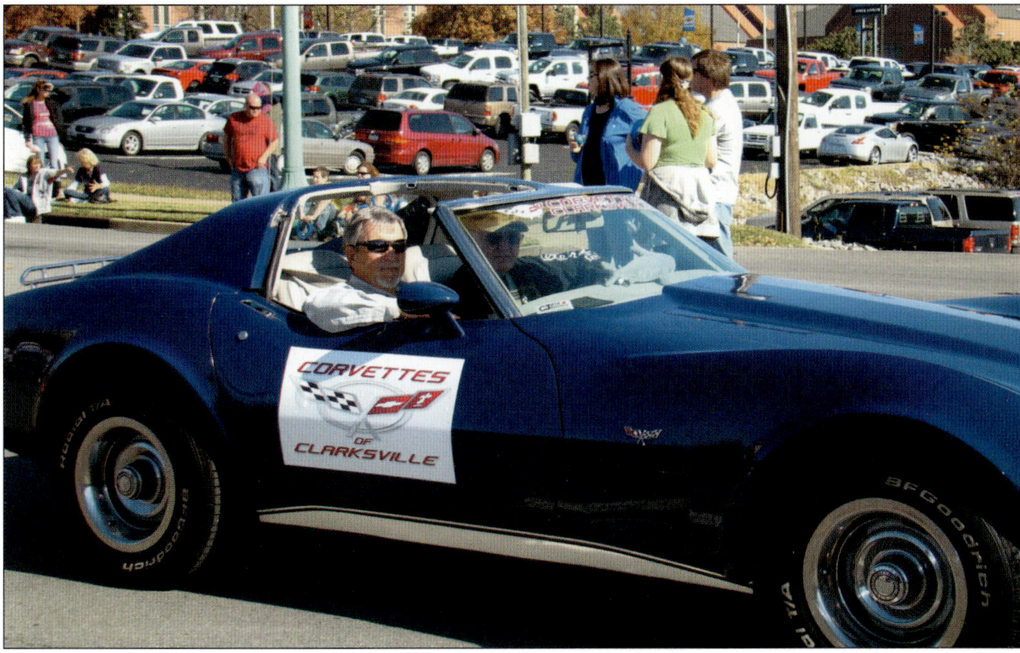

Of course, no parade is complete without a few sport cars making their way down the street, showing support for all of the men and women of the armed forces. Corvettes of Clarksville cleaned their cars for this 2013 Veterans Day parade; the owner and driver of this car is Mel Danish. (Author's collection.)

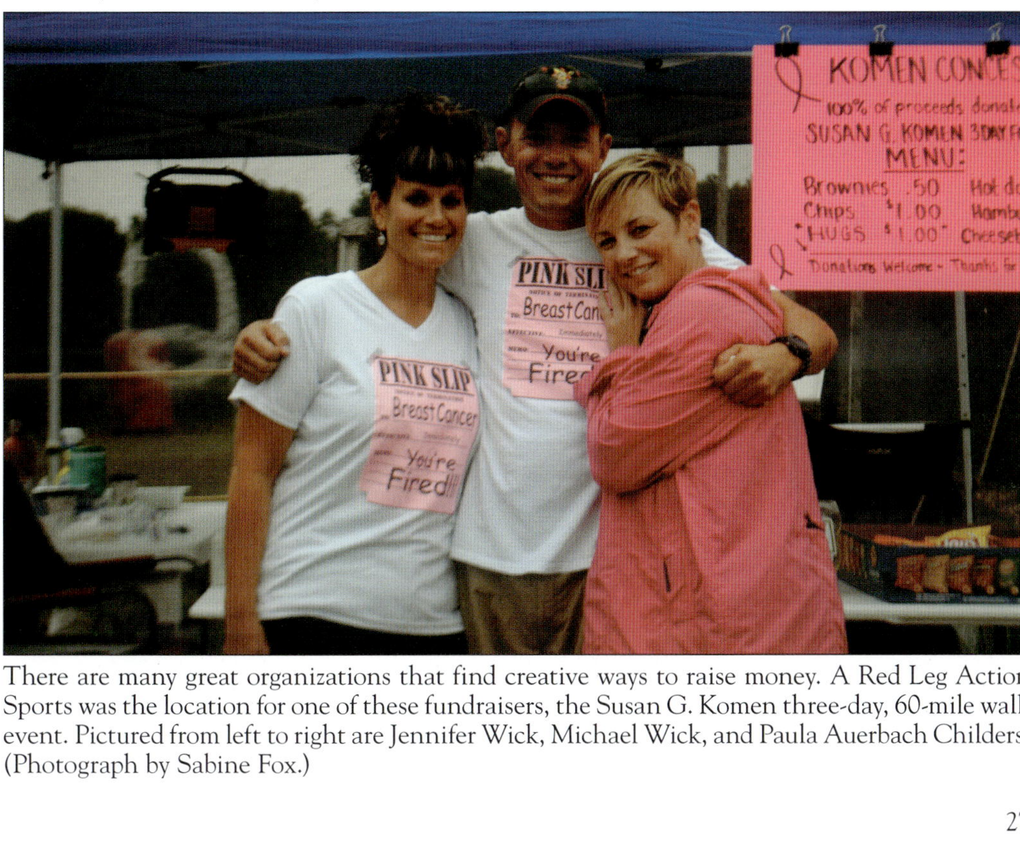

There are many great organizations that find creative ways to raise money. A Red Leg Action Sports was the location for one of these fundraisers, the Susan G. Komen three-day, 60-mile walk event. Pictured from left to right are Jennifer Wick, Michael Wick, and Paula Auerbach Childers. (Photograph by Sabine Fox.)

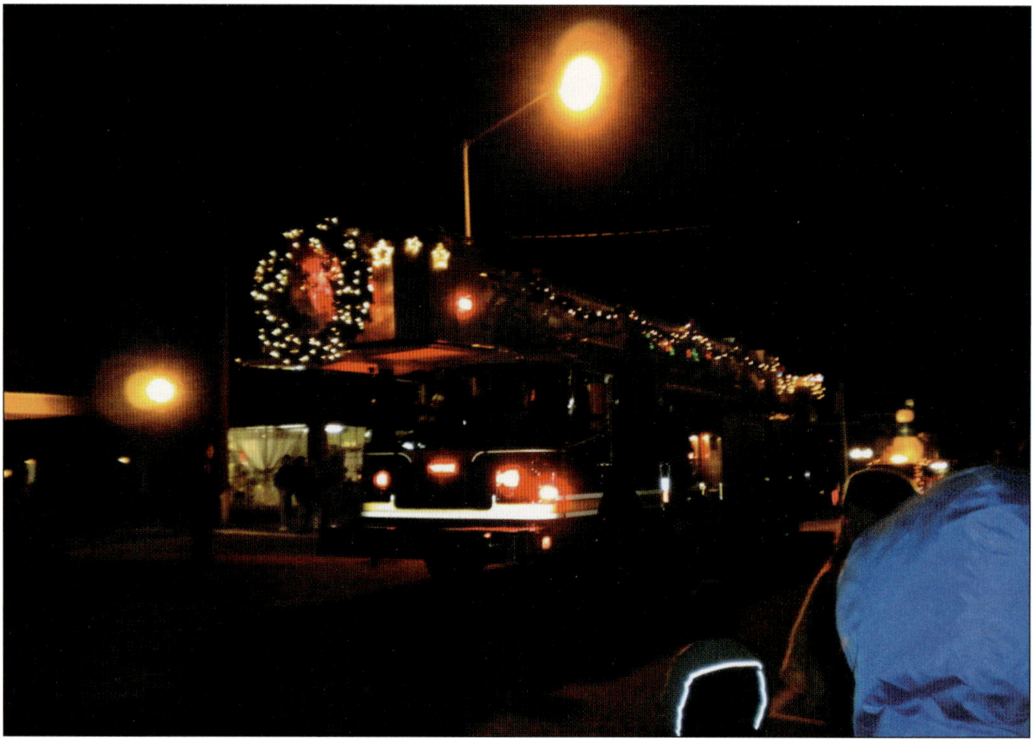

The best time to have a Christmas parade is during the nighttime hours. Above, to the sound of Christmas music, the fire truck wrapped in lights comes down the street with its horn catching the attention of spectators as they stand along the parade route. Below, members of the Montgomery County government show their festive spirit by bundling up and joining in the parade in a red truck and trailer decorated with a Christmas tree and lights. (Both photographs by Lisa Burton.)

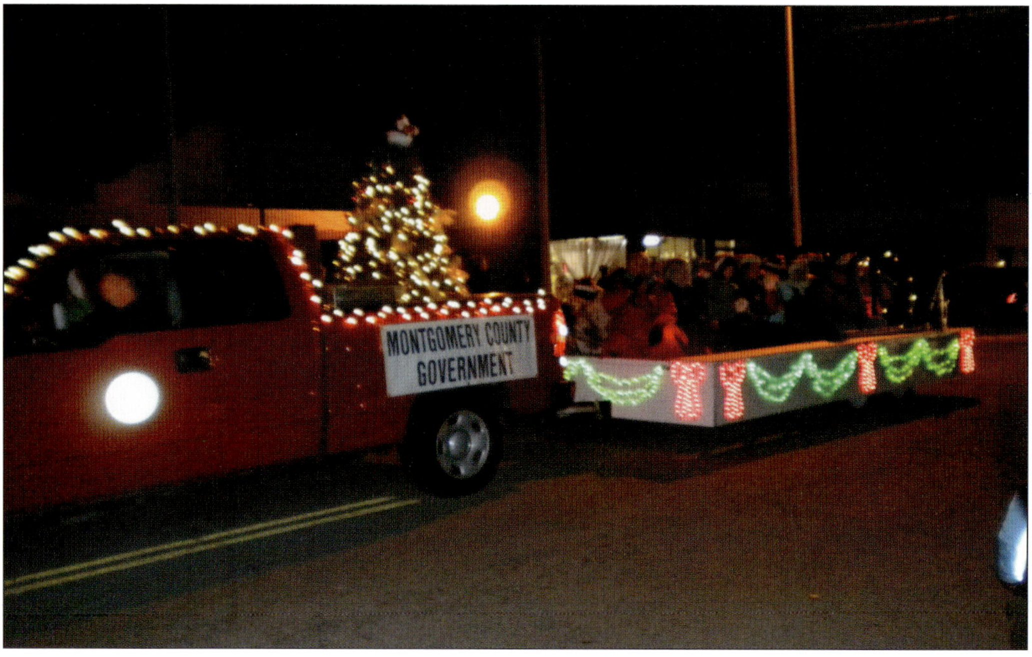

One of the most beautiful sounds during the holiday season comes from the carolers, as seen here at Hodgepodge in 2012. All the shops downtown try to bring an added touch of the holiday spirit, whether with lights and decorations, holiday sweets, or carolers outside and inside some of the businesses. During the 2012 holiday open house downtown, carolers from the Roxy spread the sounds of the season. (Courtesy of Paige King.)

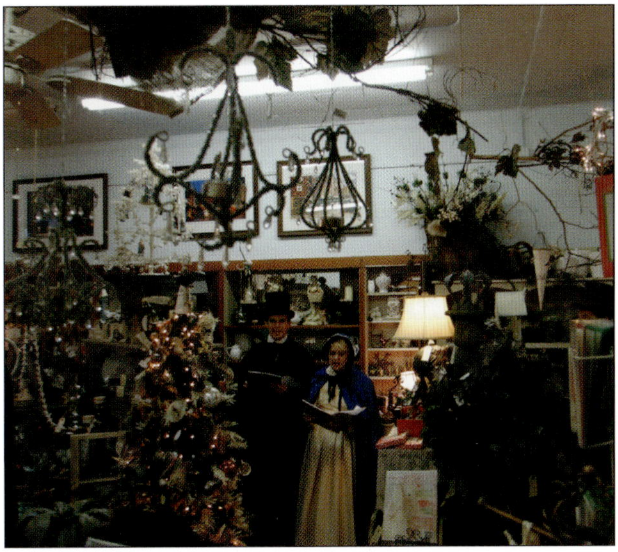

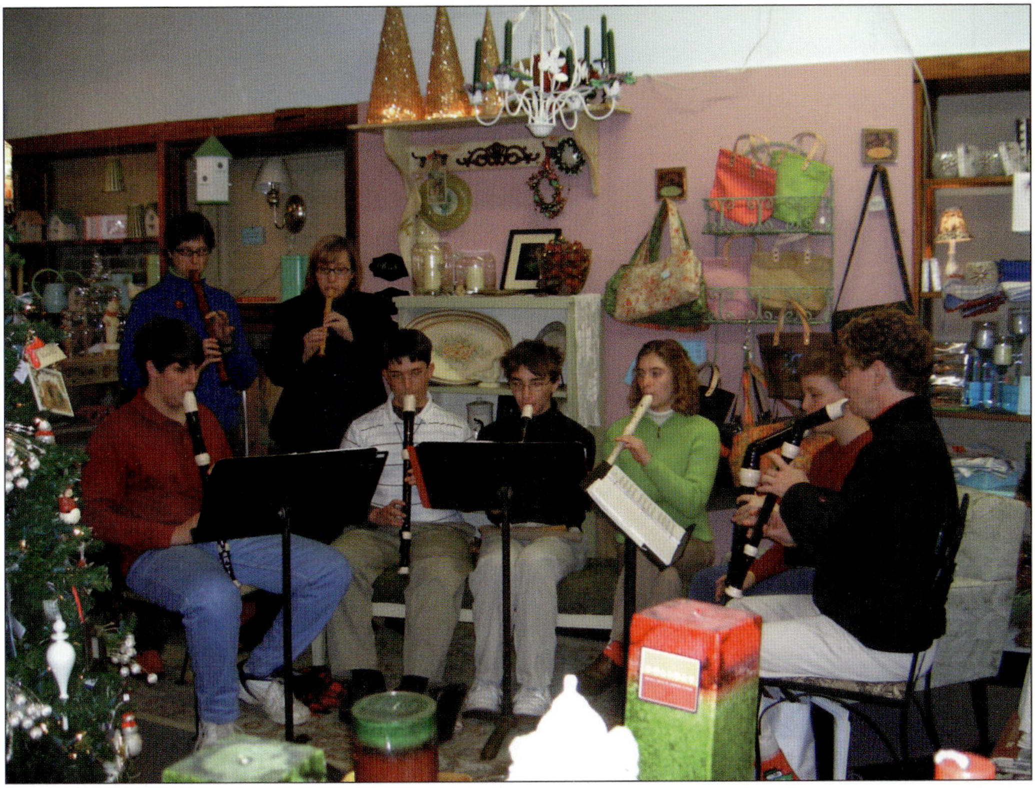

Hodgepodge continues with the holiday tradition of greeting patrons who enter the store with the sounds of the holiday season. Shop owner Paige King puts her heart into all of the holidays, and Christmas is at the top of the list. Visitors are greeted with the smell and sounds of the season and beautiful decorations. During her holiday open house in 2006, a group of performers played many holiday tunes. These students from the Clarksville Academy play their recorders with their instructor, Lisa Bishop (far right). (Courtesy of Paige King.)

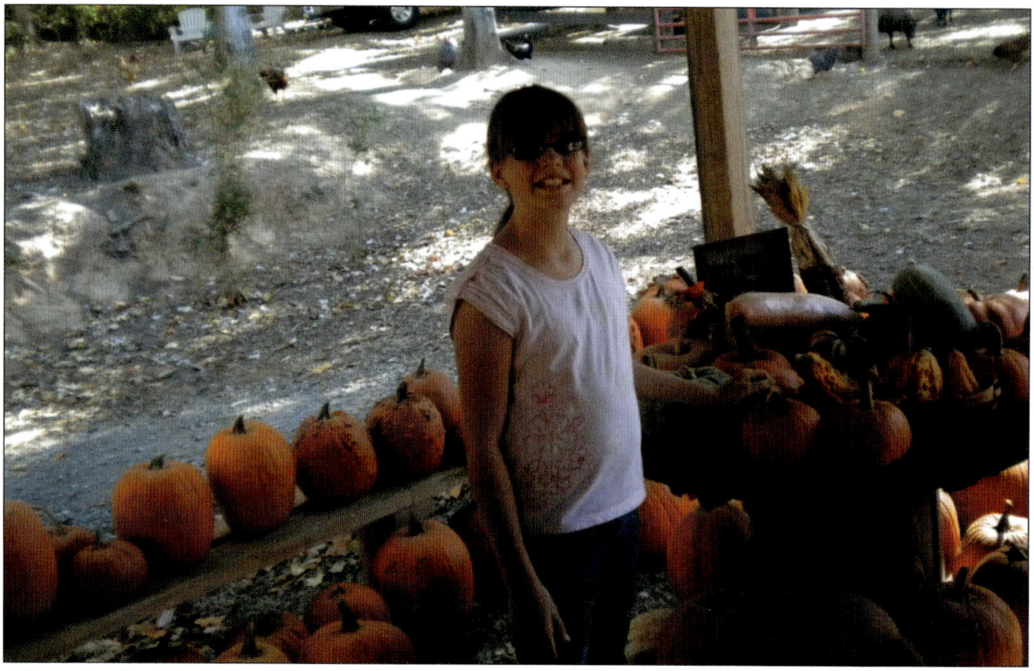

Above, Leslie Burton and her family enjoy taking a trip out to the pumpkin patch every year at the Riverview Mounds Farm. Family traditions are important to her and her family. There were so many pumpkins to choose from, but Leslie liked the smaller ones best. Below, the Burton family enjoys all of the fun to be had at the Riverview Mounds Farm on Boyd Rinehard Road. There are so many things to do, from going down slides, picking pumpkins, petting the animals, and of course watching pig racing. Pictured from left to right are four unidentified people, Sam Grimes, Charlie Grimes, Leslie Burton, Matt Burton, and Charles Moffitt. (Both photographs by Lisa Burton.)

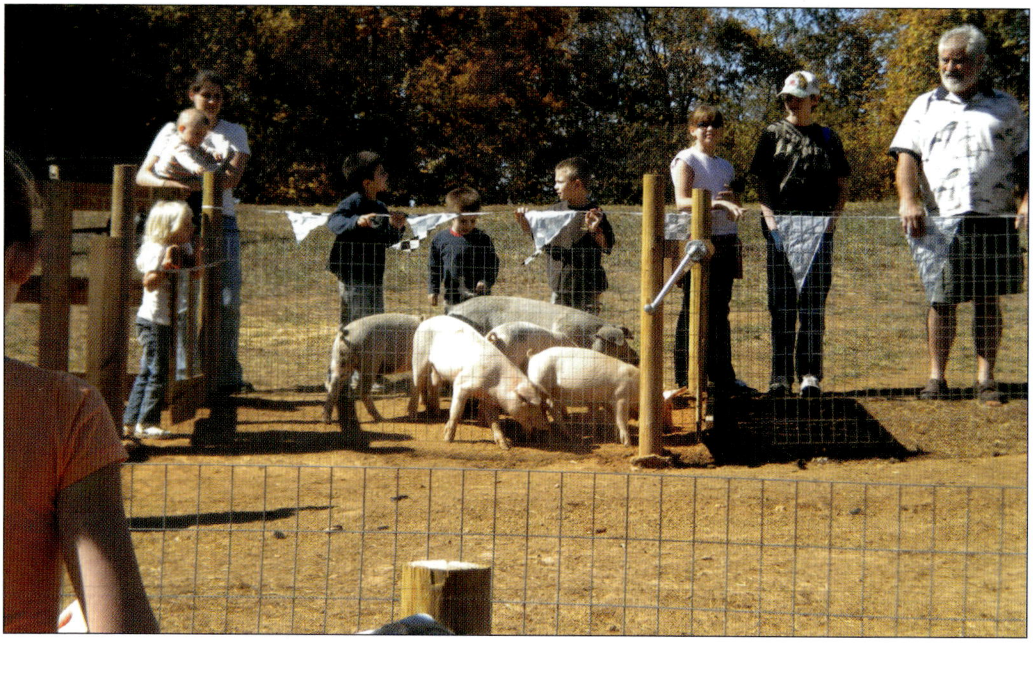

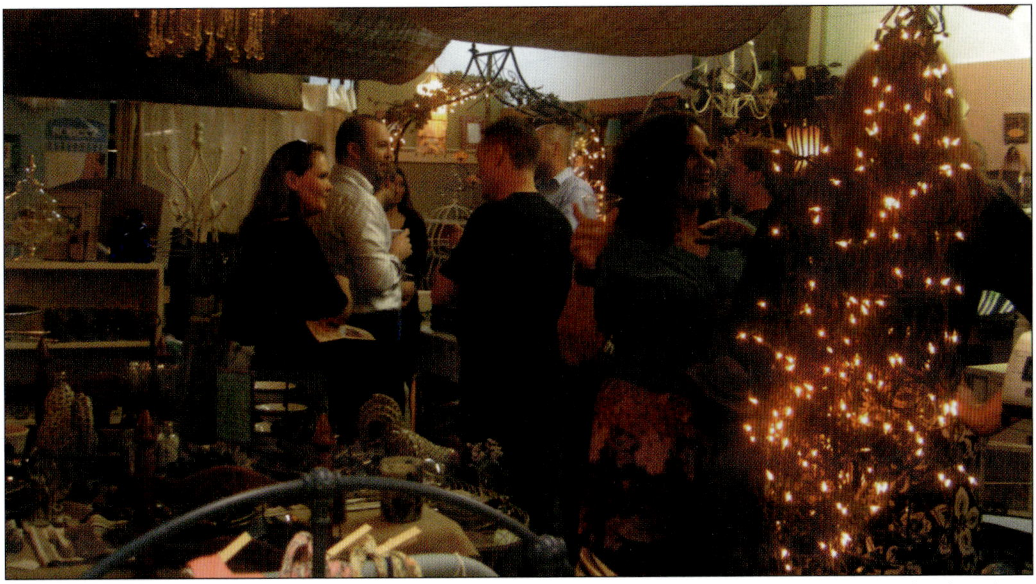

There are many artistic members of the Clarksville community, and the best way to display their talent is with the Art Walk. As seen above during one such event, patrons not only have the opportunity to stroll up and down Franklin Street and Strawberry Alley, they are also welcomed into many of the stores. This group has stopped in Hodgepodge, where shoppers can always find something in the well-designed, creative space. King offers a wide variety of home-decoration ideas and pieces with just the right "welcome home" touch. Below, local artist Reisa Peters is not only displaying her beautiful pieces of artwork, she is also creating a new piece on Strawberry Alley. (Both courtesy of Paige King.)

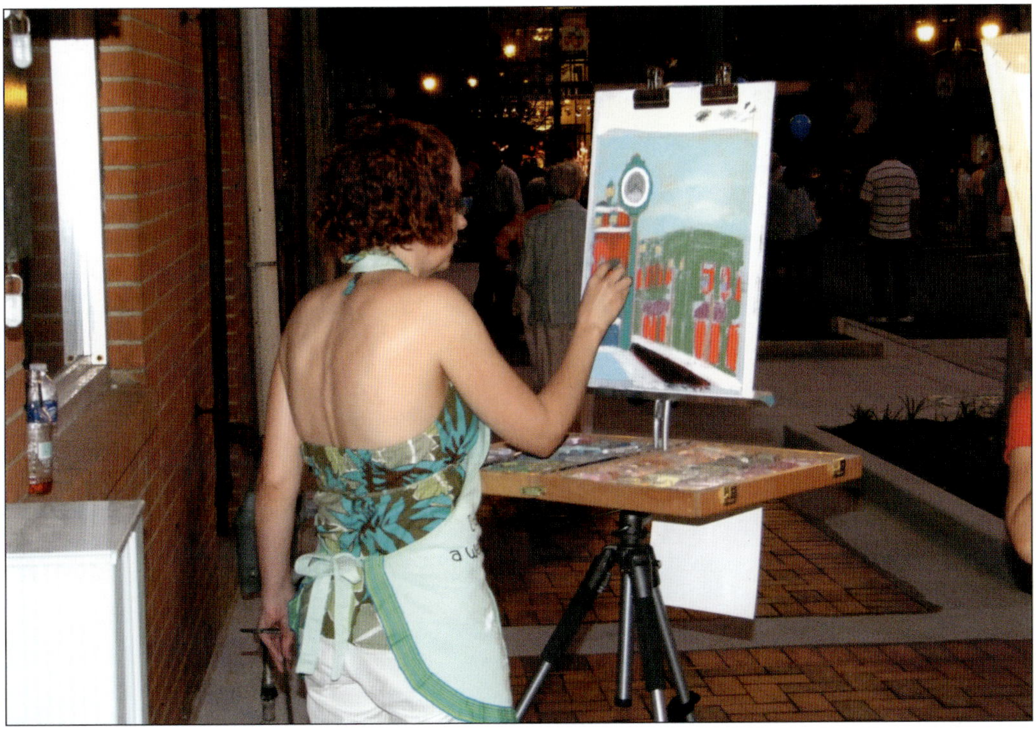

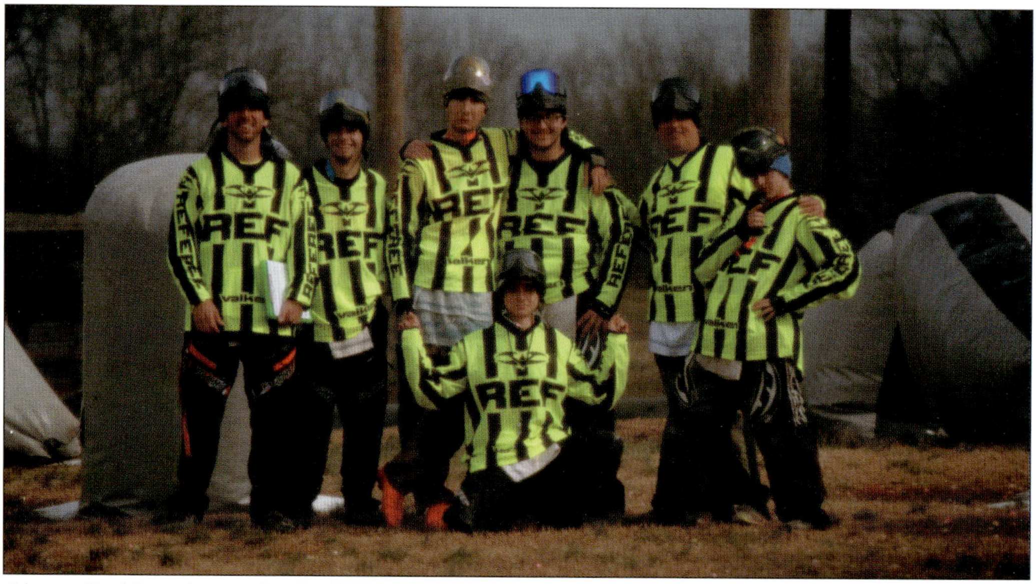

Above, Red Leg Action Sports has been around for many years and has had a few name changes, but it remains under the same owner, Chris Geiger, who considers all those who play to be like family. As with any sport, there are referees in paintball who are well trained to make calls during the games. Pictured from left to right are Jamie Lee, Liam Carreon, Dean Bechard, Kevin Haystack Nelson, Edward Fox, and Patrick Whalen, with Dalton Quinn kneeling in front. As seen below, there are numerous teams that come out and play; some prefer woodsball, while others are more focused on speedball games. Included in this group photograph are Christian Hollis, Cory Crockett, Andy Young, Edward Fox, Jamie Lee, Steve Carreon, Josh Ohler, Robert Payne, Sean Poole, Dominic Garcia, Cody Rockwood, Chance Peifer, Greg Maynard, Kevin McDonough, Tim Abair, Chris Geiger, and Zach Eby. (Both photographs by Sabina Fox.)

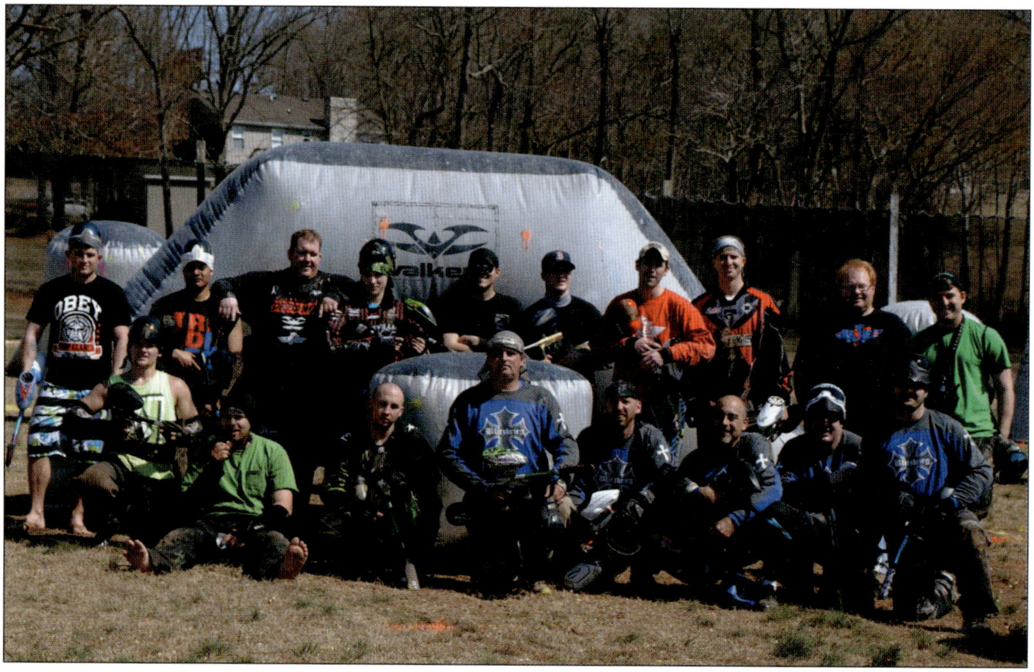

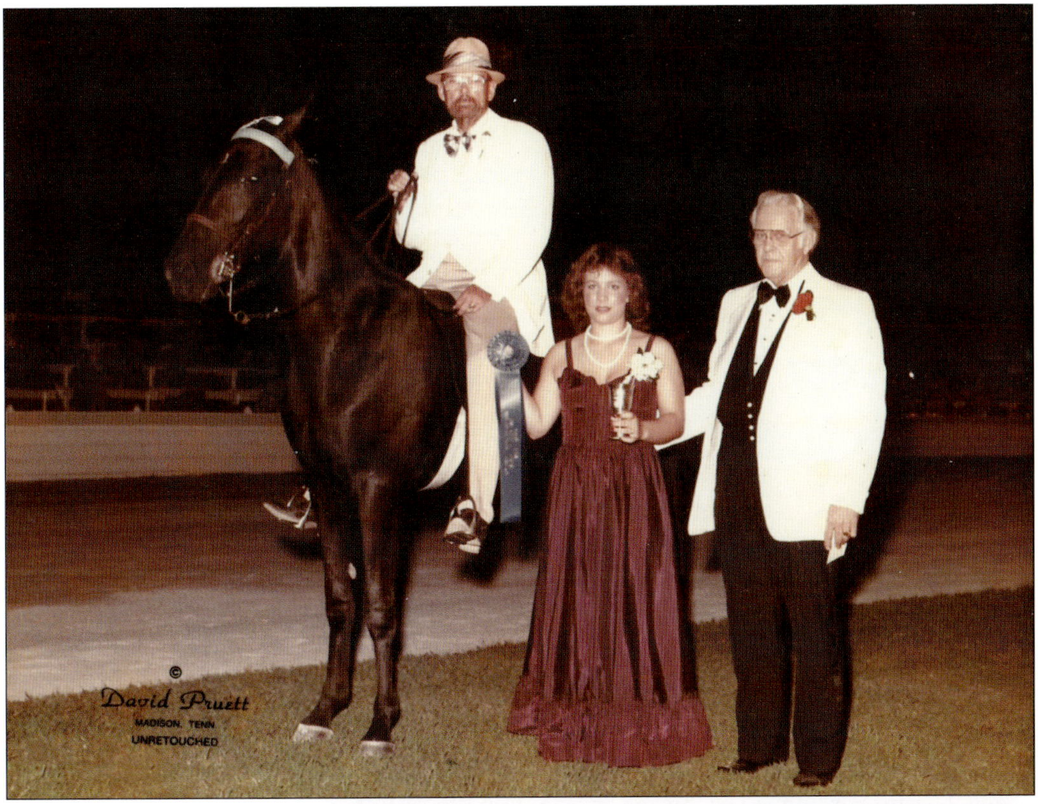

Above, W.B. Allen (left) and Darcy Hartz of Clarksville are at a horse show for Tennessee walking horses; they took first place in this 1984 event. At right, Darcy Hartz is proudly riding and showing Go Boy's Greater Glory during a 1980 Tennessee walkers horse show. (Both courtesy of Amelia Hartz.)

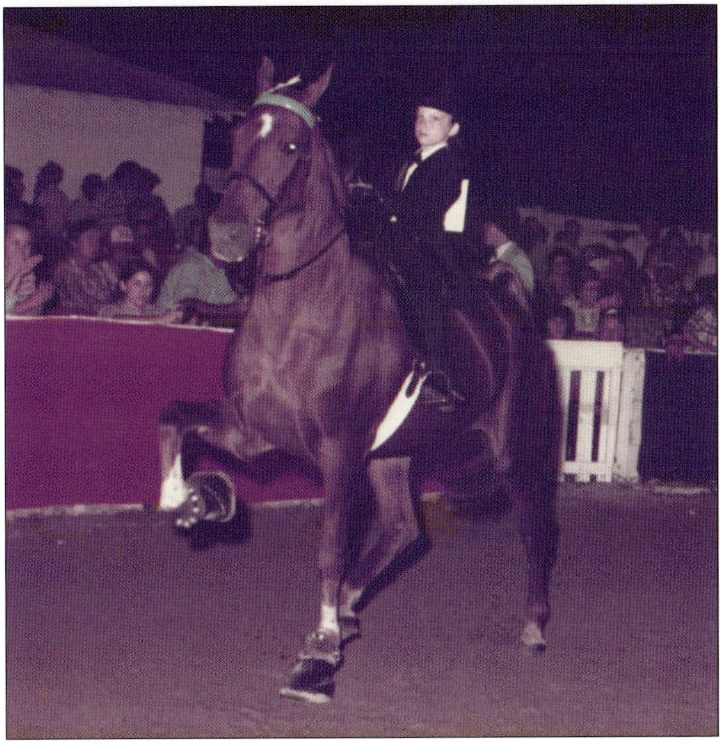

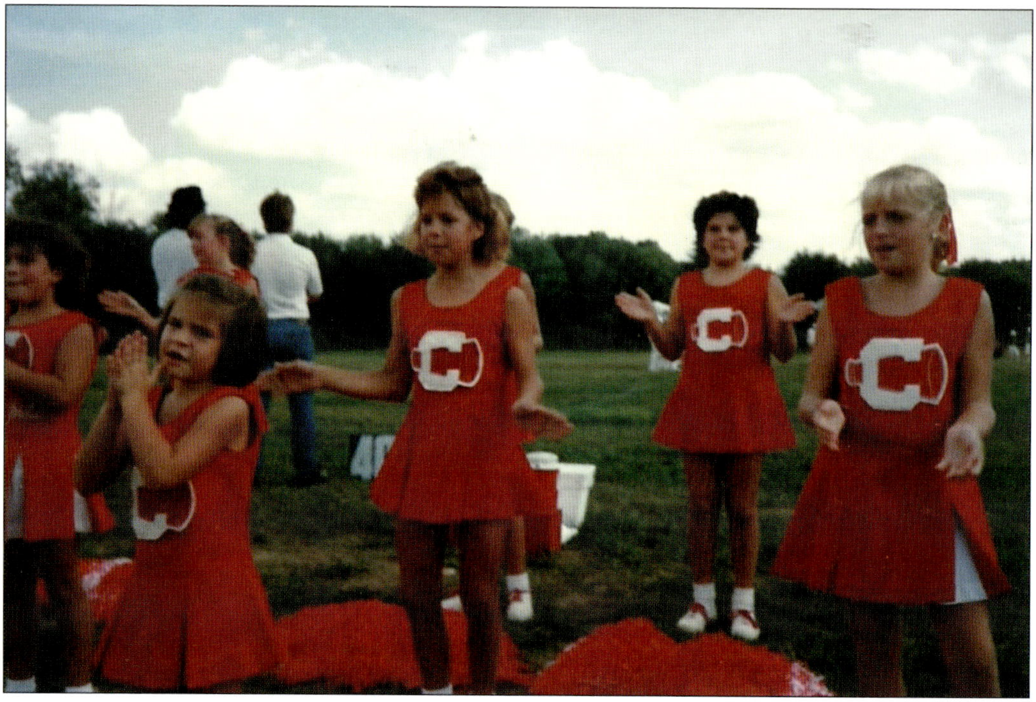

During a 1985 recreation league game at the local fairgrounds, the Cowboys cheerleaders are seen cheering, clapping, and bringing some extra spirit to the game. Pictured among the group are Kristie Rosson, Emily Hartz, Ann Halliburton, and Carrie Hartz. (Courtesy of Amelia Hartz.)

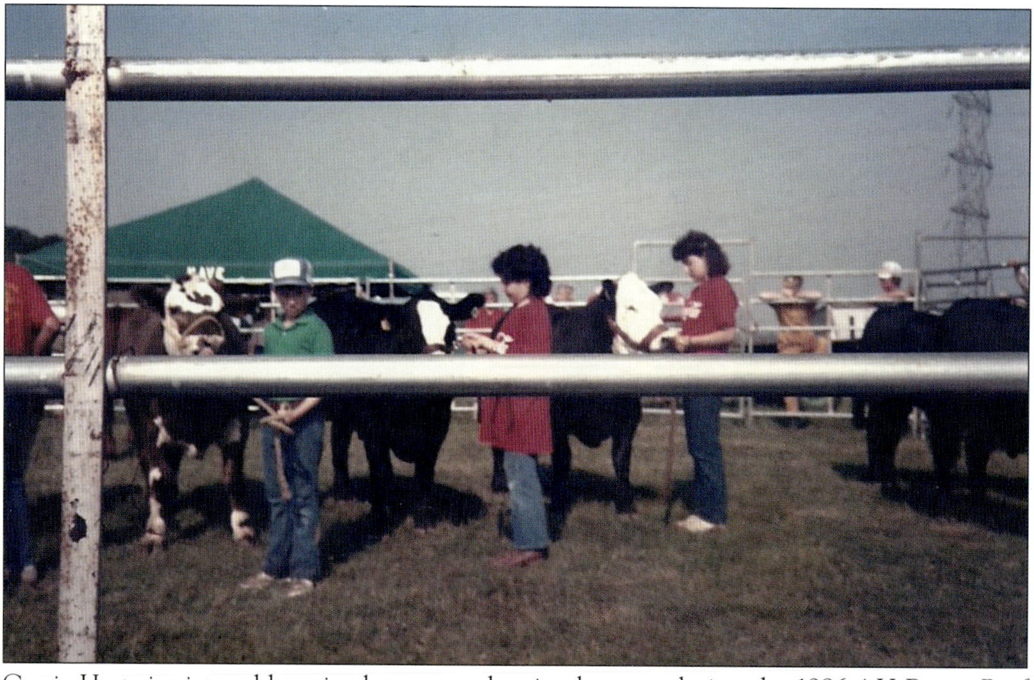

Carrie Hartz is pictured here in the center, showing her cow during the 1986 4-H Better Beef Show. (Courtesy of Amelia Hartz.)

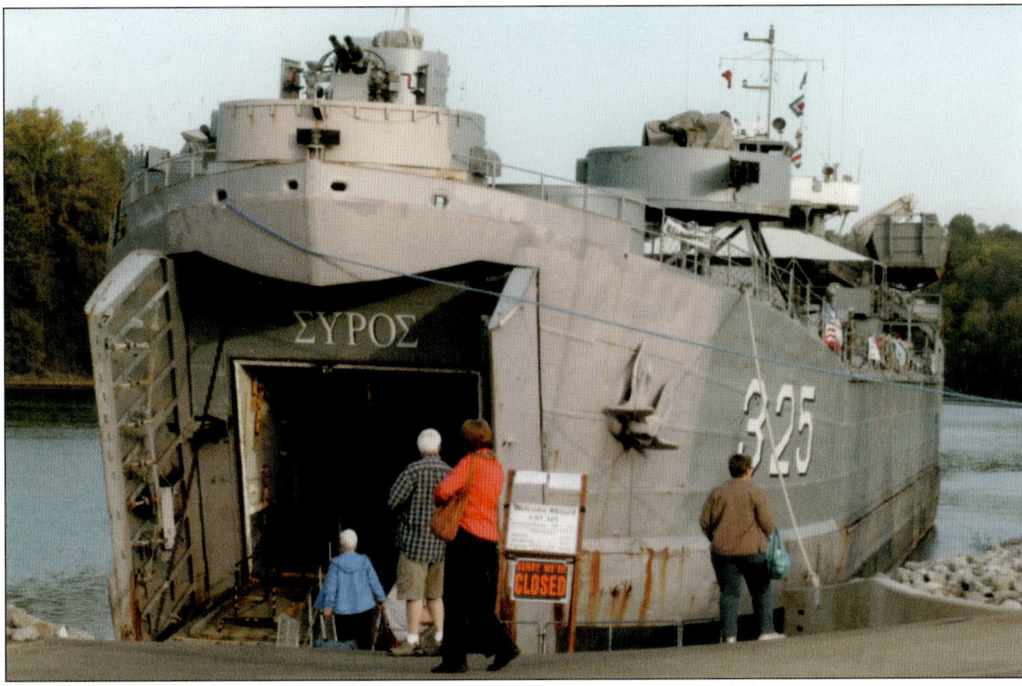

In September 2012, McGregor Park off Riverside Drive had a floating memorial museum dock along the shore. The World War II amphibious vessel LST-325 Navy ship (LST stands for "landing ship tank") was used during the D-Day invasion. Visitors were allowed aboard to tour, ask questions, and take many pictures. Returning to its home in Evansville, Indiana, the vessel ran aground in Lake Barkley, and a major effort was required to free it. (Photograph by Billyfrank Morrison.)

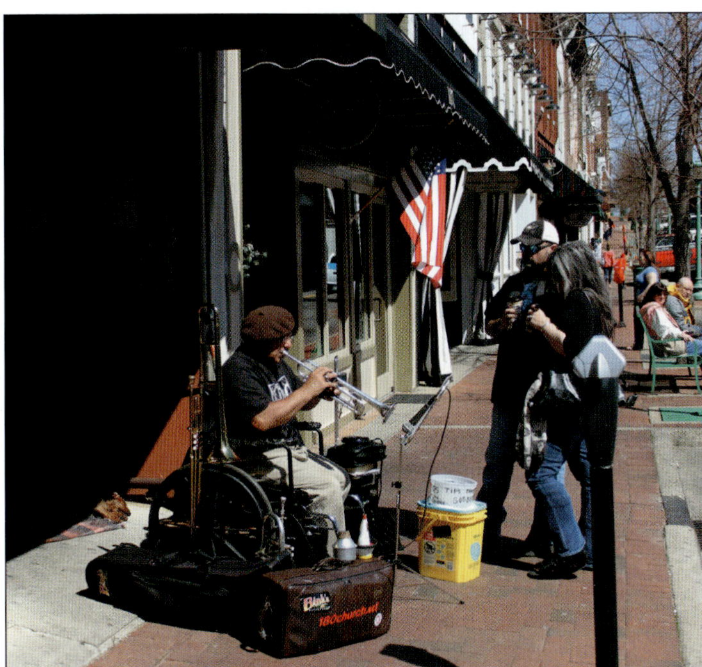

Thanks to the downtown-redevelopment project, there are many wonderful places to visit. On any given afternoon, one can find shoppers strolling through the many businesses or even be lucky enough to hear regular entertainer Ron Michaels playing his trumpet. (Author's collection.)

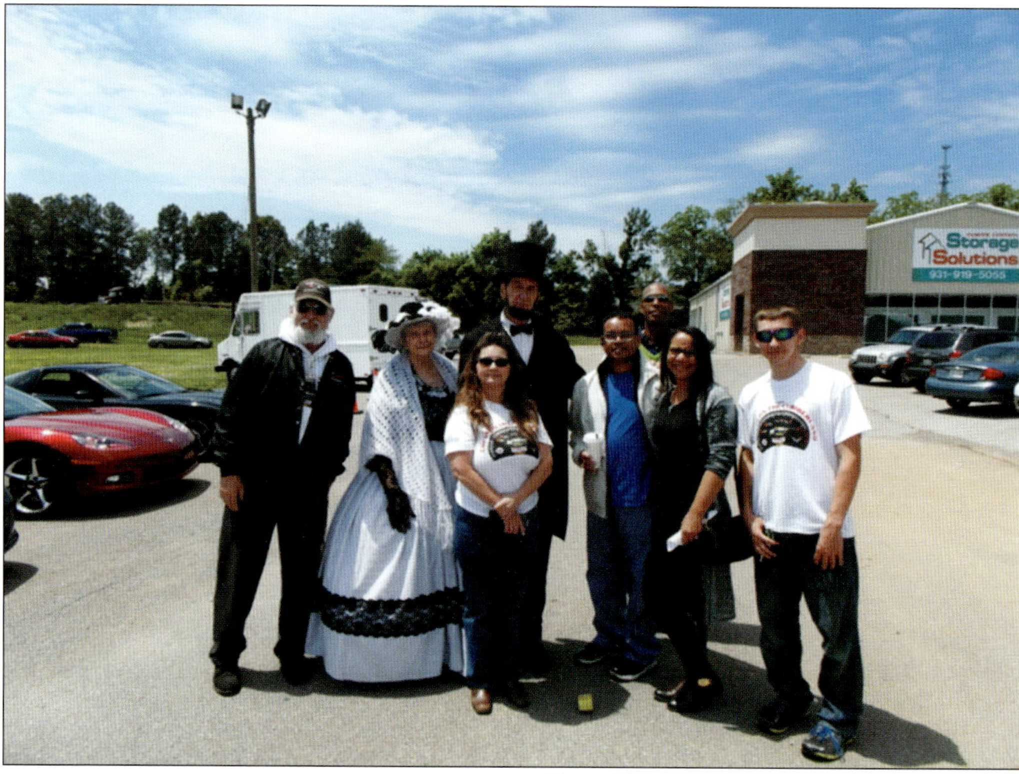

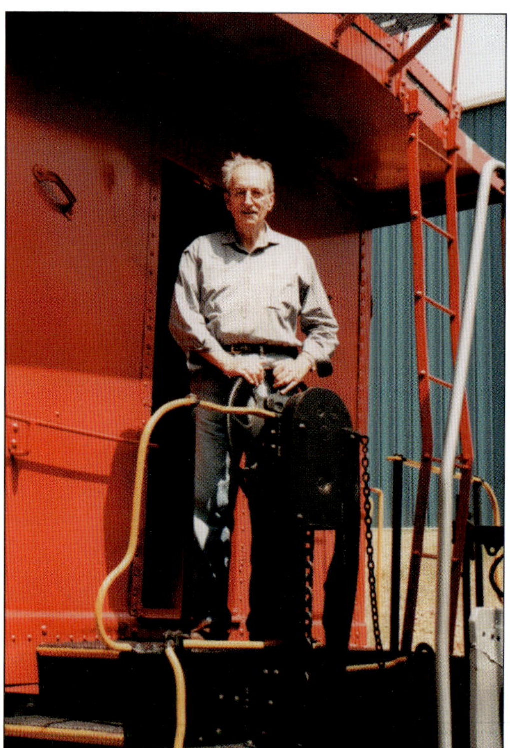

Above, Corvettes of Clarksville supports many deserving organizations and causes throughout the Clarksville community. Men and women in the armed forces are given wounded warrior rides to the Veterans Day parade. This event is for foster-care awareness, which took place in May 2014 at the LEAP plaza on Wilma Rudolph Boulevard. Those who attended enjoyed refreshments, games, face painting, an inflatable bounce house, and a demonstration of the Clarksville Zombie Hunters paintball hayride trailer. Among those pictured are Bill Bartan, Betsy Reese, and Hunter Reese. At left, during a 1996 visit to the L&N Train Station, Dr. Martin has stopped to by to visit with friends and pose for a quick photograph on the vintage caboose. Dr. Martin played a role with the restorations of the L&N Train Station. (Above, courtesy of Clarksville Corvette Club; at left, photograph by Benita Martin, courtesy of MCHS.)

Two

Views in Clarksville

It is true that over time everyone changes, but what about the scenery in the community? Some spots have changed completely, while others have needed just a little touch-up to remain in view. Through these years of changes, whether caused by the economy, weather, or just forgetfulness, Clarksville has always had community members who have worked to carry the past into the present. Because of their efforts, there is much to see when traveling through the community. Every town has some unusual, beautiful, new, or historical views, and Clarksville is no different. The historical variety in Clarksville includes not only buildings but also waterways and ships and railways and trains. There are also many pieces of art, statues, memorials, and some beautiful fountains throughout town. These pages capture the many views that locals have come to love.

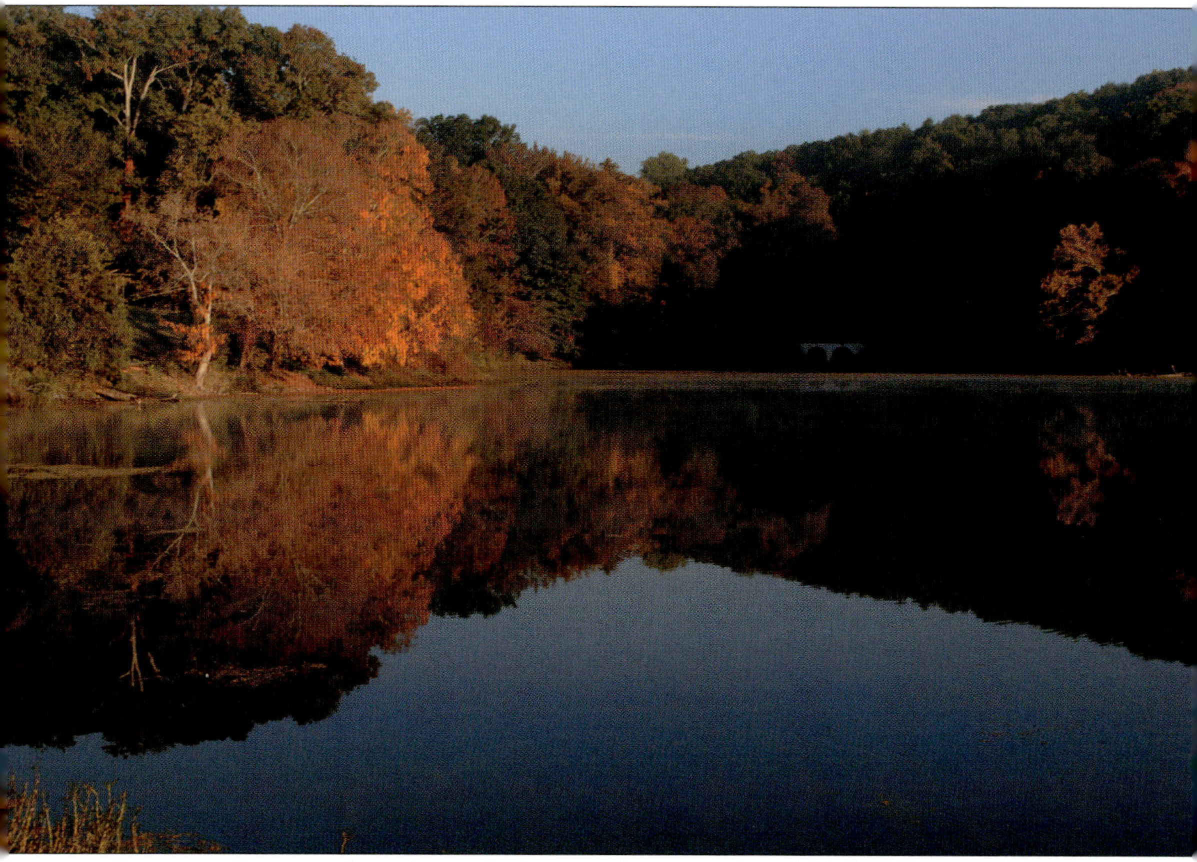

Every town has something that might be viewed as unusual, and Clarksville is not the exception to this rule. There are many beautiful things to see, including some that might not be found anywhere else, such as this breathtaking fall view overlooking the lake at Dunbar Cave. Just outside of town is Dunbar Cave State Park, where visitors can hike around and through caverns that were once mined for potassium nitrate (or saltpeter, used for gunpowder) and where live concerts were held with dancing. This was a hot spot for years, and during warmer months the cave attracted many people for many reasons. The most popular was the natural air-conditioning that the cave offered. Families would gather under overhangs for picnics and parties with music and dancing. There was also a swimming pool, a dance floor, and a bowling alley that was put in during the early 1930s. It was around this time that the Idaho Springs Hotel was built; it would later be destroyed by a fire in 1950. The pool closed in the 1960s thanks to the increase in public pools. In 2010, the park suspended public tours after a bat tested positive for white-noise syndrome. (Photograph by David Smith.)

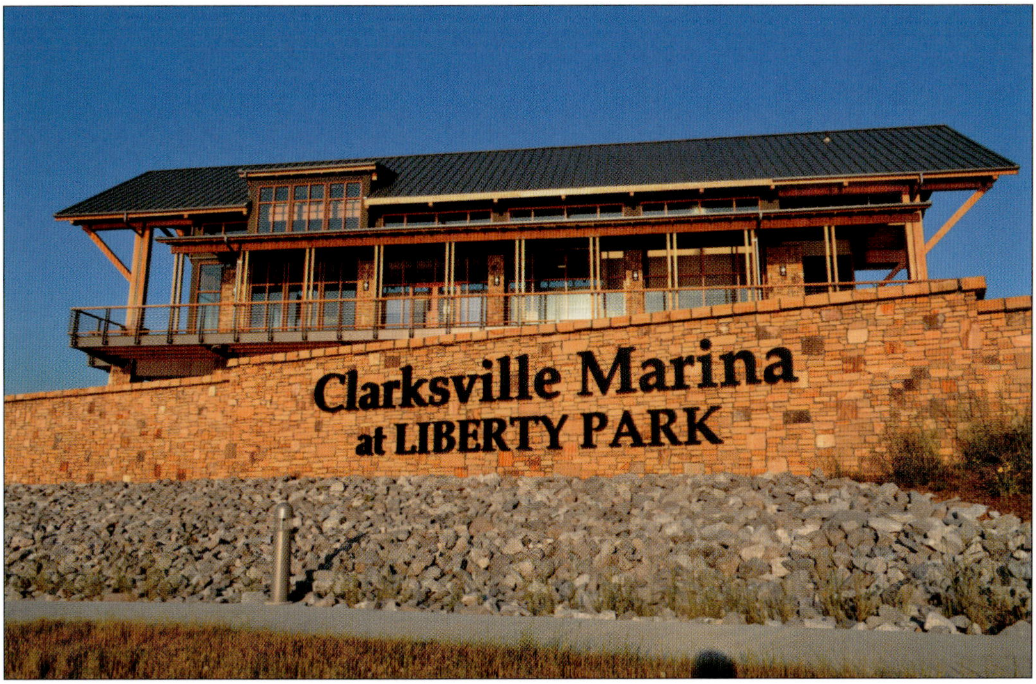

Clarksville Marina, at Liberty Park at 1190 Cumberland Drive, down by the Riverwalk, was a much-needed facility in the area. It is the perfect place for all who enjoy the outdoors and fishing. Visitors will find walking and jogging trails, biking trails, a dog park, a 10-acre fishing pond, a playground, sport fields, pavilions, and of course a four-lane boat ramp and more than 100 boat slips. Opening in 2012, it has been the host location for many family reunions, organization celebrations, and outdoor outings. (Both photographs by David Smith.)

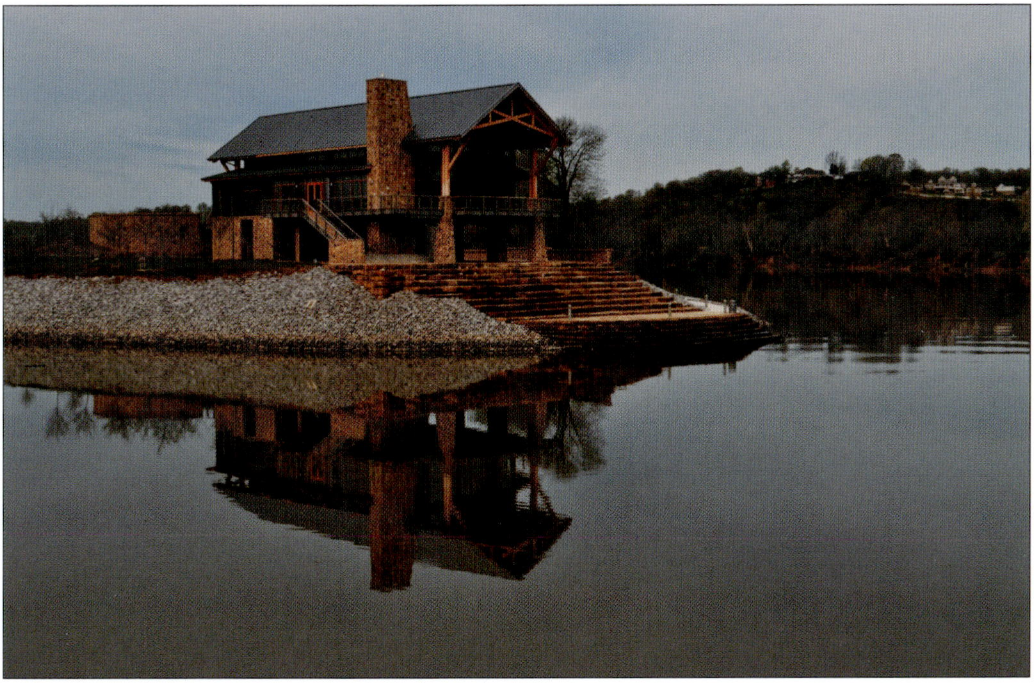

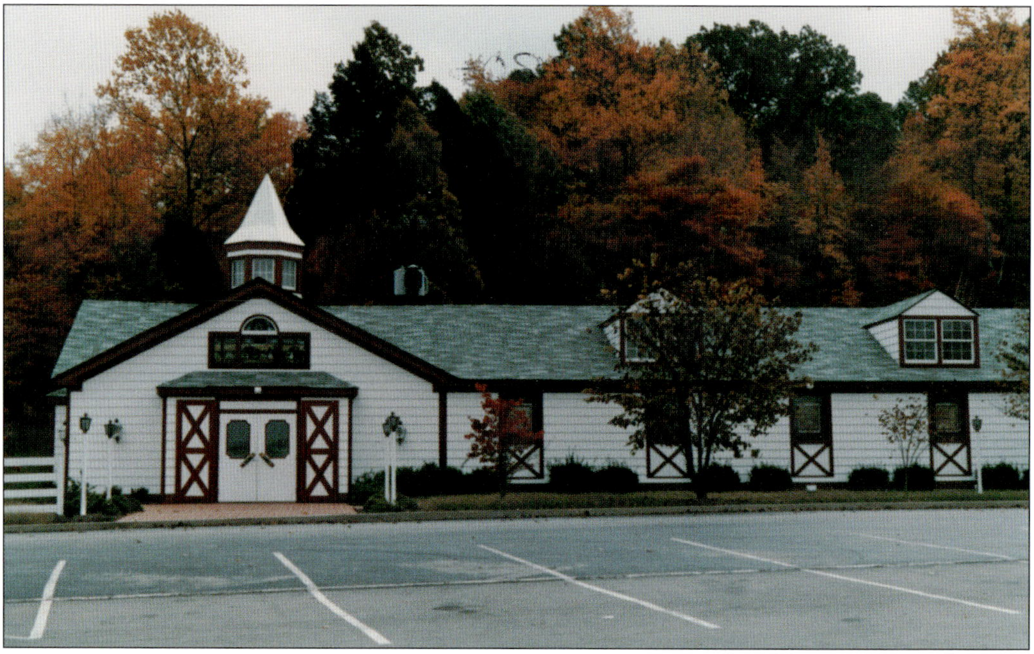

The Stables on the bypass, pictured above in 1980, was a popular place to hang out with friends and have a few drinks. Unfortunately, the Stables is no longer in business. Below, the completion of the Clarksville River Center in August 1997 was the second phase of the Cumberland Riverwalk. It is located at McGregor Park on Riverside Drive and is open every day with free admission. Inside the facility, visitors will find a permanent exhibit of the history of the Cumberland River and its aid in the development of Clarksville as a river town. (Above, courtesy of Billyfrank Morrison; below, photograph by David Smith.)

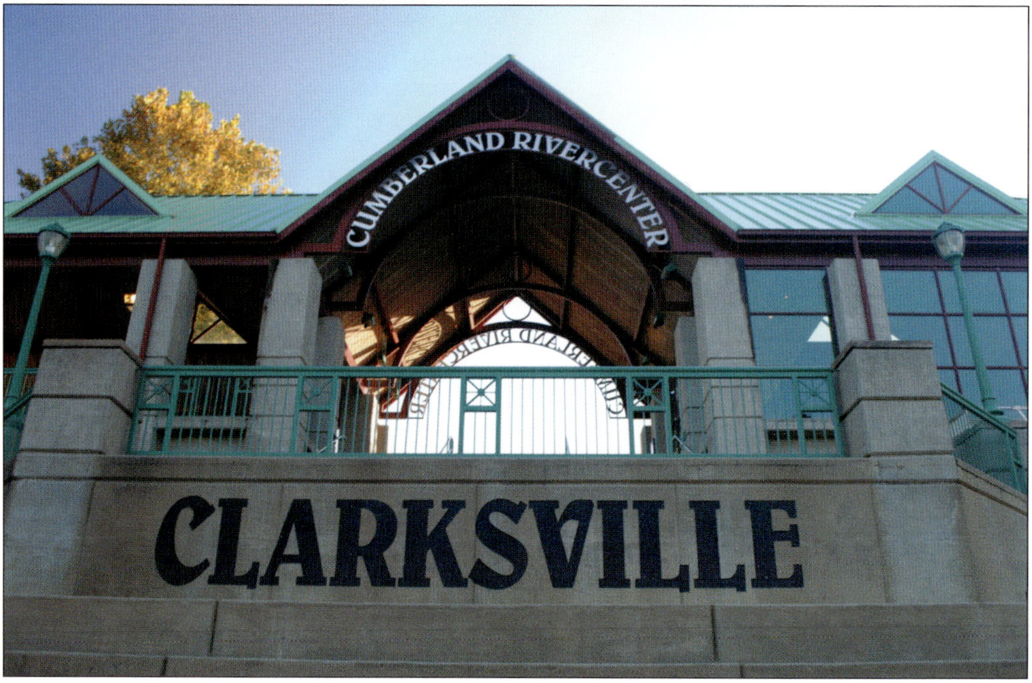

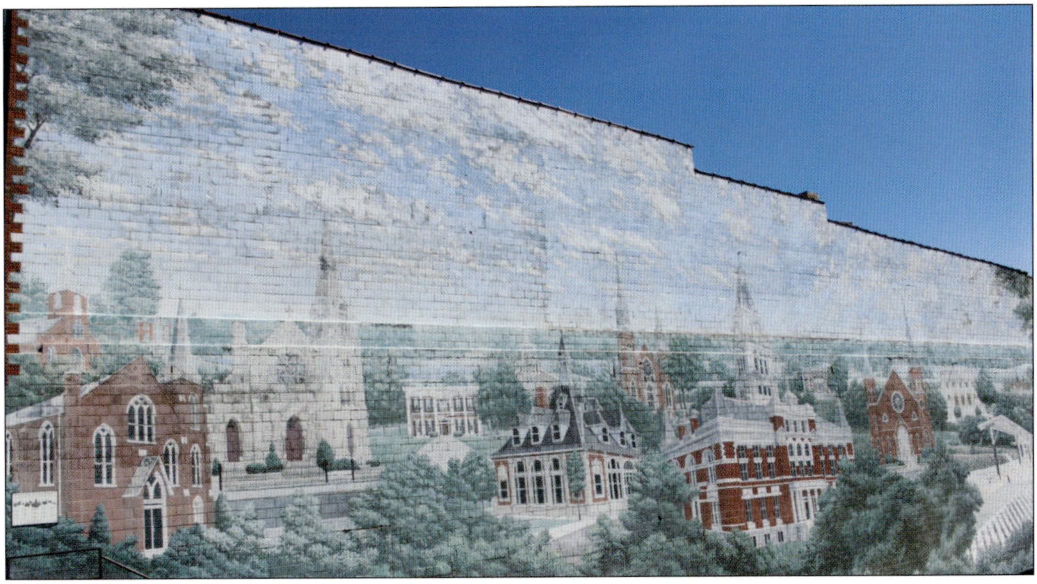

Above is one of the most photographed pieces of art in Clarksville. Titled *Bursting with Pride*, it is an eye-catching mural of historic downtown Clarksville. Local artist Ricky Deel is responsible for this informative depiction of the locations of some of Clarksville's most beautiful and historical structures, from the Smith-Trahern Mansion, constructed in 1856, to the Austin Peay State University Browning Building, built in 1927. Located next to this beautiful mural is the very informative plaque pictured below, which helps viewers name the historical buildings, find their locations on the mural, and learn some information about when they were built. (Both, author's collection.)

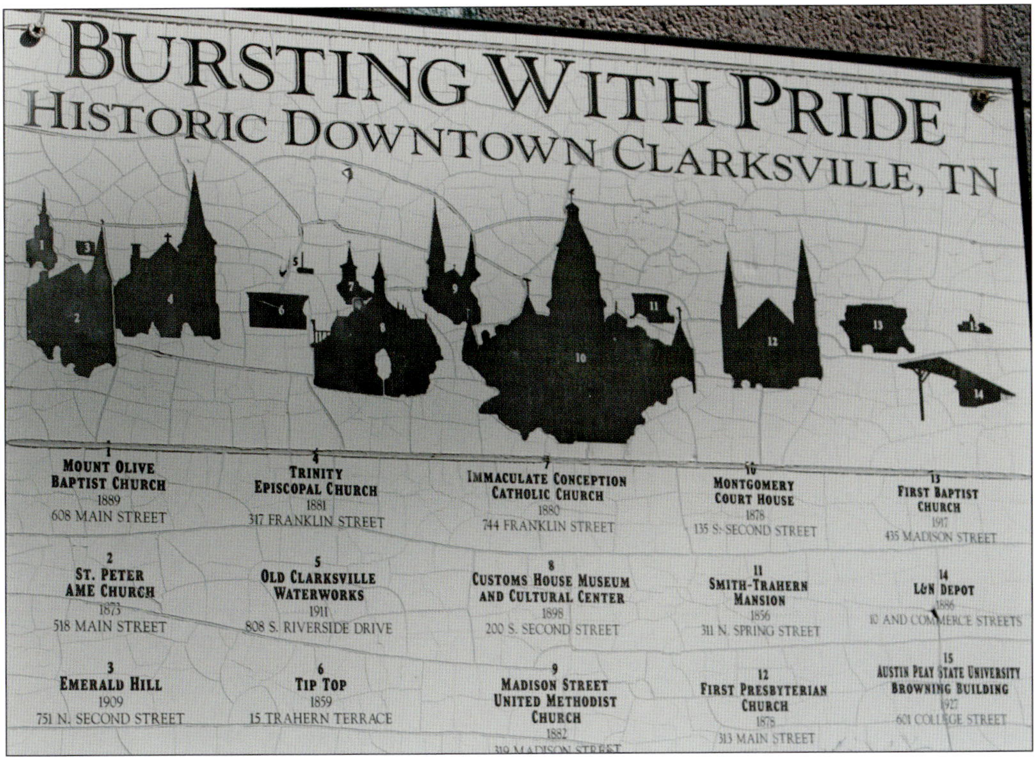

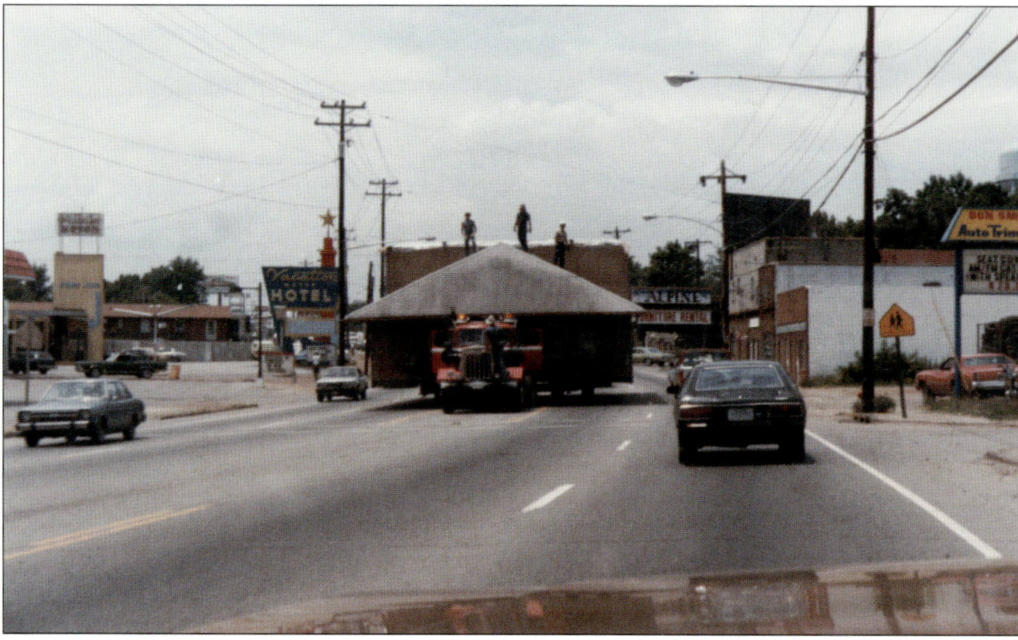

In 1980, one never knew what he or she might see while driving down the streets. Above, a house is being moved through New Providence in Clarksville. Note the men on top of the house; they were required to keep their balance while lifting phone or power lines over the roof during the move. Below, it is obvious that creativity is a necessity in advertisement. What better way to run for school office then to campaign on a local school bus: "Voted Dave Cook for School Board." (Both photographs by Billyfrank Morrison.)

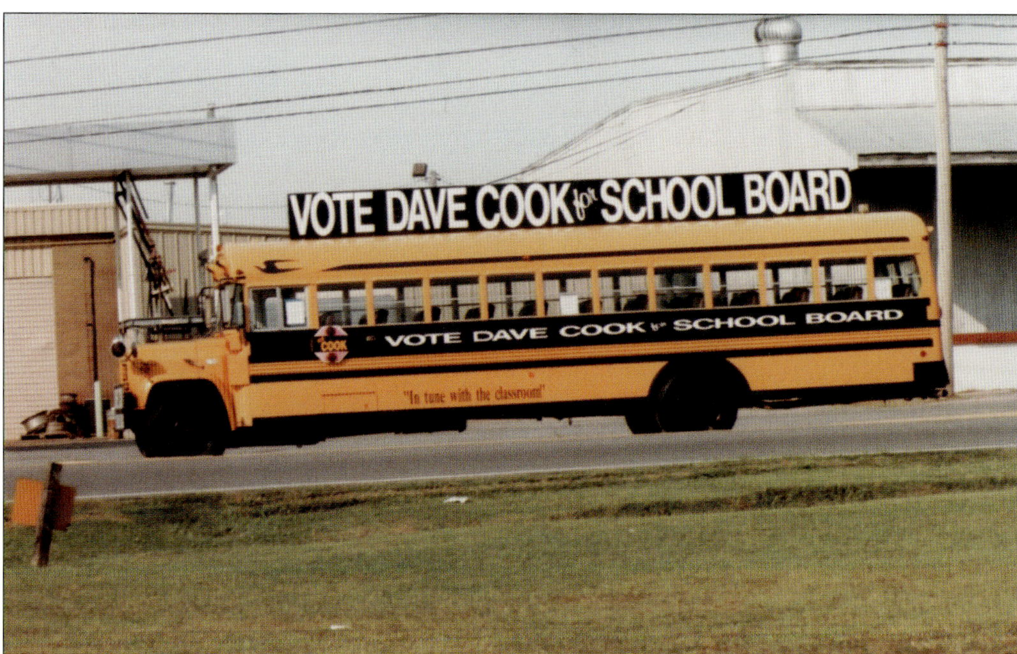

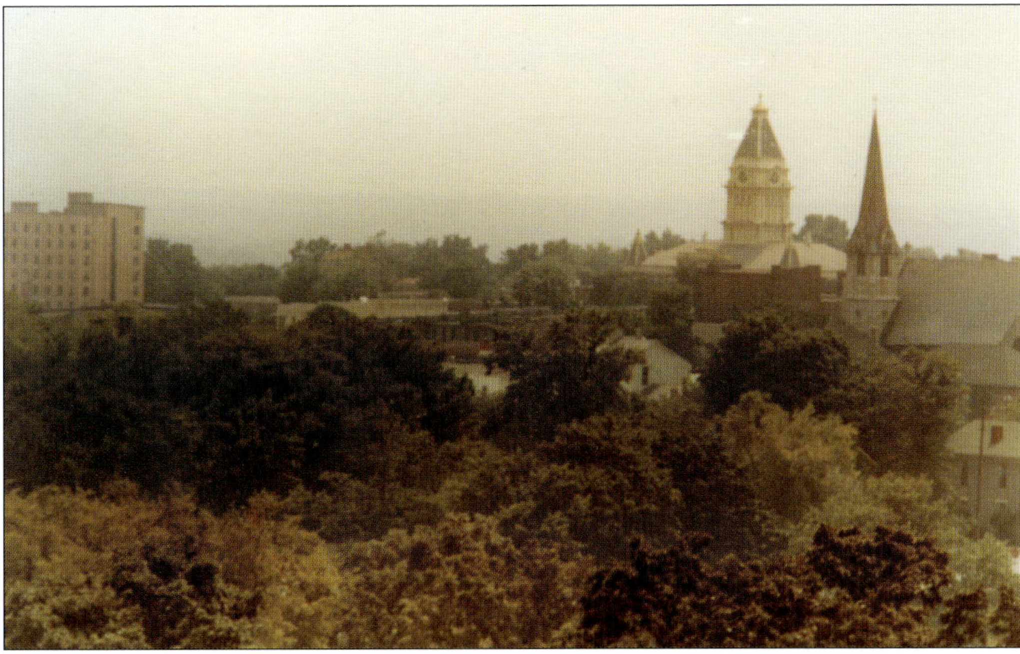

This 1969 photograph was taken from a perfect location to capture a view of the building tops. Some of the structures are recognizable: Riverfront Hotel is off to the left, the top of the Montgomery County Courthouse is in the center, and to the right is the Trinity Episcopal Church on Franklin Street. (Courtesy of Austin Peay State University.)

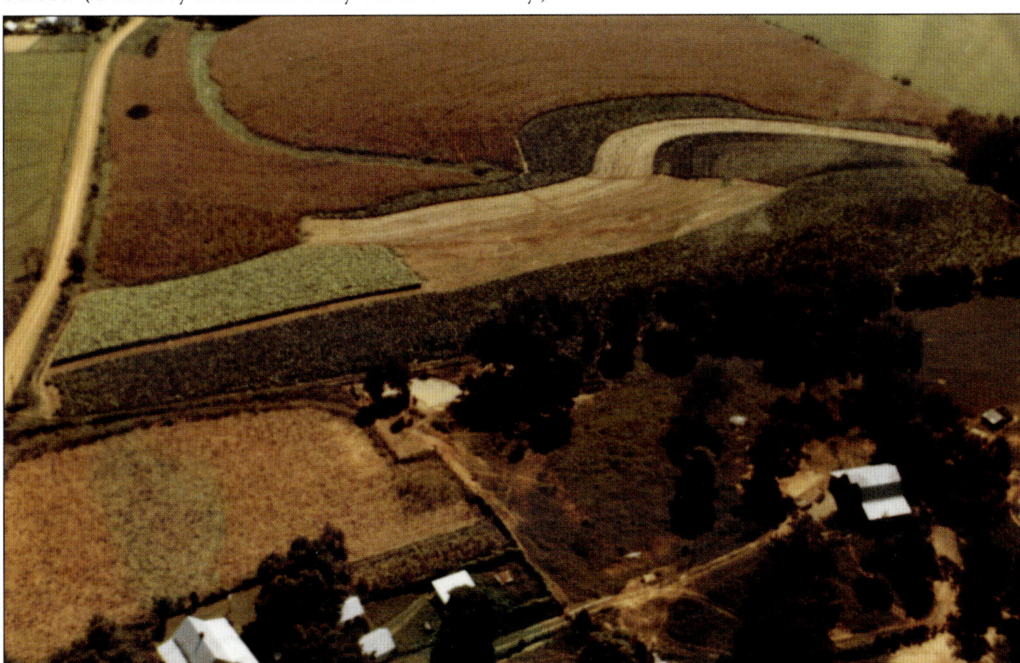

This is an aerial shot of some of the farmland in Clarksville. Farms not only grew corn, mustard seeds, and soybeans, but also tobacco. One thing that has not changed over the years is the farming industry out in Clarksville's countryside. (Courtesy of Austin Peay State University.)

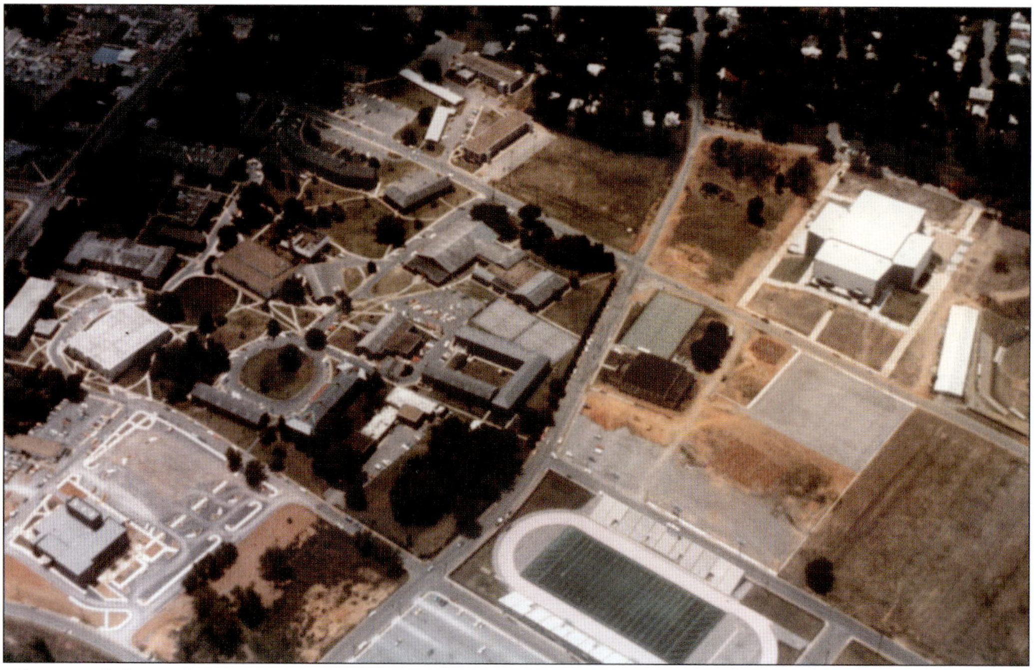

The aerial shot of Austin Peay State University above shows a good view of what was then known as Municipal Stadium. The stadium opened in 1946 with 5,500 seats; it would not be until 1970 that APSU obtained one-third ownership of the stadium. APSU became the sole owner of the stadium after the 1993 season, upon which the school renovated the facility by placing artificial turf on the field, adding an eight-lane track, and changing the name to Governors Stadium, as it is known today. Shown are the completed, updated stadium, some new parking lots on the campus grounds, and the ever-growing campus. It is easy to see in this photograph the multiple sidewalks on the campus connecting buildings. Below is a nice bird's-eye view of Austin Peay State University, taken in the late 1960s, that shows the growing campus, College Street running in front of the university, and Governors Stadium, among other features. Behind the university are rising, muddy waters of the Little Fork River. (Both courtesy of Austin Peay State University.)

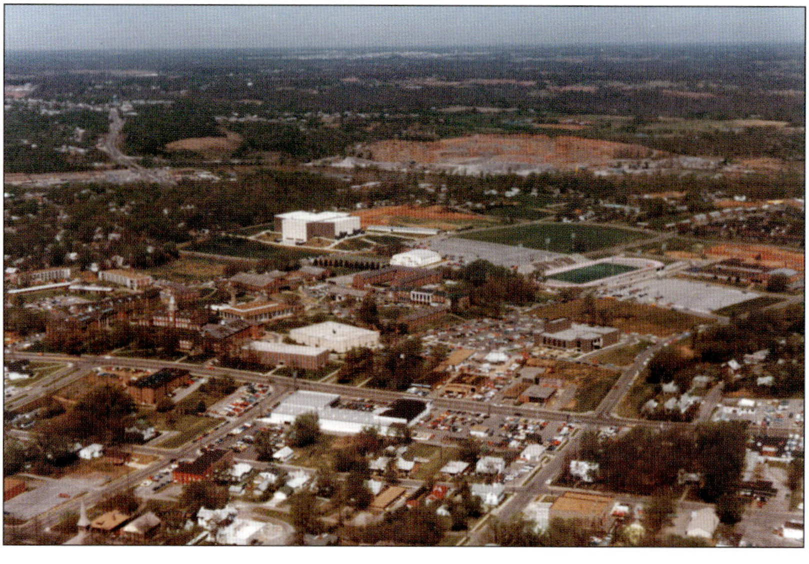

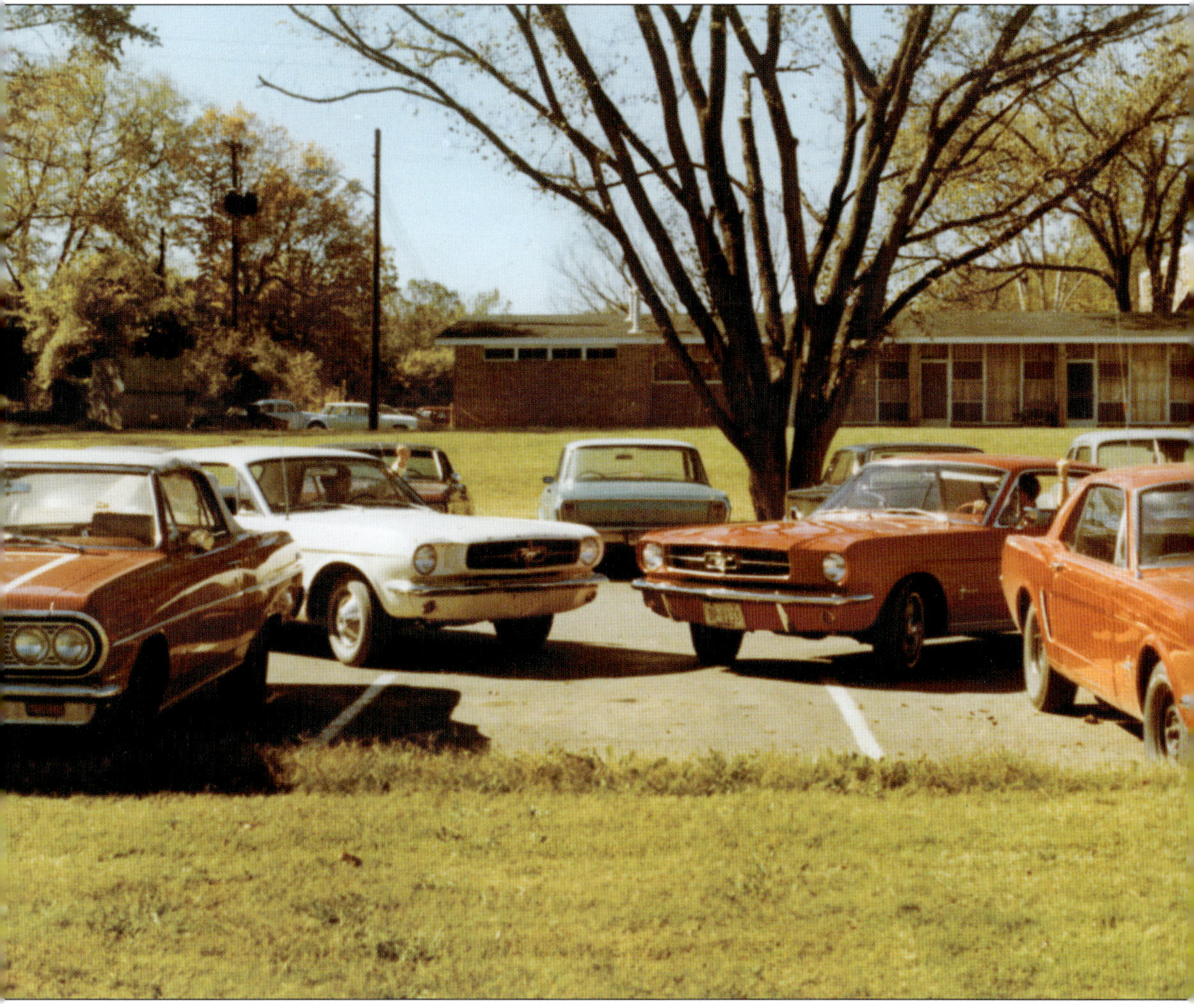

Some things never change, including the lack of parking spaces at Austin Peay State University. Here, two unidentified students desire the same parking space in their 1968 Mustangs. This photograph was taken in October 1969 by a fellow student. Today, students still battle over parking spaces on campus. (Courtesy of Austin Peay State University.)

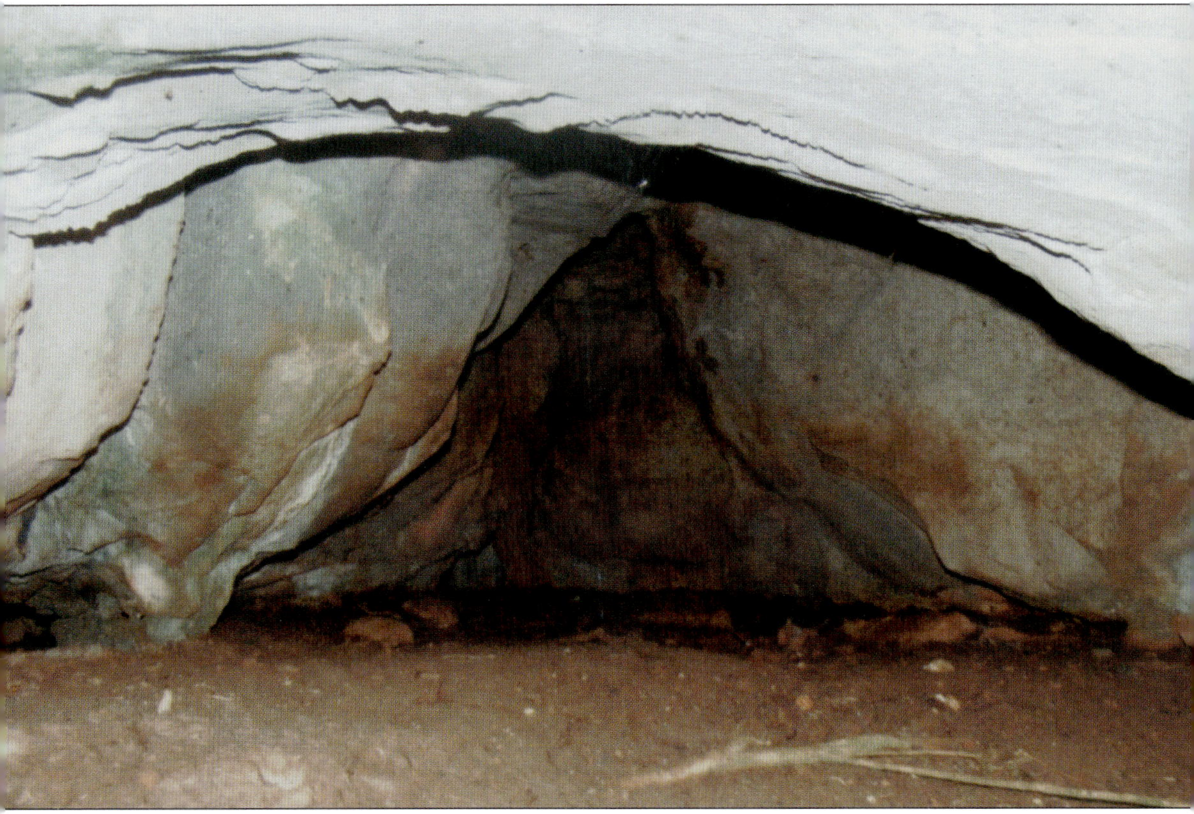

Some people might remember the stories of the Gus Hite and his infamous train robbery. Hite was the cousin of the Frank and Jessie James, and he wanted to emulate his cousins' career paths. He had many aliases, including "Babe," "Hall," and "Red Horse," and he was a feared robber and murderer. In 1897, he killed officer James Green, and the *Clarksville Times* reported that he escaped the Tennessee State Penitentiary while serving 15 years for his crimes. This image shows the cave that served as the hideout after one of his criminal acts. It is found on the Garner Griffey farm in Clarksville that was incorporated into the Fort Campbell Military Reserve. (Courtesy of Amelia Allan Hertz.)

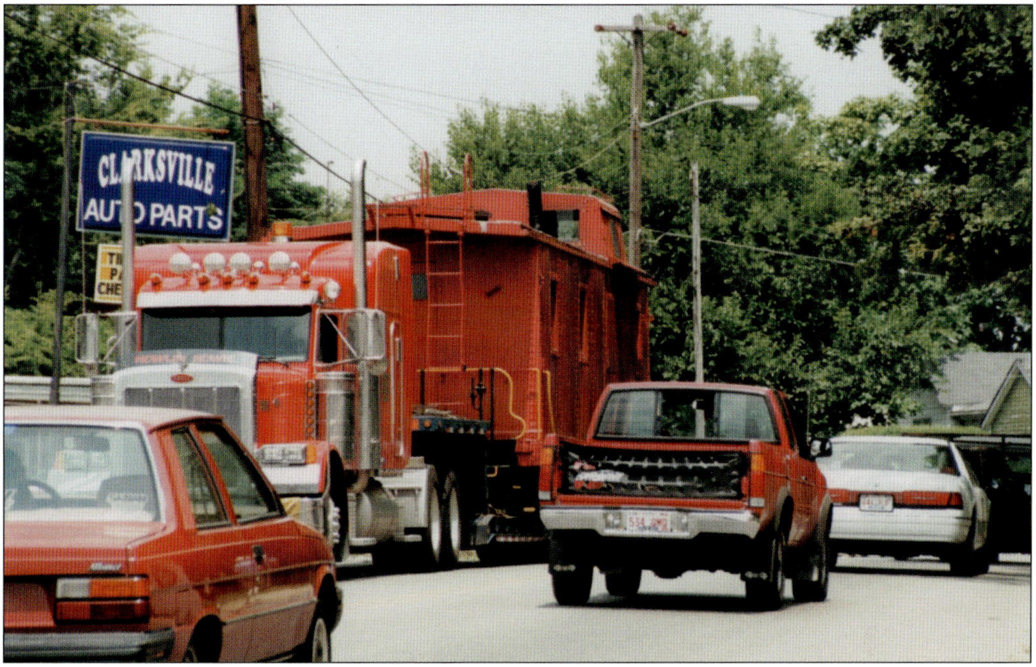

Above, the L&N Train Station receives a vintage caboose. Contributed by Toney Smith, it is a great addition to the station and serves as the backdrop for wedding, prom, family, and senior-year photographs. The delivery put the finishing touches on a piece of history in Clarksville that everyone can continue to explore. Below, the placement of the vintage caboose on Tenth Street at the L&N Train Station was a long-awaited task. (Both photographs by Benita Martin, courtesy of MCHS.)

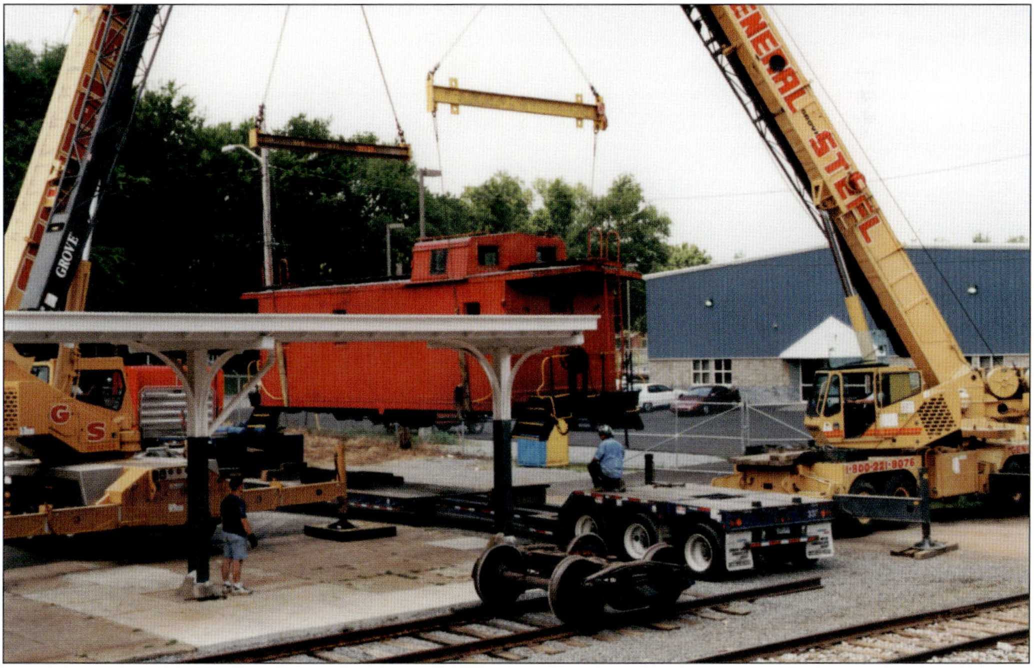

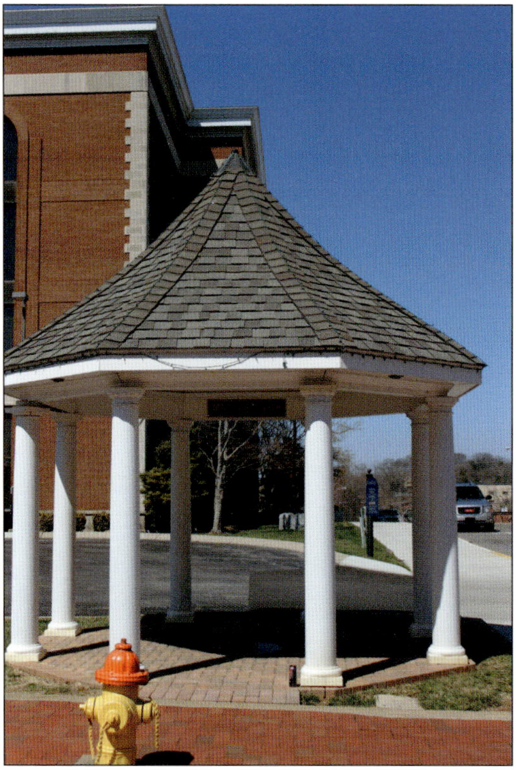

The gazebo at left was dedicated to the memory of Mary Jo Dozier, who had strong family roots in Clarksville. She was the first city councilwoman and served for 28 years, from 1974 to 2002. Below, this family-run dairy farm is still in business and continues to bear the same name it has had for years. The Hinton Haven dairy farm has been in operation since 1928, when David Hinton was owner. (At left, author's collection; below, photograph by Jeremy Rodesky.)

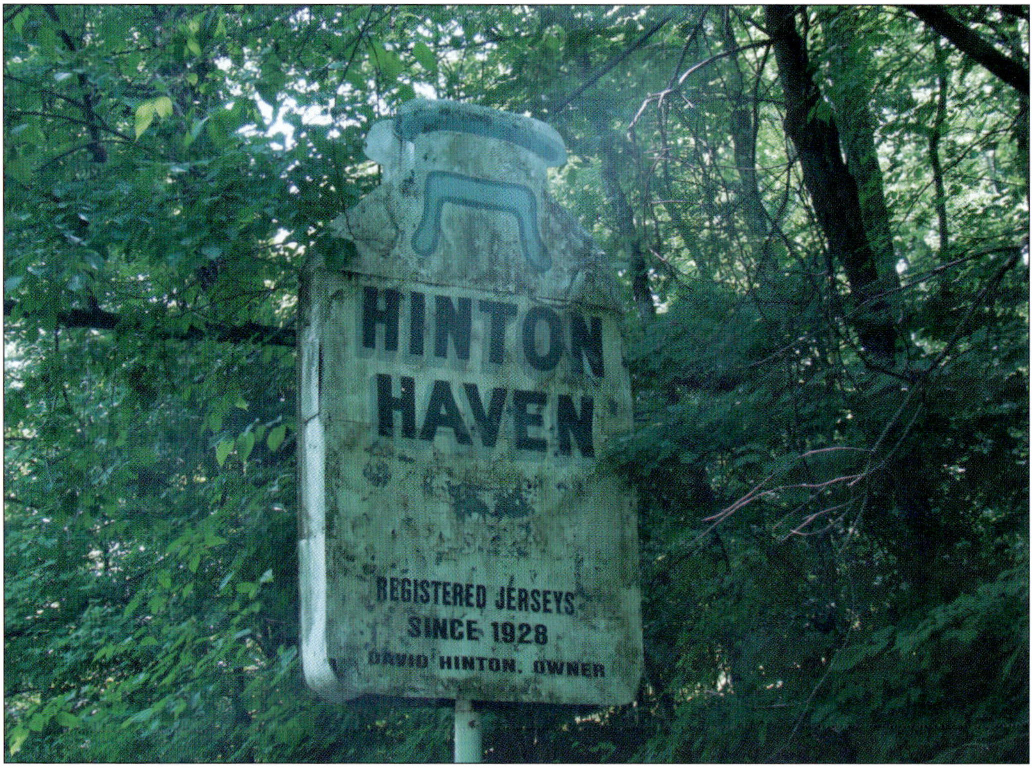

This historic marker stands outside the Old Post House and explains in detail its historical relevance. The marker states that the site was not only used as a stagecoach stop between Nashville and towns along the Ohio River but that it also served as a place of residence and as a post office. (Courtesy of Gail Longton.)

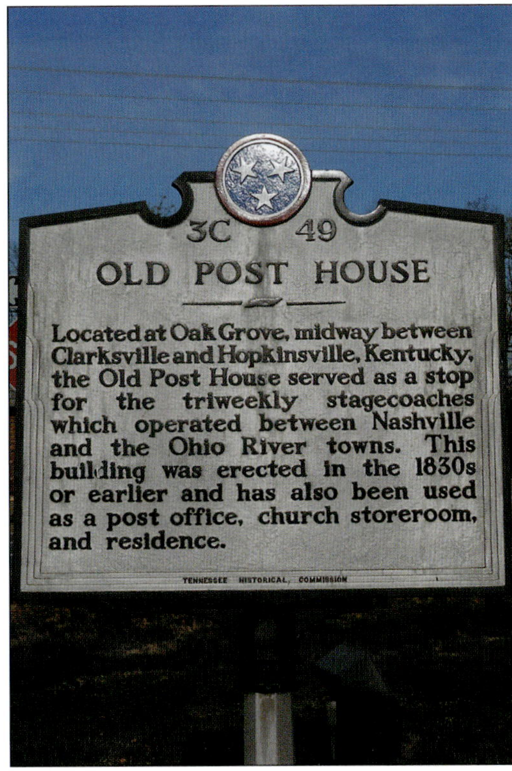

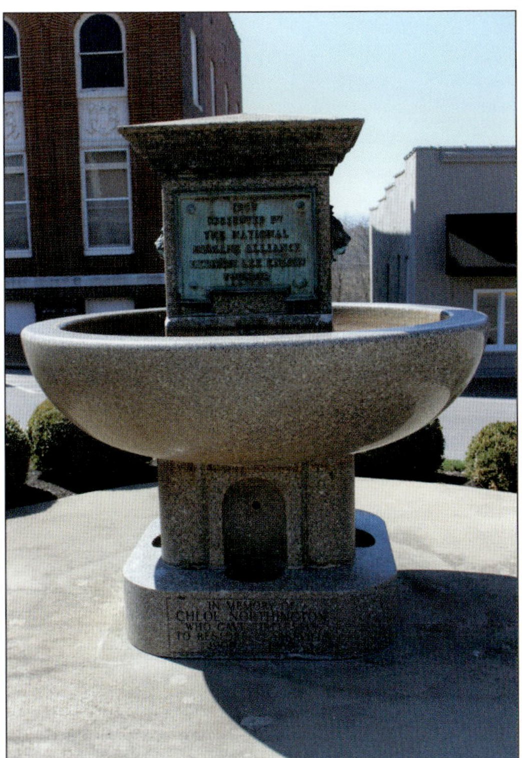

The top portion of this fountain was presented to National Humane Alliance founder Hermon Lee Ensign. The base is in memory of Chloe Northington, who passed away in 1989. The inscription states that she gave tirelessly in restoring Clarksville. (Author's collection.)

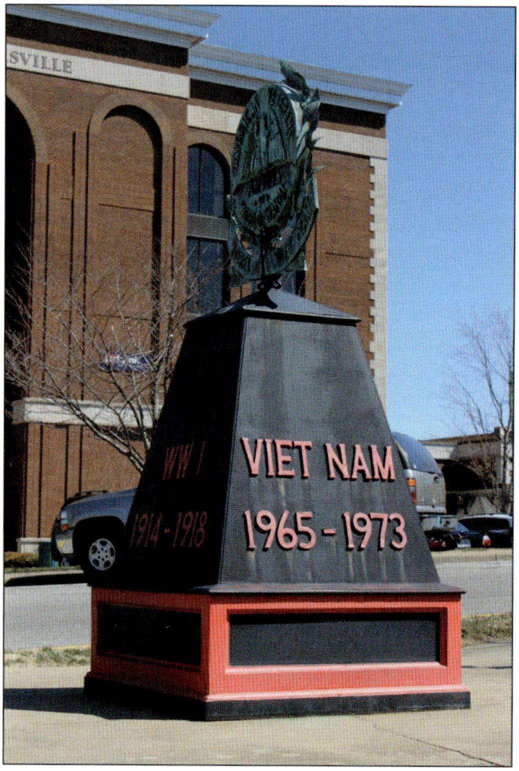

There is a unique, four-sided American Veterans of World Wars memorial in downtown Clarksville. It states the names of each conflict fought, along with the years: "WWI 1914–1918," "WWII 1939–1945," "Korea 1950–1953," and "Viet Nam 1965–1973." (Both author's collection.)

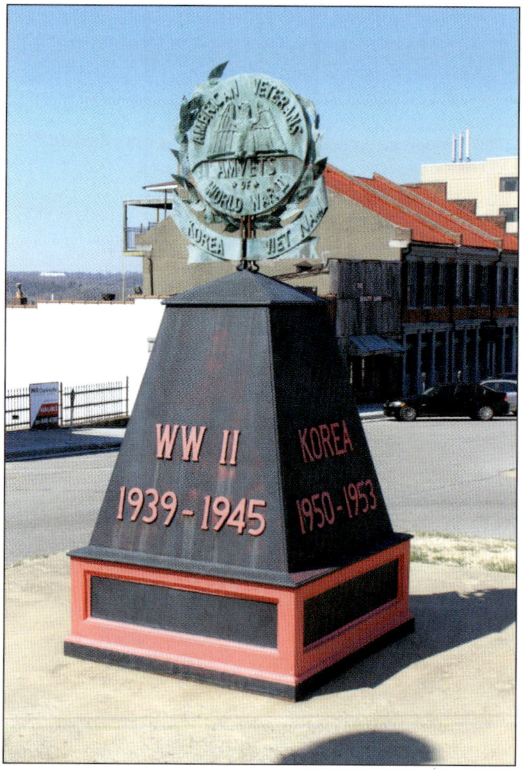

Outside of US Bank in historic downtown Clarksville is a statue of the man for whom Montgomery County was named, John Montgomery. It was erected on Main Street in 2002 and stands tall, as shown in the image at right. Another interesting historical figure that has a monument dedicated him is Col. Valentine Sevier, who defended the earlier settlers of the community. This memorial, seen below, was erected by the Capt. William Edmiston Chapter of the Daughters of the American Revolution. (At right, author's collection; below, courtesy of Gail Longton.)

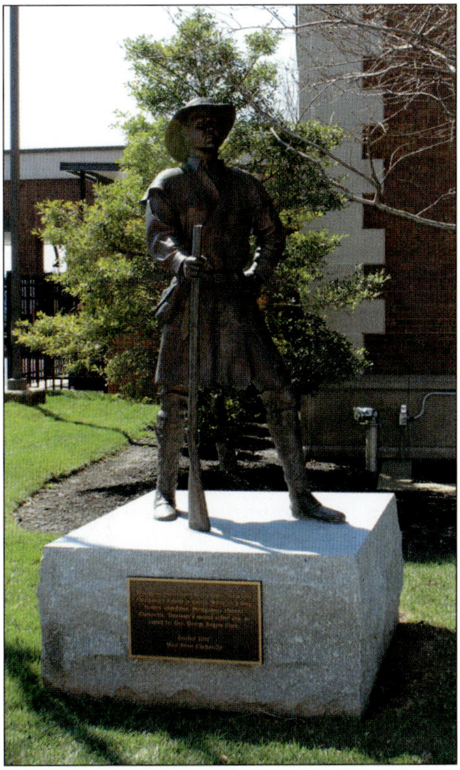

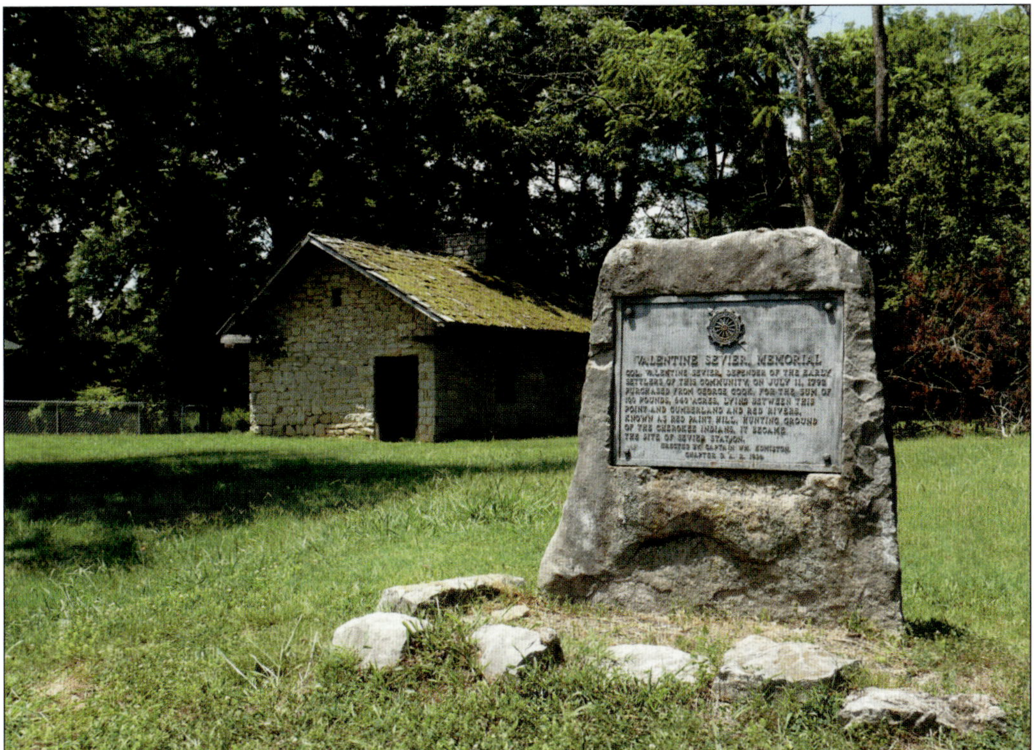

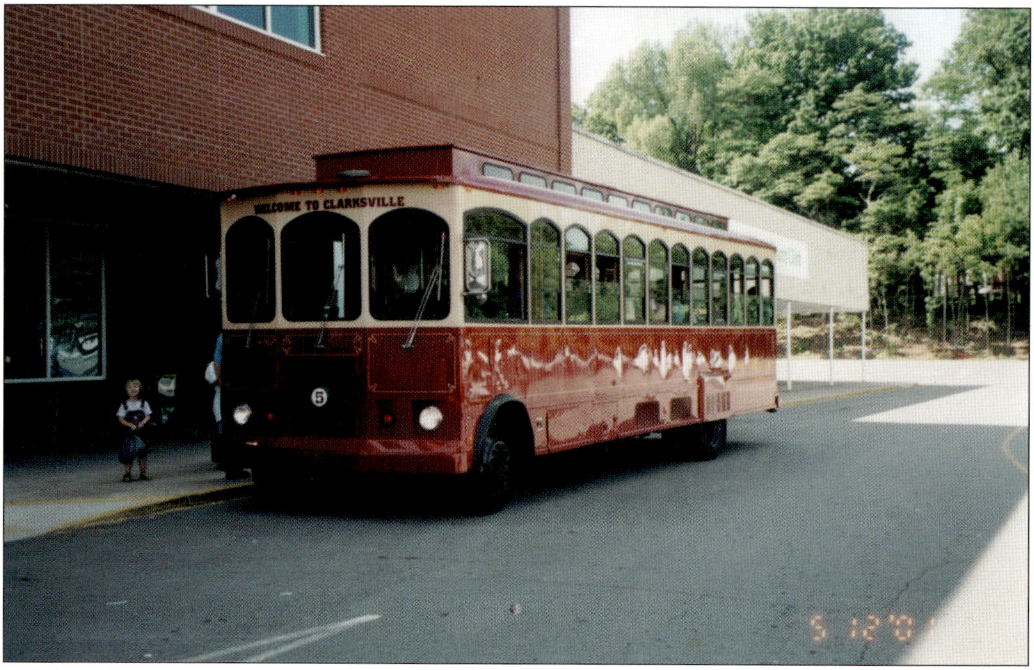

While walking around Clarksville and visiting the historical district or taking a trip down to the Riverwalk, it is no surprise to see a red trolley driving around, as shown above. When walking along the riverbank, one might catch a glimpse of history making its way up and down the river, as shown below. By the 1820s, pedestrians were sure to have caught a glimpse of a steamboat carrying oats, cotton, tobacco, or even soybeans down the river. The first steamboat to travel the Cumberland River was the *General Jackson*, and the river is still used today for transportation and recreation. (Both photographs by Billyfrank Morrison.)

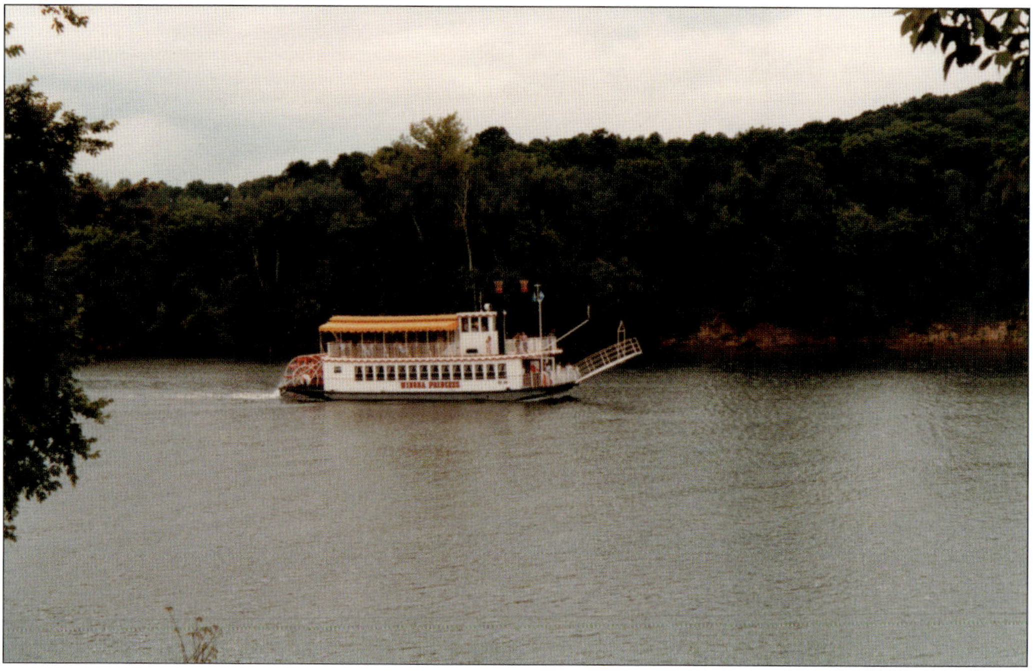

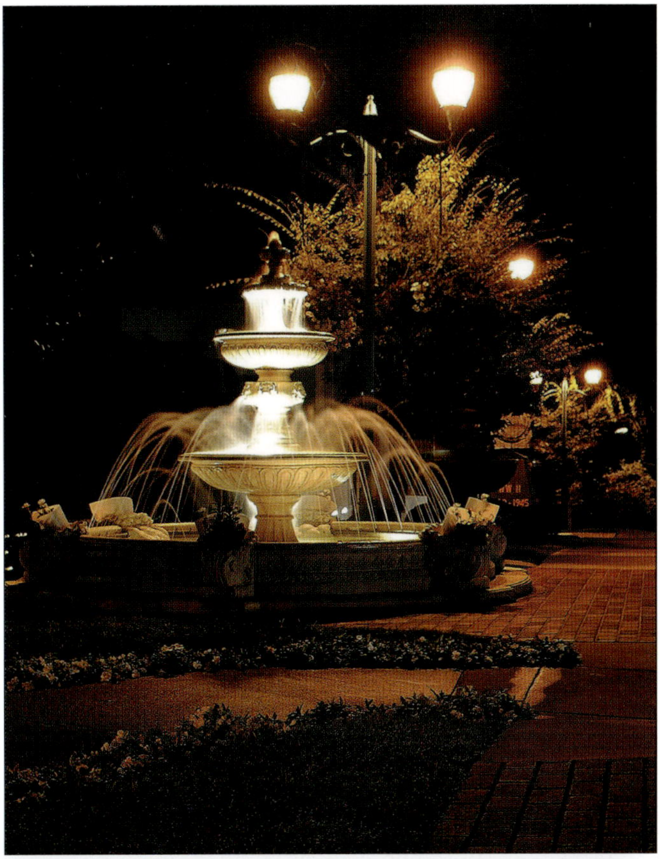

This is a beautiful fountain to visit, both at night while lit up and during the day. It can be found in the miniature park that was dedicated in honor of the nation's bicentennial in 1976. Situated in front of city hall on the public square, the fountain was donated by F&M Bank in 2008. (Both photographs by David Smith.)

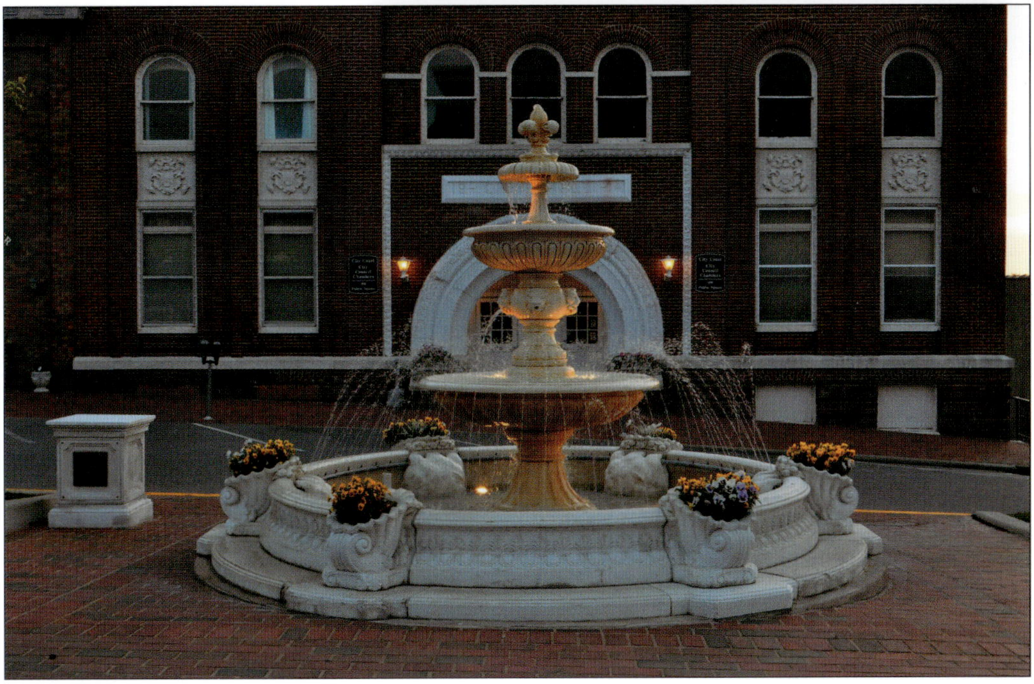

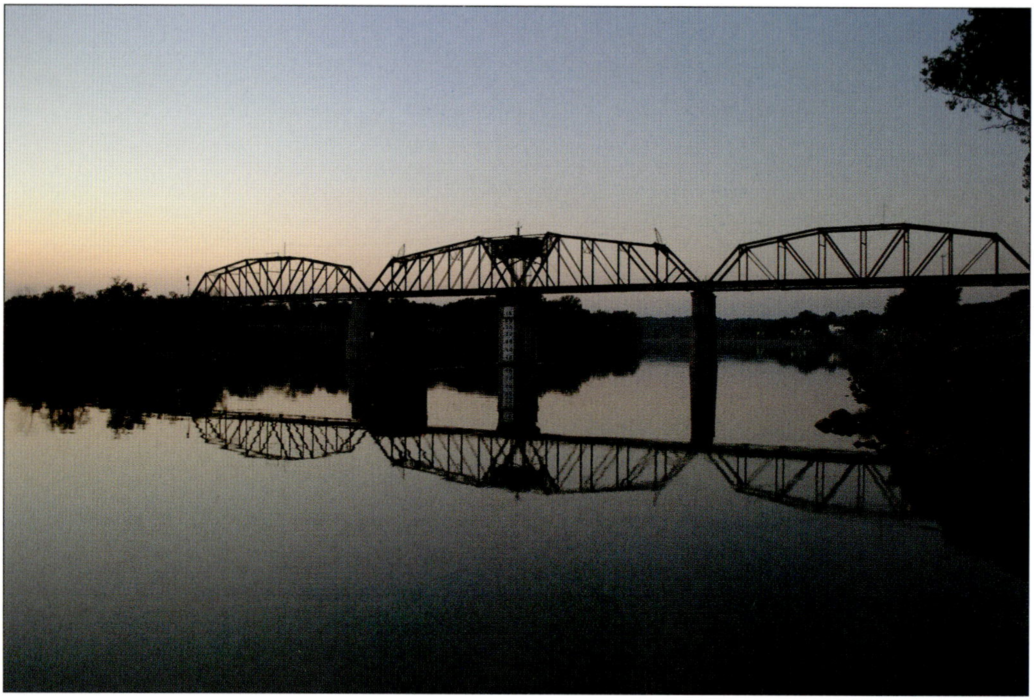

Above, the L&N Turn Bridge has faced years of weather, war, and constant use. It was once set ablaze by Confederate soldiers to prevent the movement of Union forces. It carried trains over the Cumberland River while they were transporting agricultural products and passenger cars. Passenger service stopped in 1966, but transportation of agriculture continues today. After years of wear and tear from weather and use, the bridge was in need of a good cleaning and face lift, as shown below. (Above, photograph by David Smith; below, photograph by Joe Sweeten.)

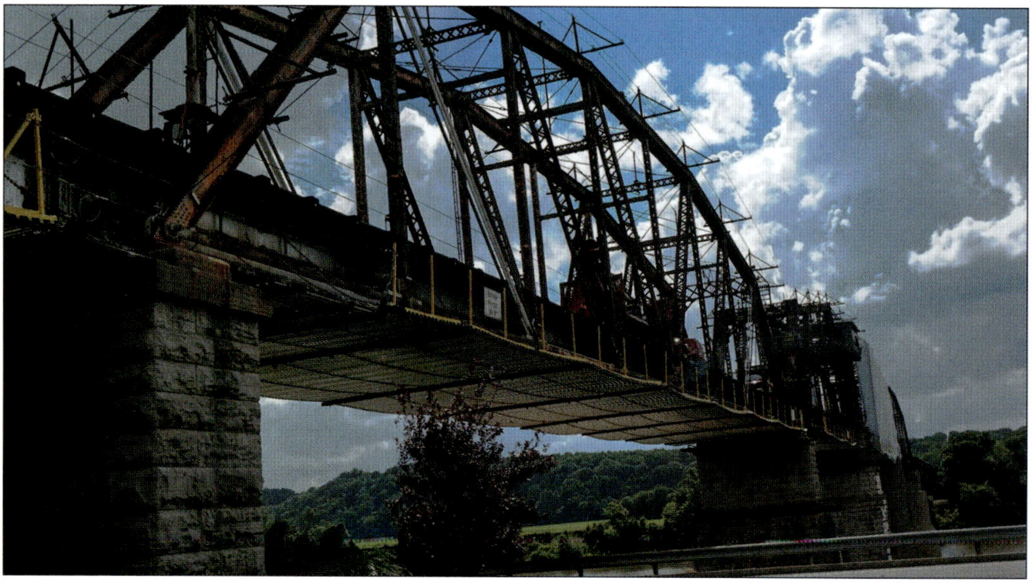

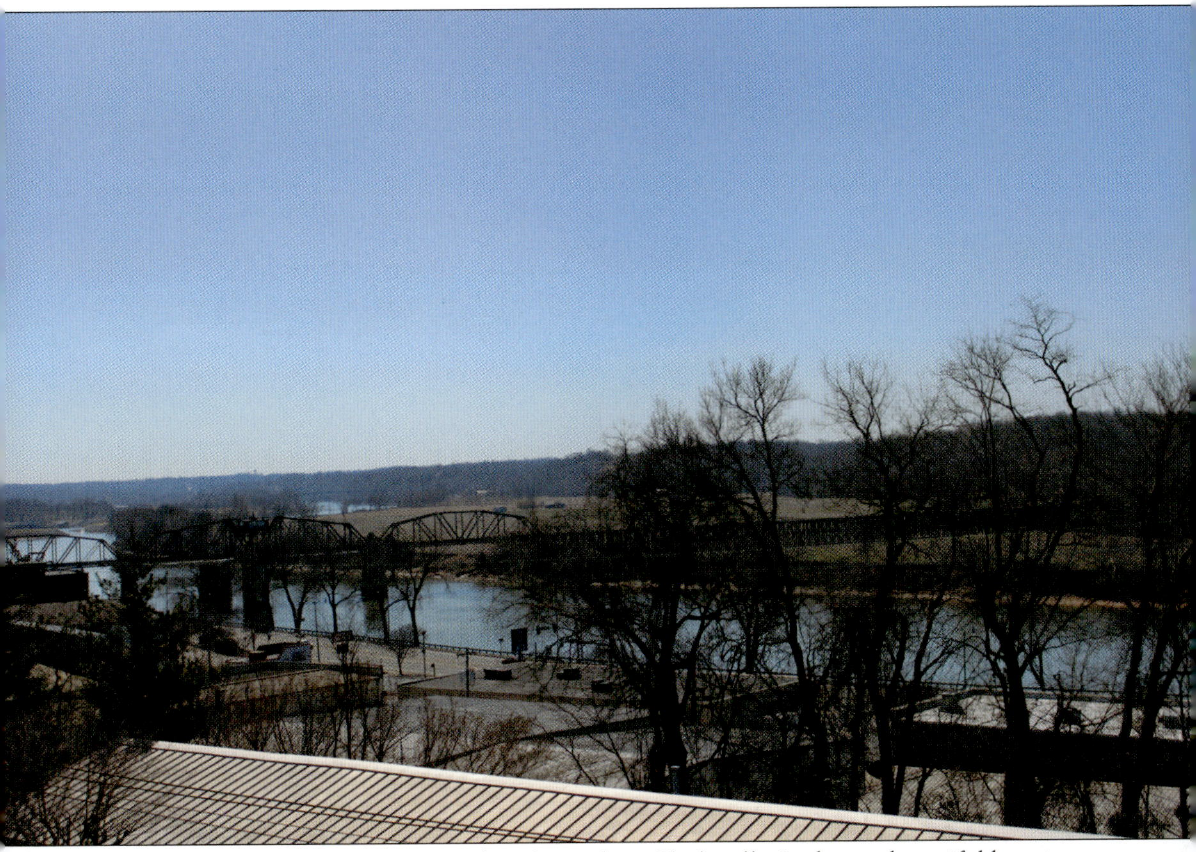

In 1989, F&M Bank had its expansion ideas focused on Clarksville. It chose a beautiful location here on Franklin Street with a view that looks out over the Cumberland River. This was taken from the F&M Bank parking lot in the late winter of 2014. (Author's collection.)

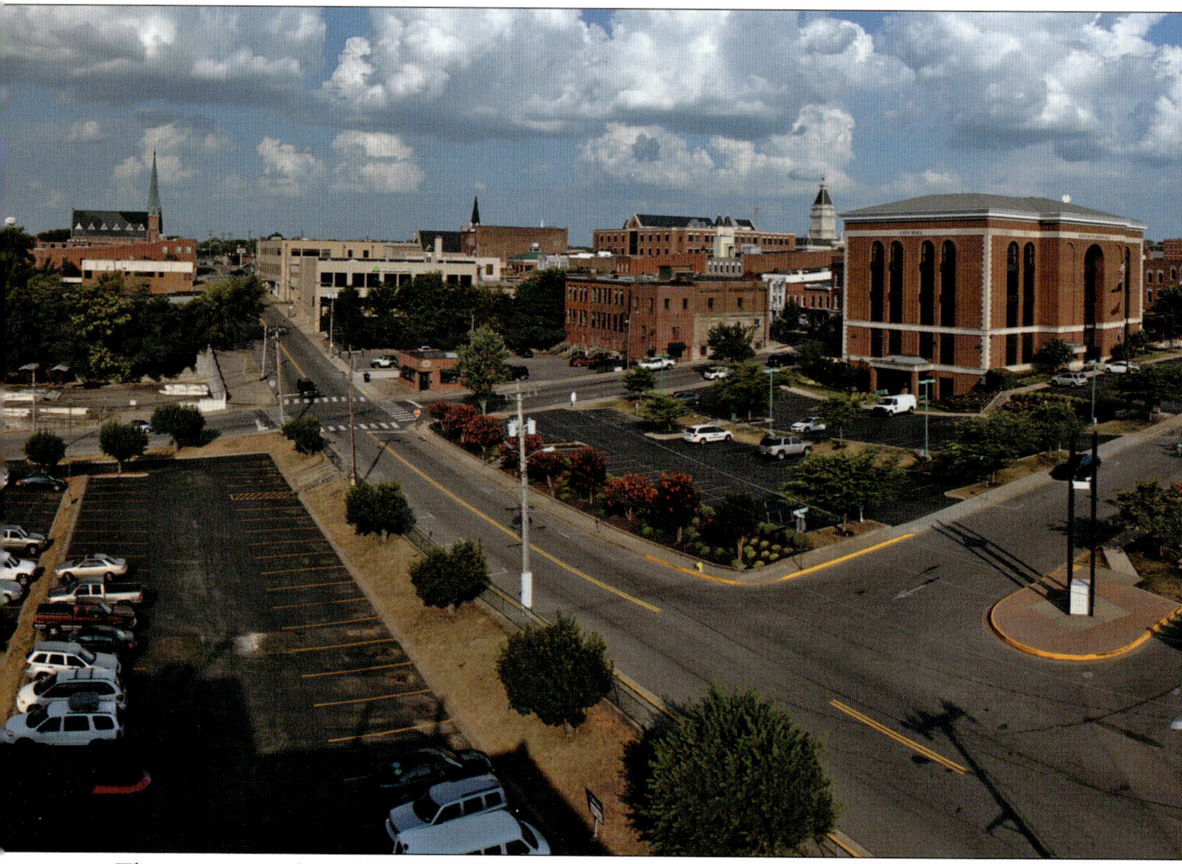

This panoramic shot of downtown Clarksville was taken on a clear day, and it is pretty easy to pick

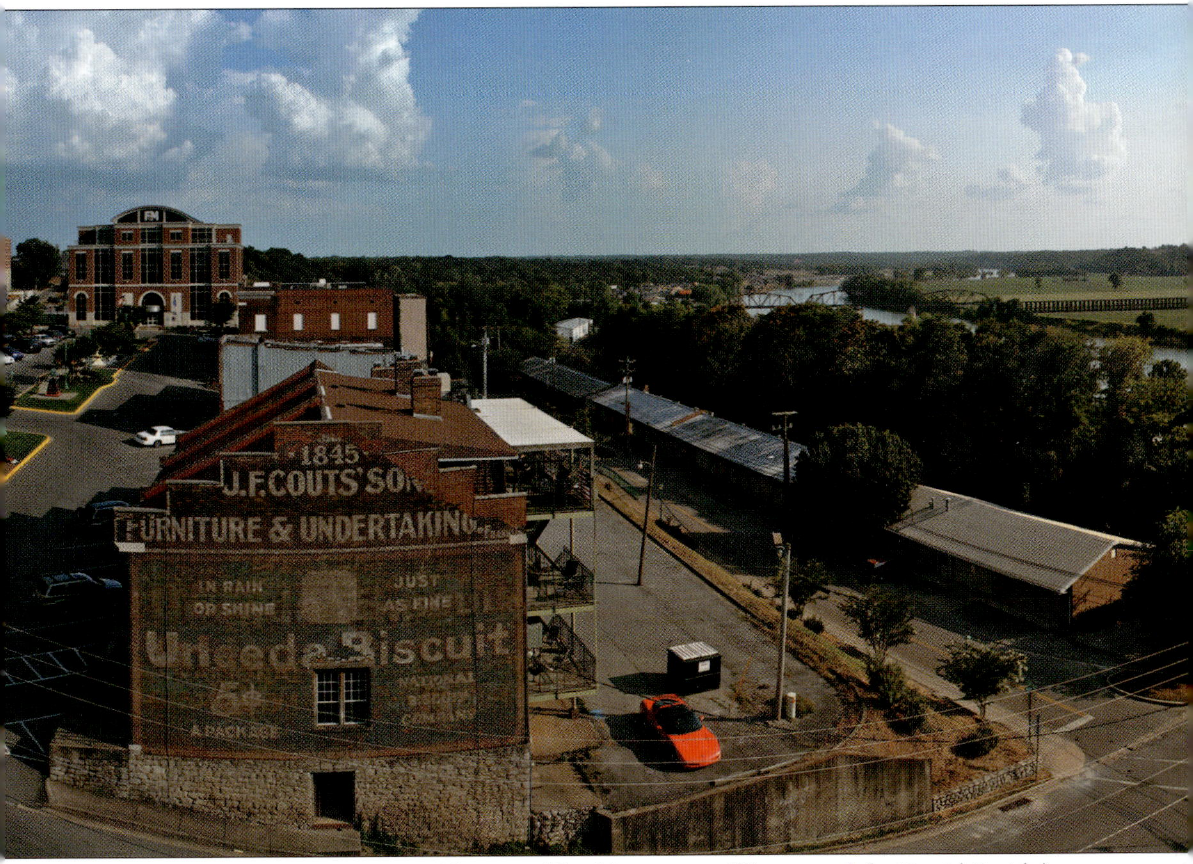

out some of the major structures and historical buildings in it. (Photograph by David Smith.)

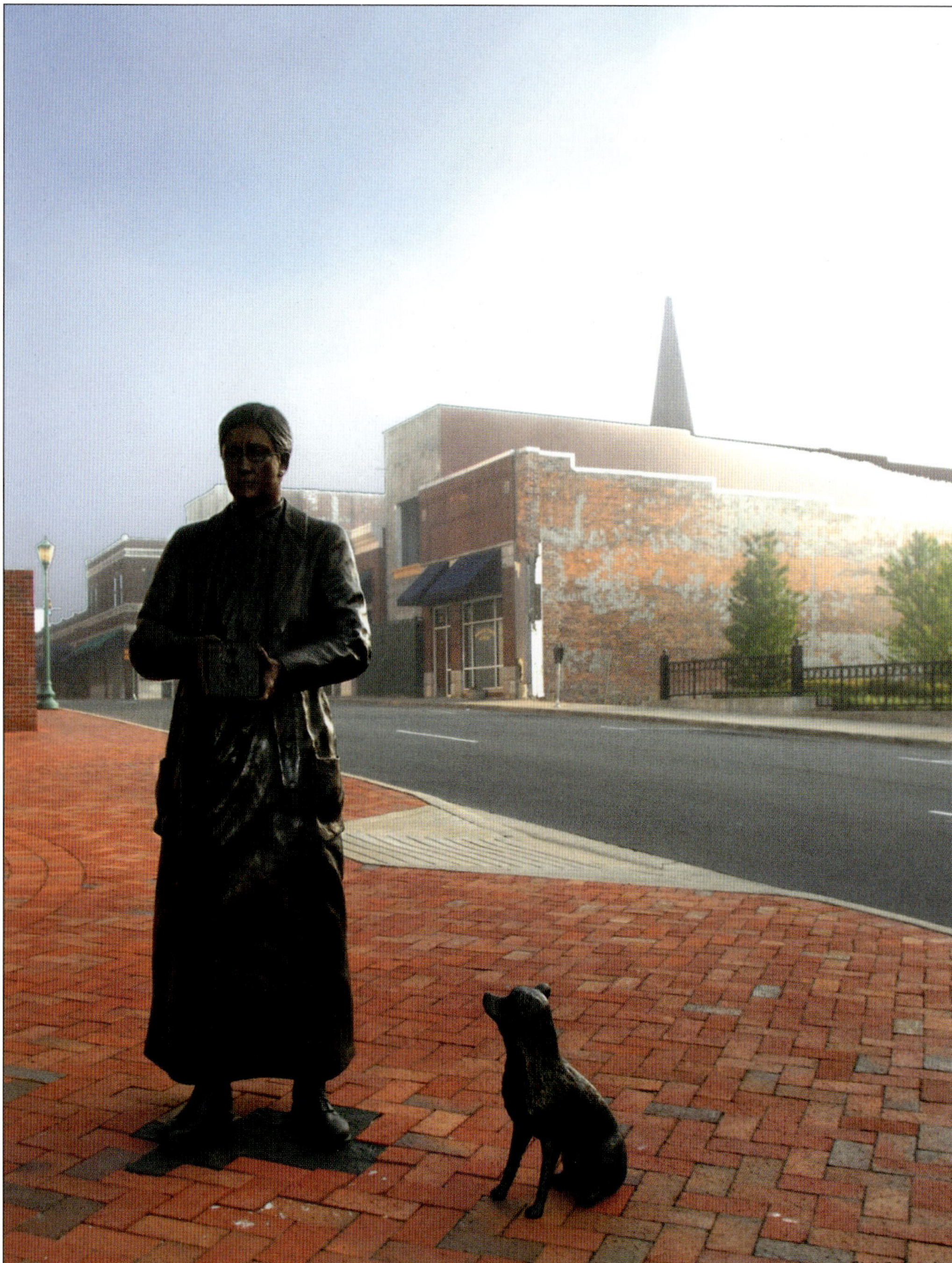

This is a bronze statue of Nora Witzel, a pioneer in photography during the early 20th century. Most of her work dates to between 1920 and 1940, and she was what some would call a rebel. She would walking around town with her camera and her partner, her dog Nettie, snapping photographs. Andrea Lugar was the creator of this piece of art, which can be seen while walking through the historic areas of downtown Clarksville. (Photograph by Clifton Whittaker.)

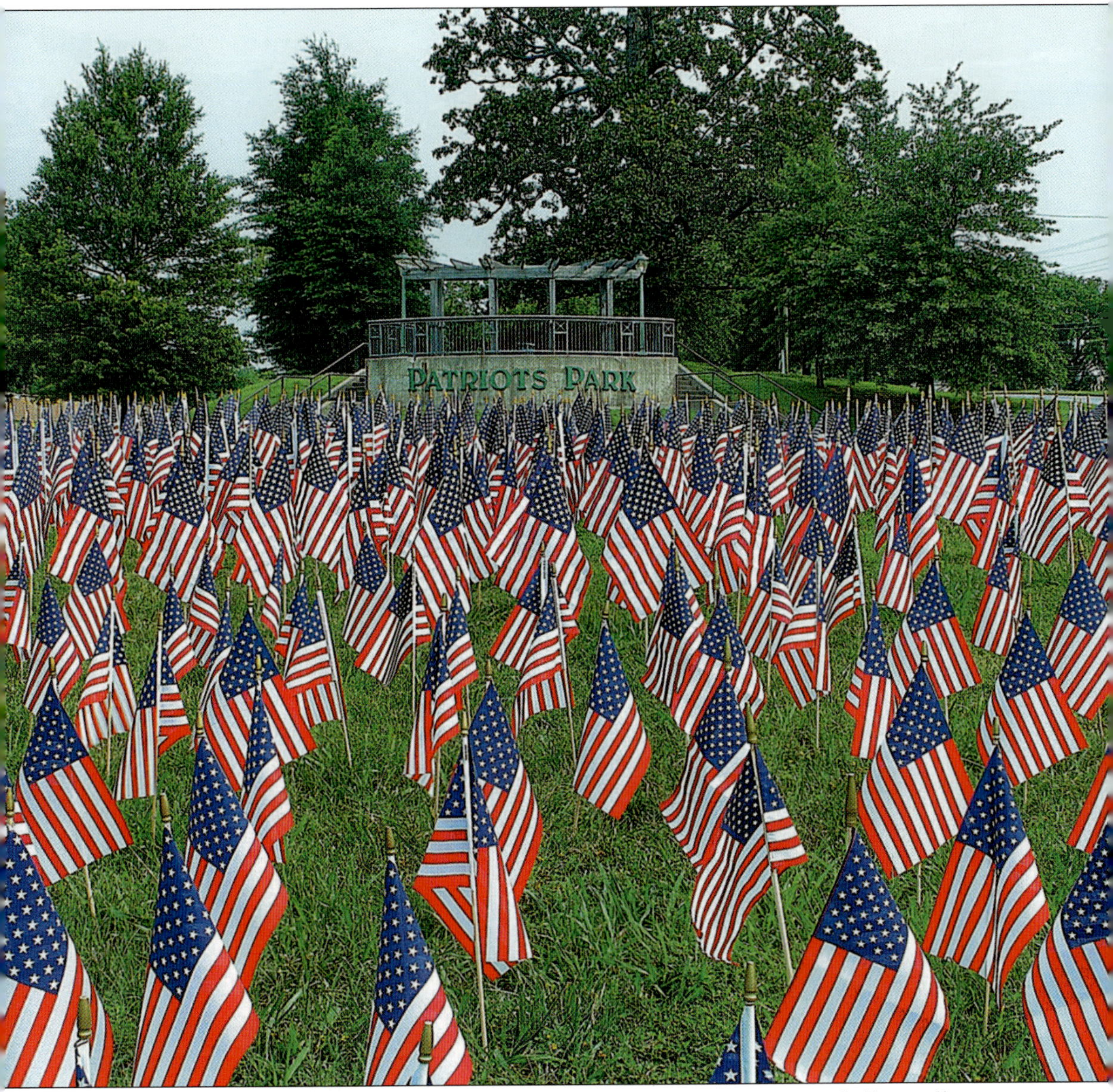

While traveling up Fort Campbell Boulevard toward Gate 3 of the Fort Campbell installation, a park of military respect sits to the left. Patriots Park is a 3.5–acre site between the north and south lanes of US Route 41a. It features a walking path, benches, and two monuments: the Purple Heart Monument for Combat Wounded Veterans and the POW/MIA Monument. During patriotic holidays, small flags are placed to symbolize the fallen soldiers of Fort Campbell. (Photograph by David Smith.)

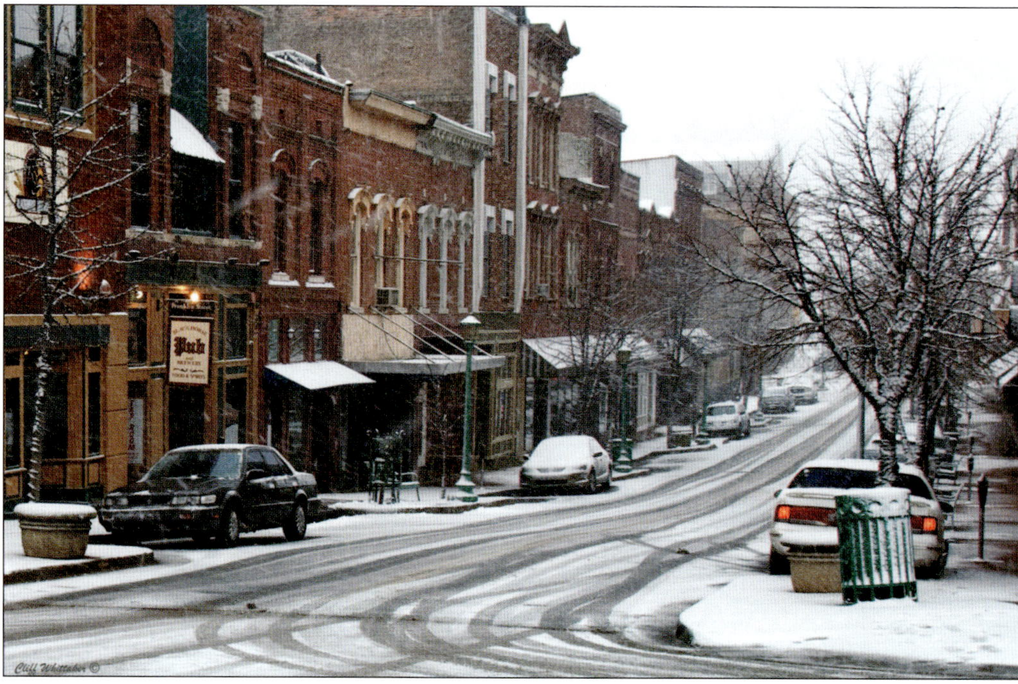

Living in Clarksville brings the joy of celebrating all four seasons of the year. This winter storm came through downtown with a slow and steady snowfall. The Blackhorse Pub is noticeable on the left, and during this storm customers are sitting inside enjoying the warmth and great food. Opening in 1992, the pub continues to bring customers down to Franklin Street, serving up excellent dishes and freshly brewed, handcrafted beer. (Photograph by Clifton Whittaker.)

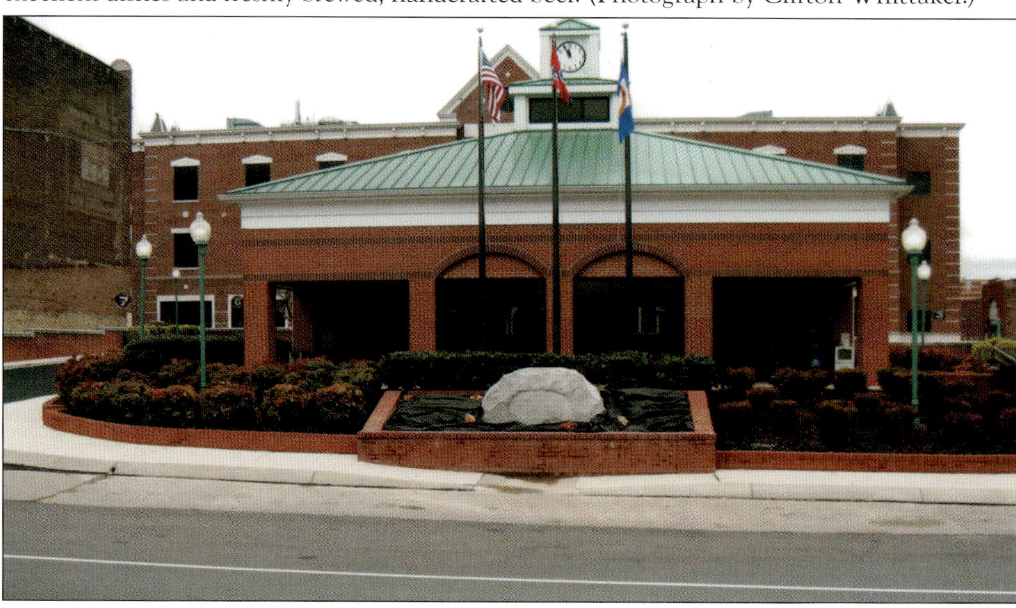

Pictured in 2010, the Clarksville city bus terminal is awaiting the arrival of the *Clarksville Doughboy*. The statue was dedicated in June 1929. After years of decay and simple neglect, it was restored by Scott Wise and rededicated in April of 2010 at this transit station on Legion Street. (Photograph by Billyfrank Morrison.)

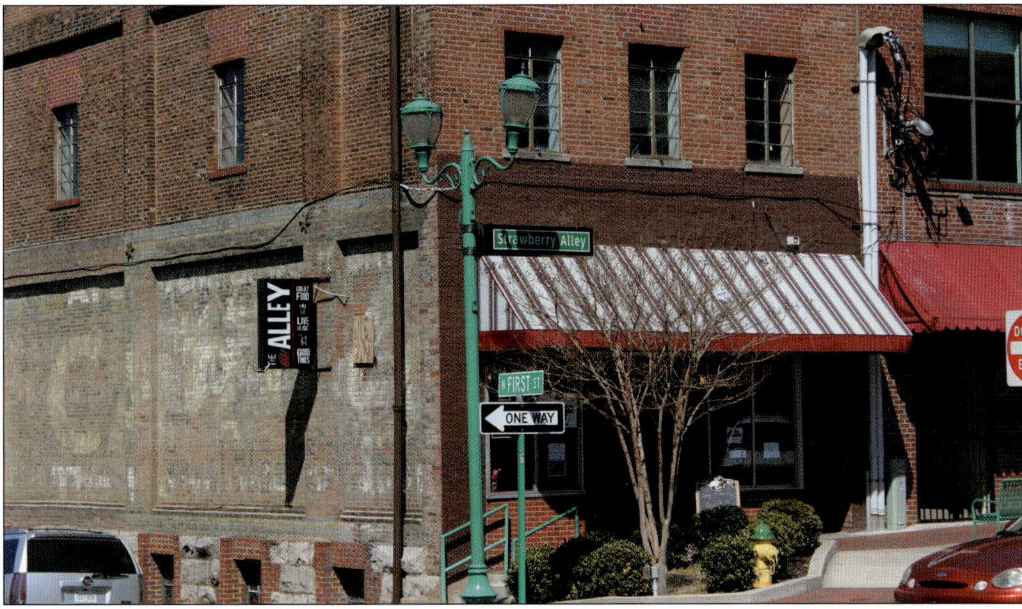

Strawberry Alley in downtown Clarksville brings many visitors to its shops. The name is in honor of the wife of Clarksville's first mayor, James Elder, because the street was built across her strawberry patch. During the Art Walk, which takes place the first Thursday of the month from 5:00 p.m. until 8:00 p.m., rain or shine, participants will find local artists out drawing, painting, and even playing musical instruments. While visiting the street, one can enjoy baked goods from George the Cake Guy, lunch at Kooka's Nest, and live music with great food on the weekends at the Alley. (Author's collection.)

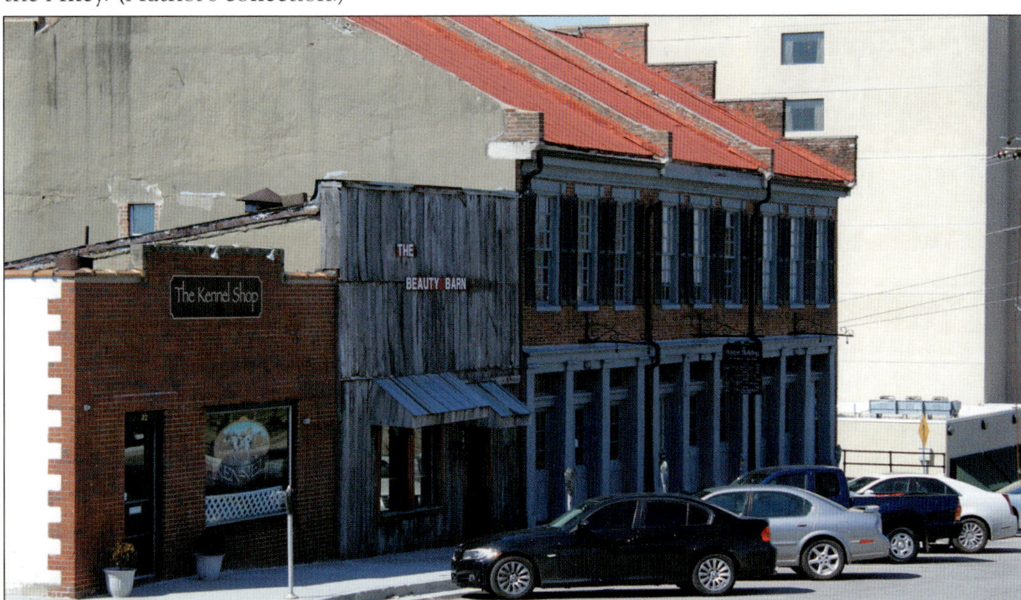

Many who walk through downtown are told about the side of the Poston Building. Its front and other storefronts capture history and are well worth visiting. Its eye-catching advertisements were put in place in the 1870s. These three buildings were constructed by John Poston in 1842. (Author's collection.)

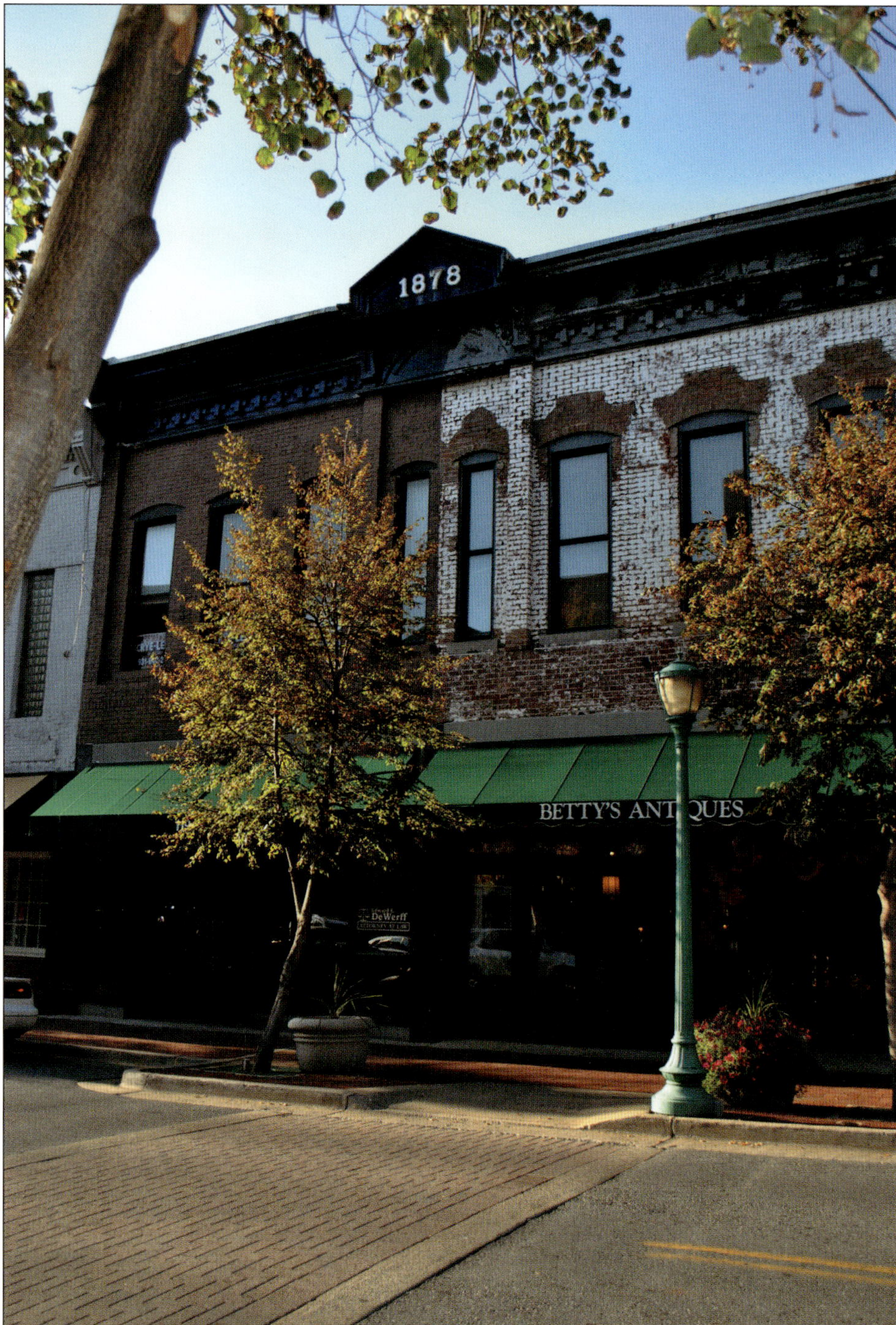

When walking down Franklin Street, it is important not only to peruse the interior of the stores but to also pay attention to the exteriors of the buildings and their architecture. For instance, Betty's Antiques is dated to 1878, and the years of wear on the weathered brick and the beautiful details still visible on the front roof just add to the desire to enter. Betty's Antiques has been in business for over 30 years, offering some beautiful pieces. (Photograph by David Smith.)

Three

Fort Campbell

The town of Clarksville has a big heart, and it opens its arms to welcome the many families using it as a temporary home while moving around with the military. Once known as Camp Clarksville, it was feared at one point that the installation would disappear or close after World War I. But, that was not the case, with the arrival of the Airborne Division in 1949 and the redesign in April 1950. It was during this time that Camp Clarksville received not only a redesign but also a change in name, becoming what is now known as Fort Campbell. From 1950 to 1962, paratroopers were seen going through the airborne course. Then, in 1956, the reactivation of the 101st Airborne Division, also known as the "Screaming Eagles," took place. Fort Campbell suffered its largest, most devastating loss in December 1985. A plane taking off from Newfoundland, carrying military personnel from a peacekeeping assignment in Egypt that was headed back to Fort Campbell, crashed—the 248 service members and eight crew members aboard were lost.

Fort Campbell has played host to many famous faces, both in pop culture and in the political field. Presidents Johnson, Bush, Reagan, and current commander in chief President Obama are just a few of the political figures who have visited the families and soldiers of Fort Campbell. There have also been a few visits by some of the first ladies, including Nancy Reagan, Barbara Bush, and most recently Michelle Obama, who was joined by Dr. Jill Biden. The photographs in this chapter give a peek into what can be seen on the installation and the love and support military families offer.

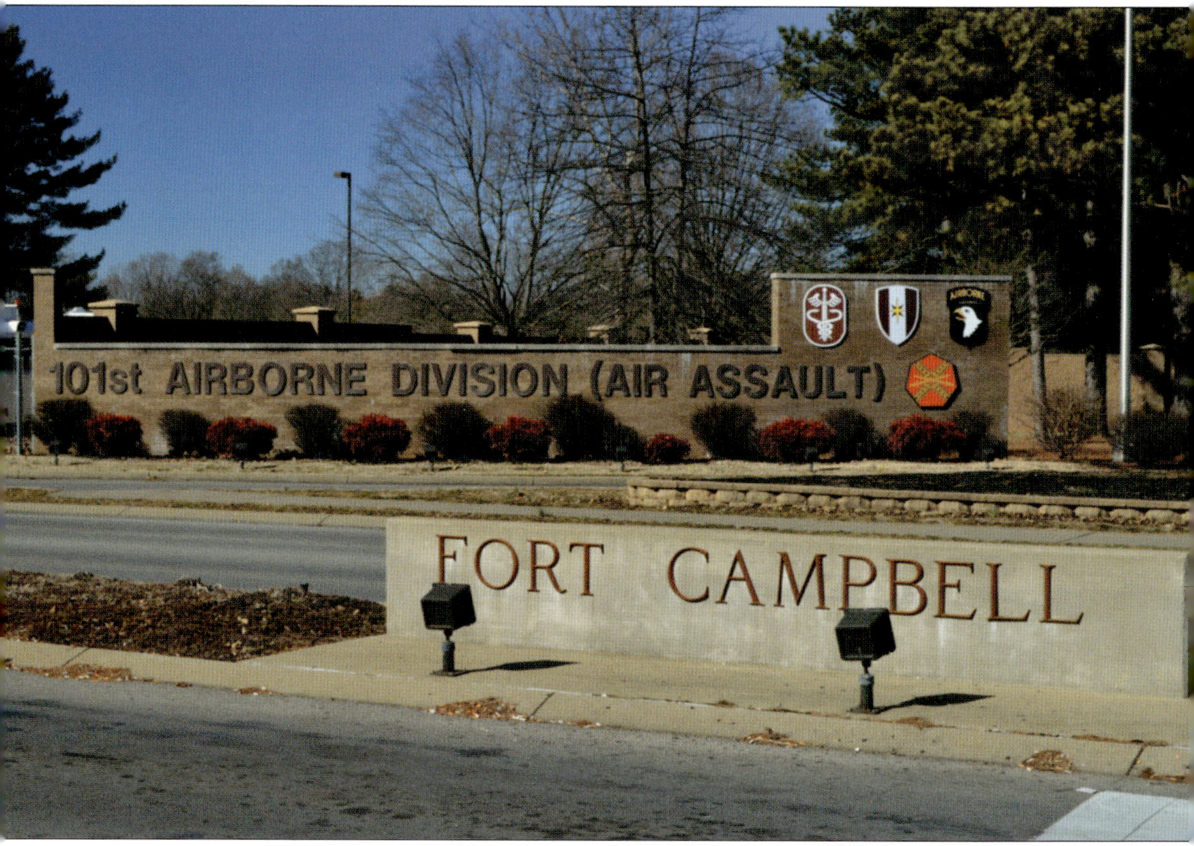

One of the biggest changes that came to Clarksville was the 1942 construction of Camp Campbell, now known as Fort Campbell, home of the 101st Airborne Division. The families are always welcomed to the Clarksville community, and with the constant rotation that soldiers and their families go through, this location is often referred to as "home" for many. (Photograph by David Smith.)

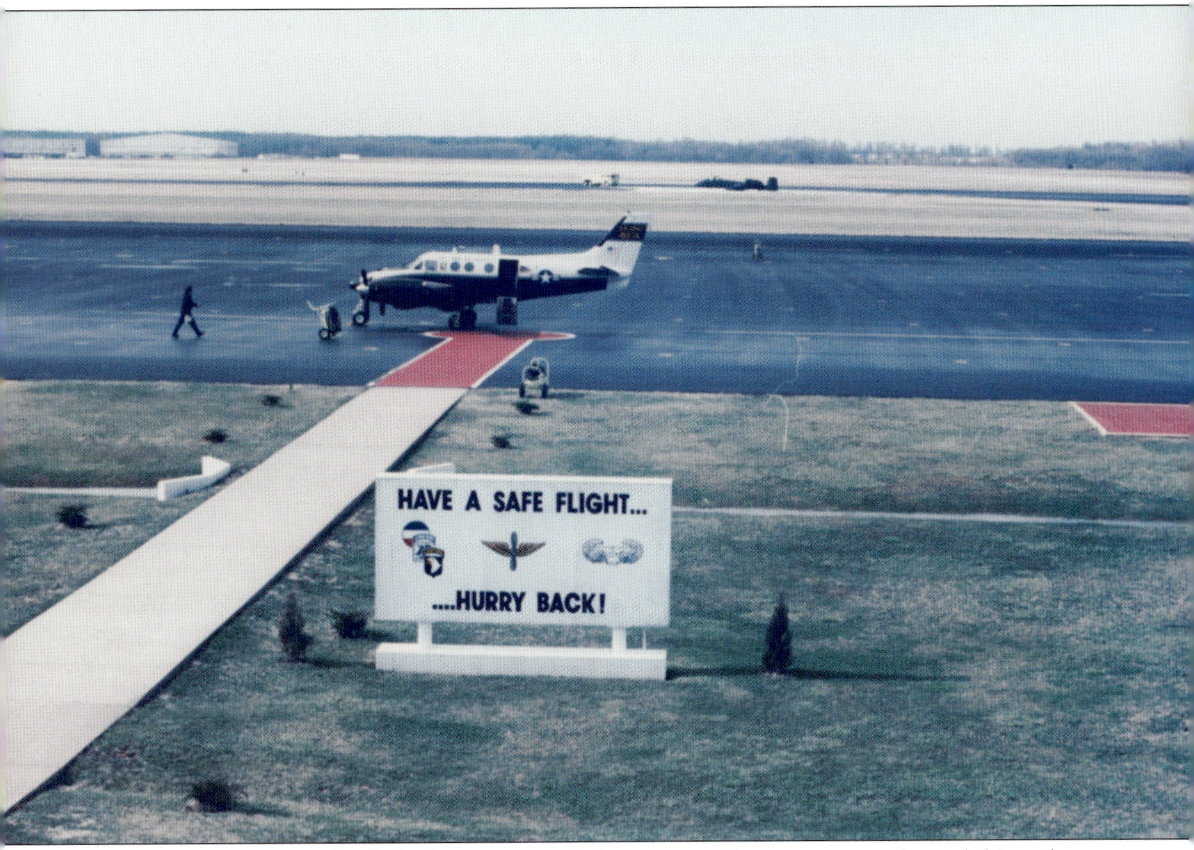

While walking out onto the flight line, one might have many things running through his or her mind. This is one of those reminders posted for those about to board aircraft: "Have a Safe Flight . . . Hurry Back!" Waiting to be boarded is an MC-12. In this distance, one aircraft has had a mishap. (Photograph by Billyfrank Morrison.)

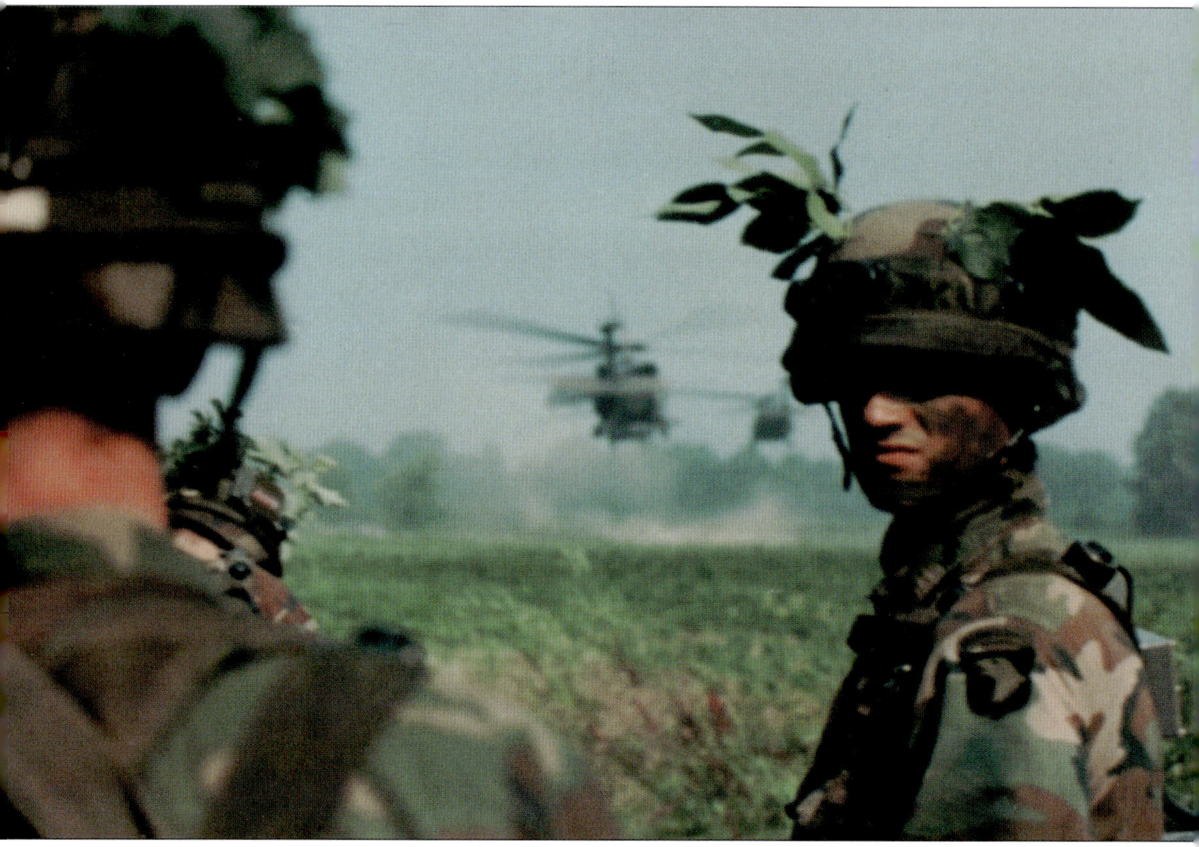

Dressed in BDUs (battle dress uniforms), with camouflage on their faces and leaves in their "steel pots" (helmets), these two unidentified soldiers are pictured during one of the many training exercises that take place on the installation. As with most exercises, there was frequently the sight or sound of an aircraft flying above, like the UH-60 Black Hawk in the background. (Photograph by Billyfrank Morrison.)

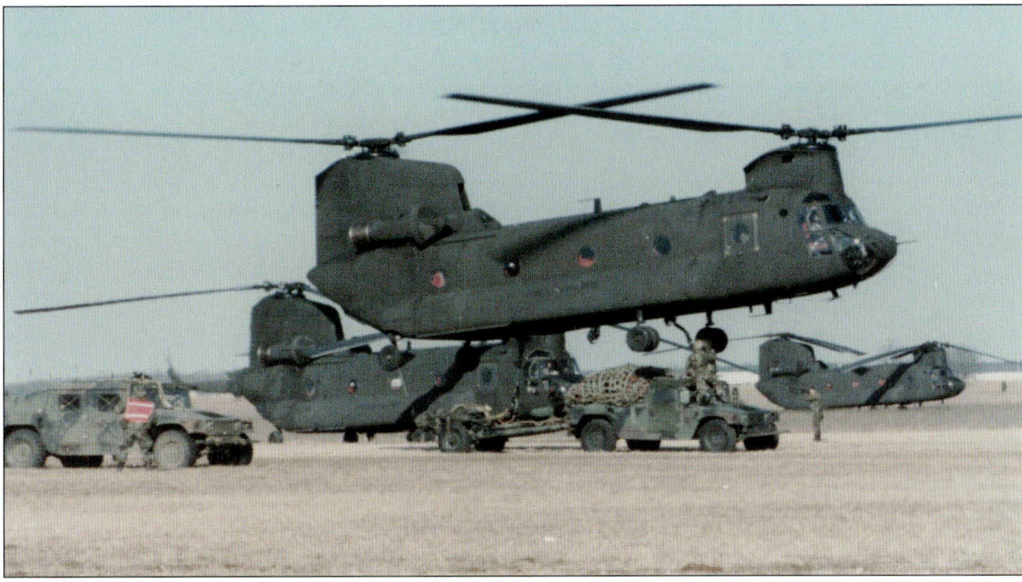

During an October 1980 exercise on the installation, three twin-engine CH-47 Chinook helicopters are going through the steps of loading and carrying equipment. Above, one is hovering near cargo to be hoisted, while the other two helicopters wait their turn. Soldiers on the ground are there for safety, locking the load for the Chinook to carry. Below, one of the Chinook tandem-rotor, heavy-lift helicopters is transporting a securely locked jeep during an exercise. Once it arrives at its drop-off point, a member of the flight crew will release the jeep to the ground. The Chinook's primary role includes movement of troops, artillery placement, and resupplying battlefields. (Both photographs by Billyfrank Morrison.)

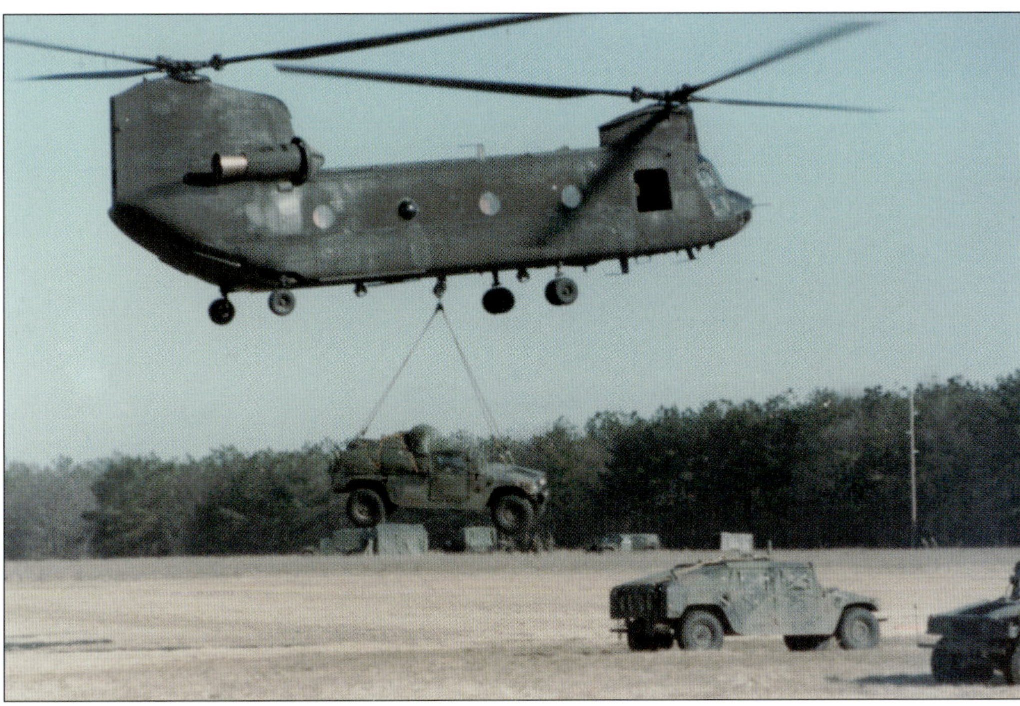

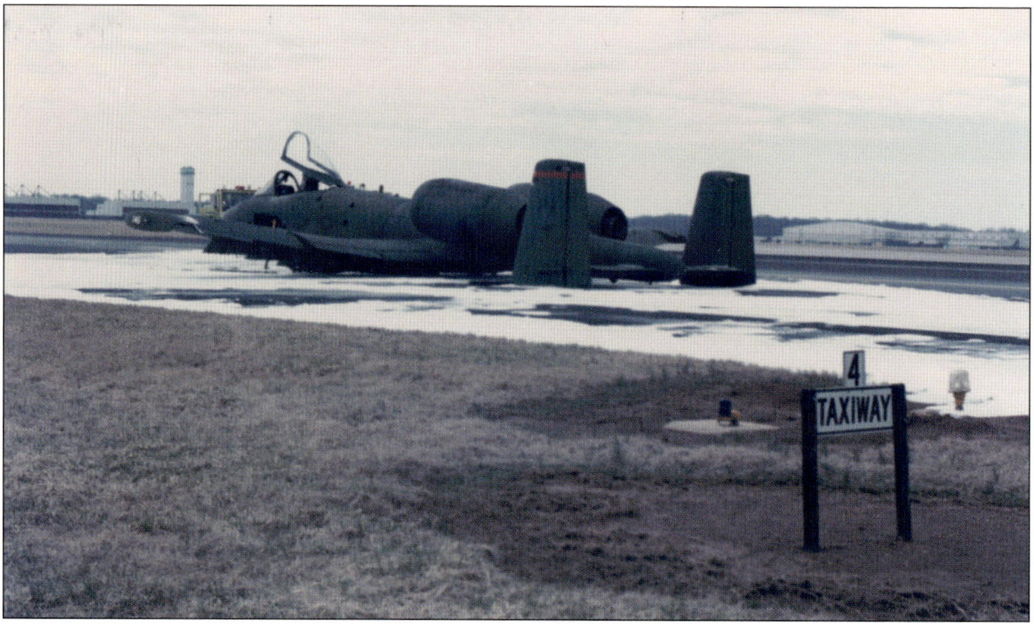

On page 65, it is mentioned that an aircraft had a mishap. The Air Force A-10 Warthog encountered a mechanical issue with the landing gear—it would not come down. The aircraft had to make an emergency landing on its belly, as shown above. Below, awaiting the Air Force A-10 Warthog aircraft during its emergency landing is the emergency response team. At the aircraft's final stopping point, the installation fire department sprayed foam on the belly of the aircraft and the landing strip. The flight landed safely without any injury during this cold month of January. (Both photographs by Billyfrank Morrison.)

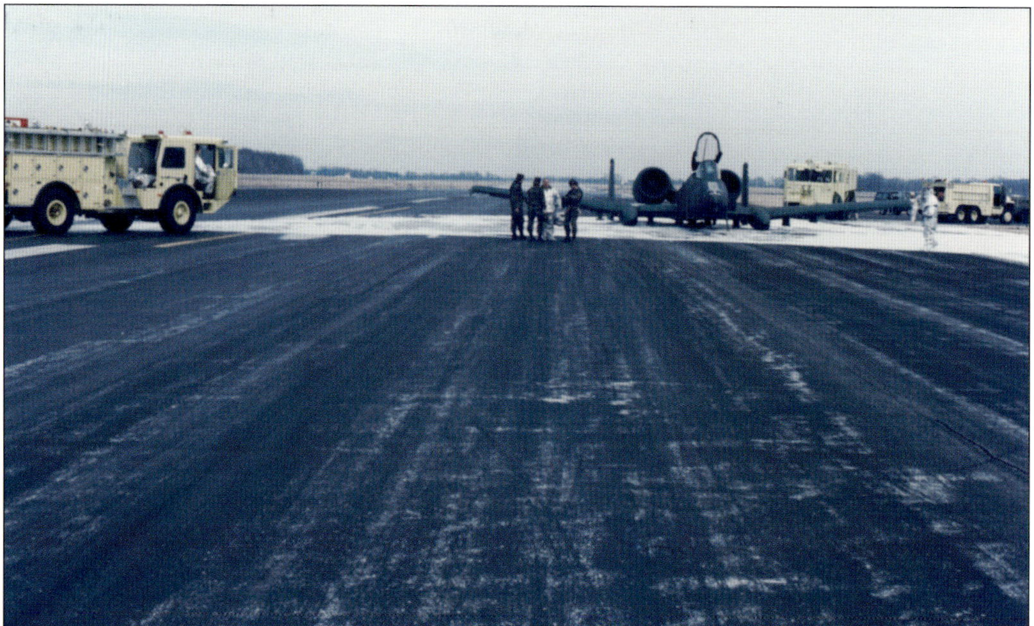

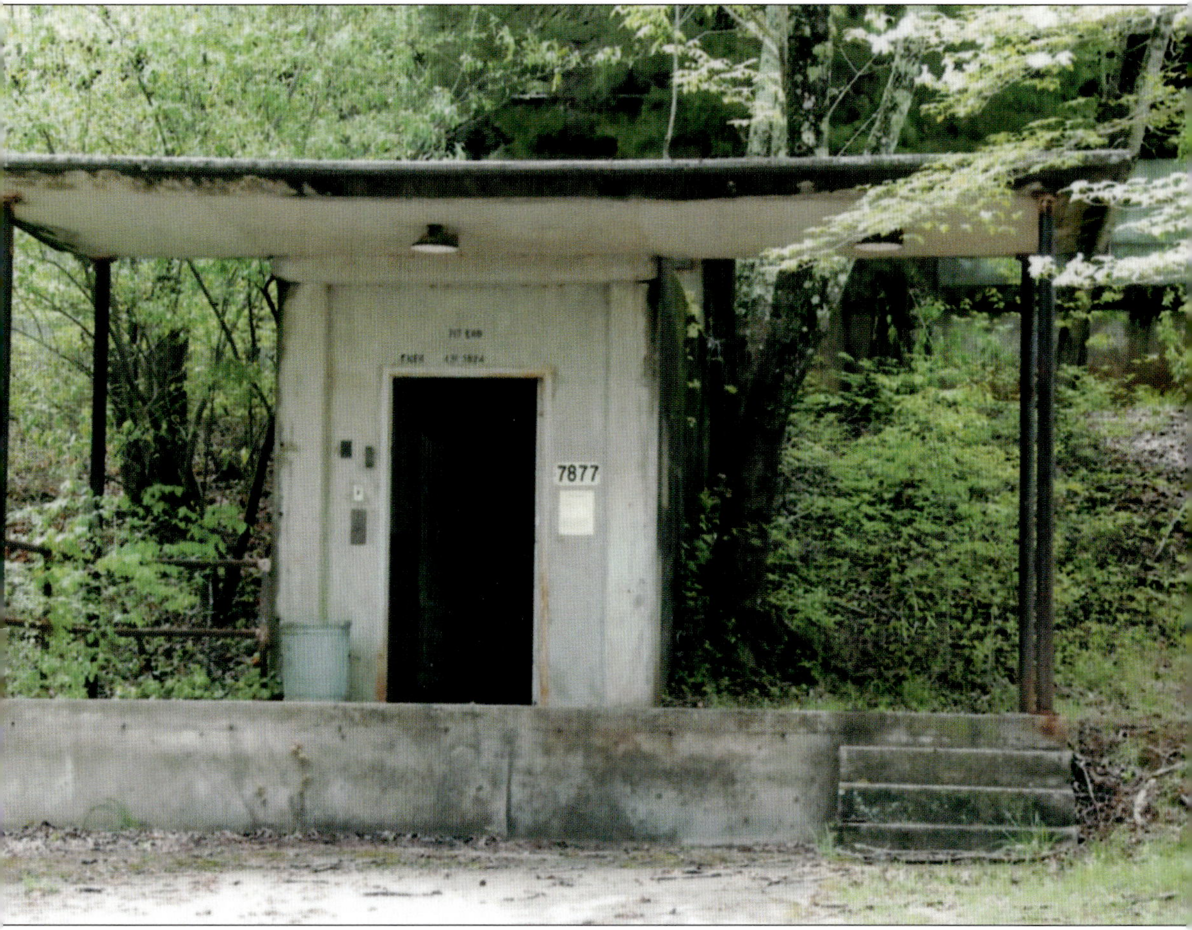

One of the unique structures on the Clarksville base is the Birdcage, where nuclear weapons were secretly stored without the community even knowing it existed. Recently, the Fort Campbell installation and Clarksville acknowledged the location and opened it to the public, allowing visitors to take tours and photographs. This image was taken during a visit in 2013. (Photograph by Billyfrank Morrison.)

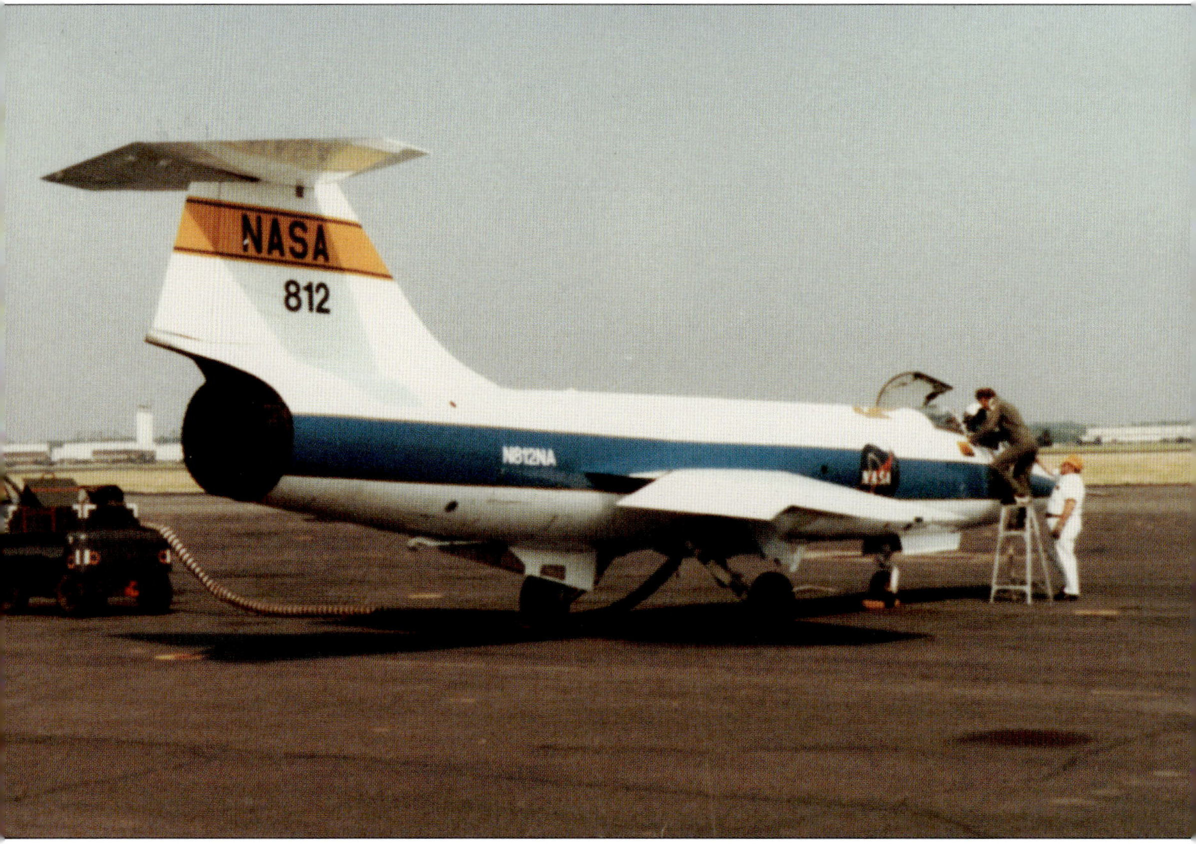

The airfields at Fort Campbell have been used in numerous exercises. Surprising to some, one of the most common uses was when NASA would fly to the installation, using the airfields and other parts of the base to conduct exercises along with some test flights. (Photograph by Billyfrank Morrison.)

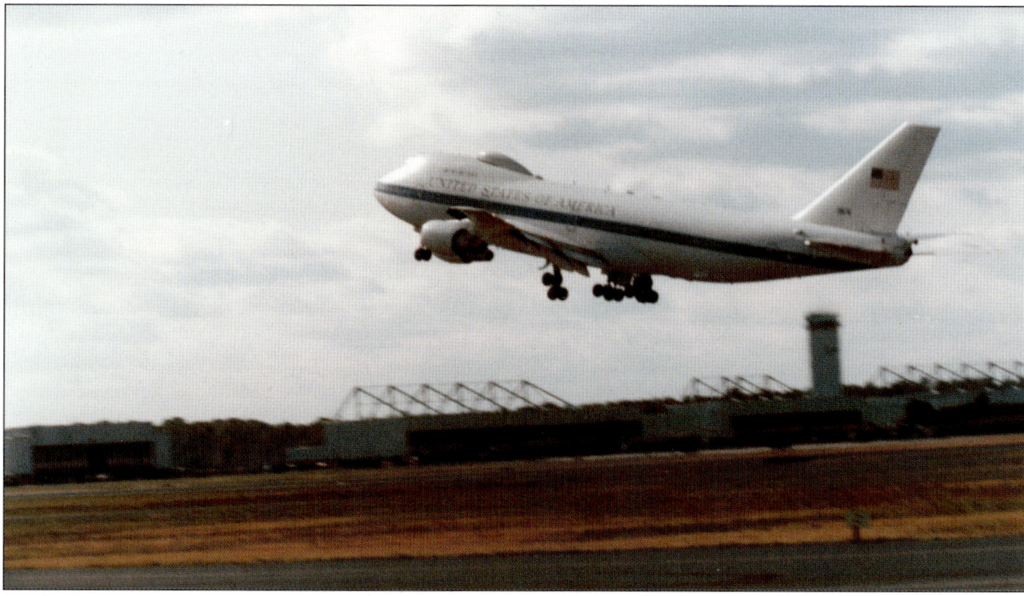

With the numerous political figures visiting Fort Campbell over the years, it was pretty common to see government aircraft. Shown here is a plane taking flight and leaving the Campbell Army Airfield. It was taken during one of First Lady Barbara Bush's visits. (Photograph by Billyfrank Morrison.)

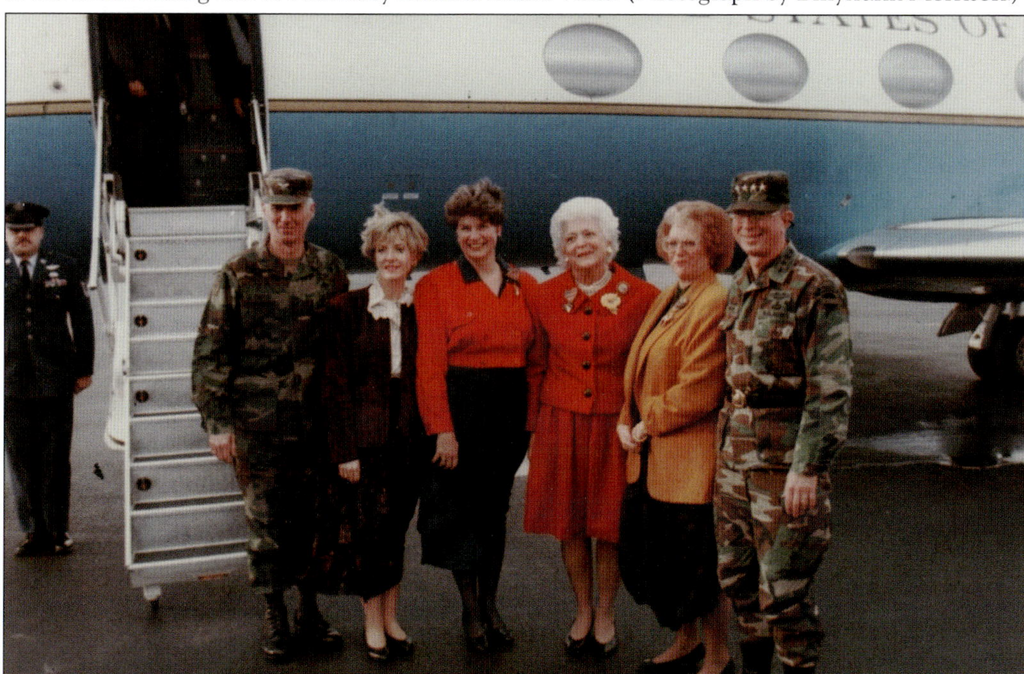

Campbell Army Airfield has welcomed many political figures, including first ladies. This is just one of the three trips First Lady Barbara Bush made to the installation. During this February 1991 visit, she met privately with some relatives of the troops before speaking with a crowd of more than 3,000. Pictured from left to right are Col. John Seymon, Mary Seymon, unidentified, First Lady Barbara Bush, unidentified, and an unidentified four-star general. (Photograph by Billyfrank Morrison.)

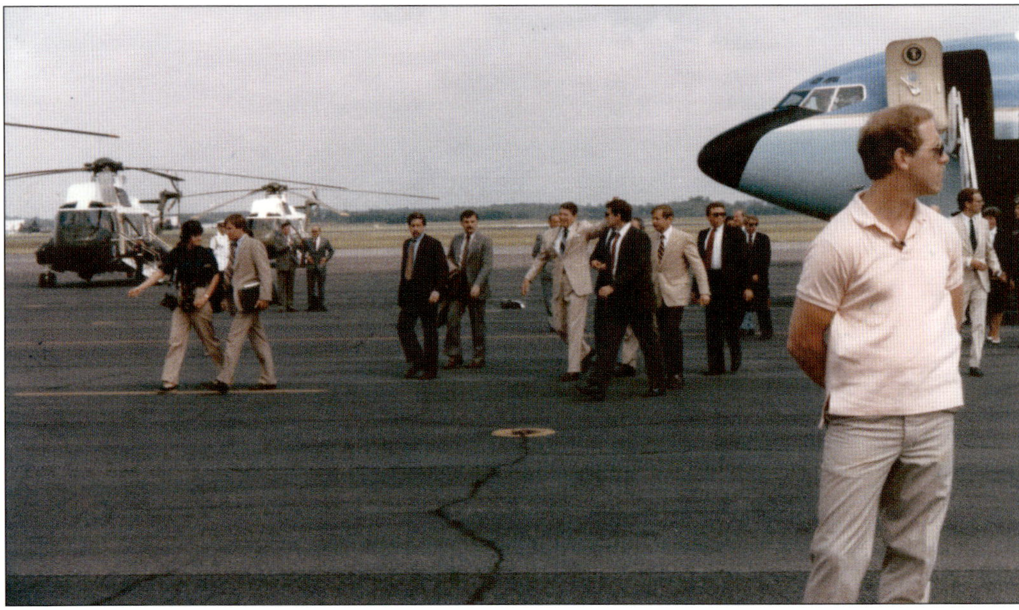

Fort Campbell has played the host to many political figures throughout the years. Both of these photographs were taken during a visit from the 40th president of the United States, Ronald Reagan. Many people remember the speech President Reagan gave to the families at Fort Campbell. On December 12, 1985, while returning home after a peacekeeping mission in Egypt, 248 soldiers died when their flight crashed in Newfoundland. Above, Pres. Ronald Reagan steps off Air Force One and is greeted by local photographers, media, and military personnel at the Campbell Army Airfield. Below, after speaking with local reports, he is escorted off the airfield to tour the Fort Campbell installation and meet with some soldiers. (Both photographs by Billyfrank Morrison.)

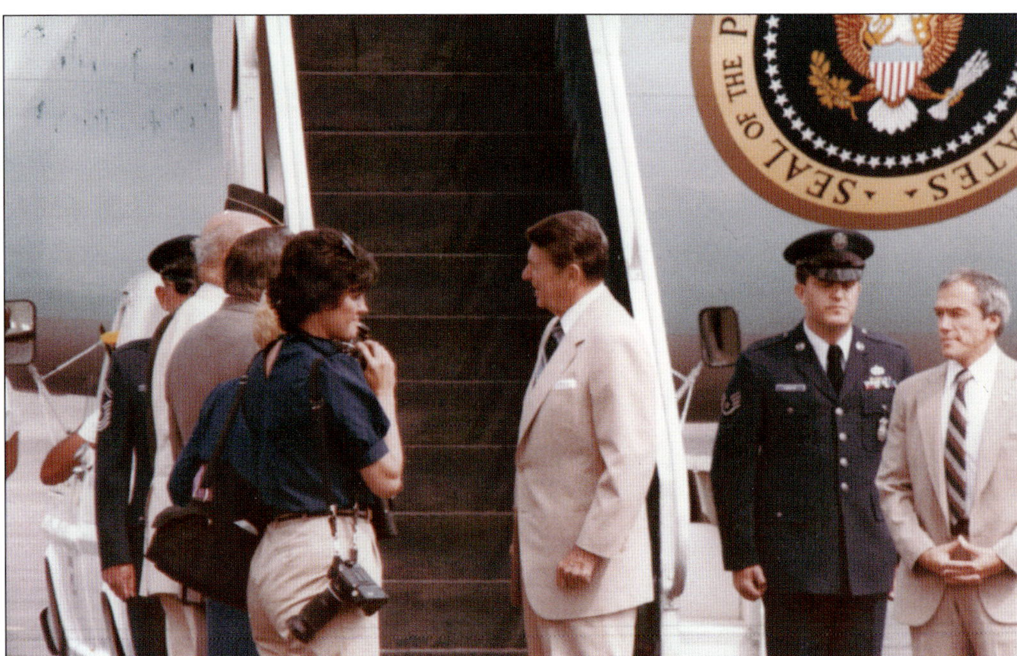

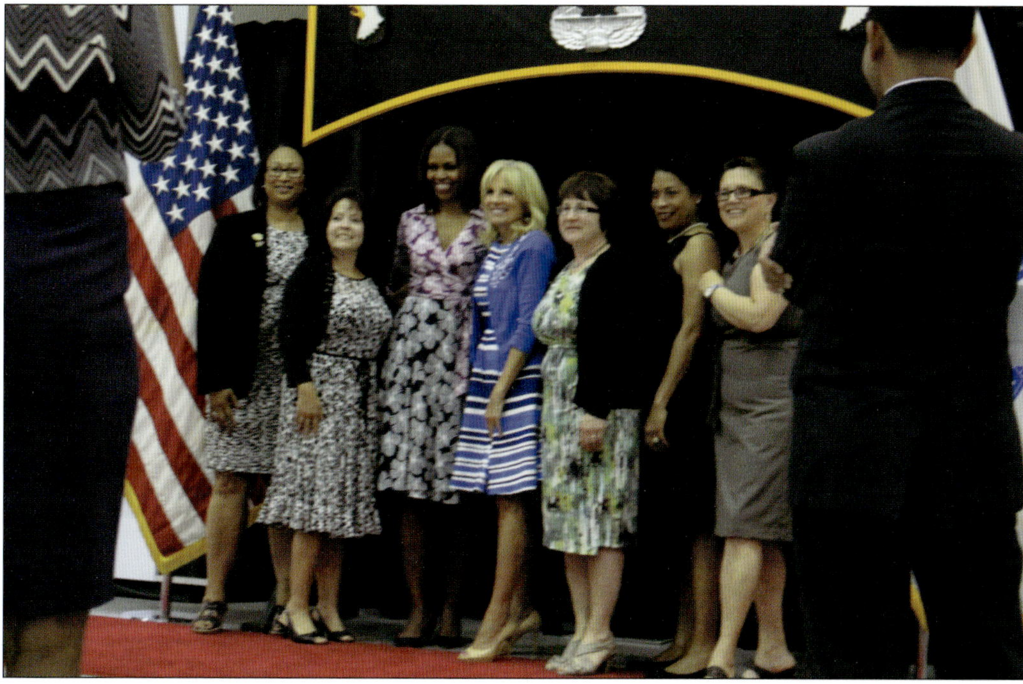

One of the most recent visits by political figures was from First Lady Michelle Obama and Dr. Jill Biden. They made a surprise visit to a few military spouses, with an up-close-and-personal greeting. Following the event, they spoke with some of the soldiers on the installation about a program geared toward helping veterans find work after their service. Above, seven ladies pose for a photograph with the First Lady Michelle Obama and Dr. Jill Biden. From left to right are Veronica Martin, unidentified, Michelle Obama, Jill Biden, and three unidentified women. Below, all of the ladies who attended the greeting were able to personally meet both guests after their inspiring speeches. The first lady is chatting with Veronica Martin. (Both courtesy of Veronica Martin.)

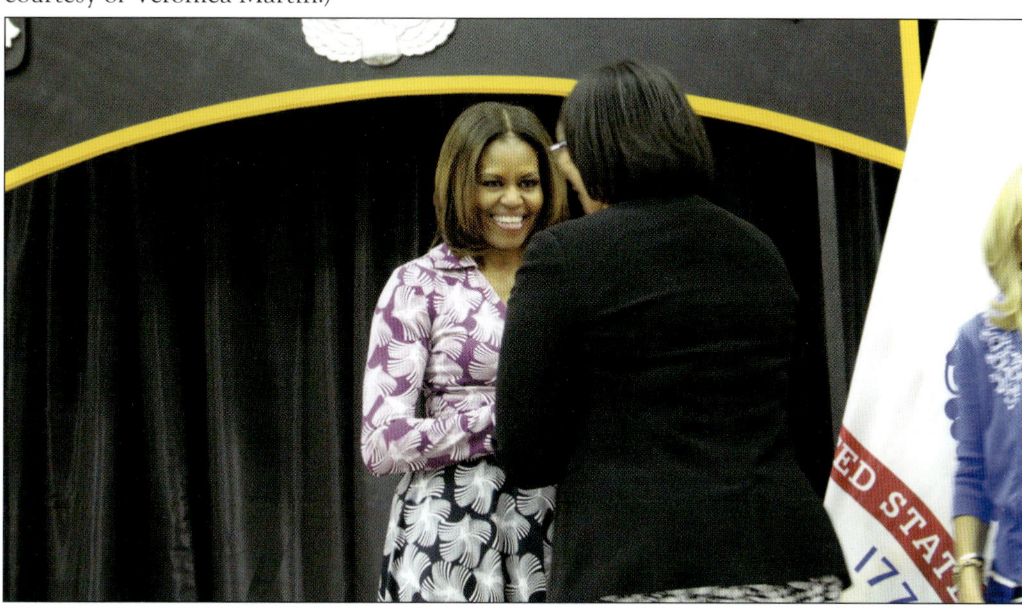

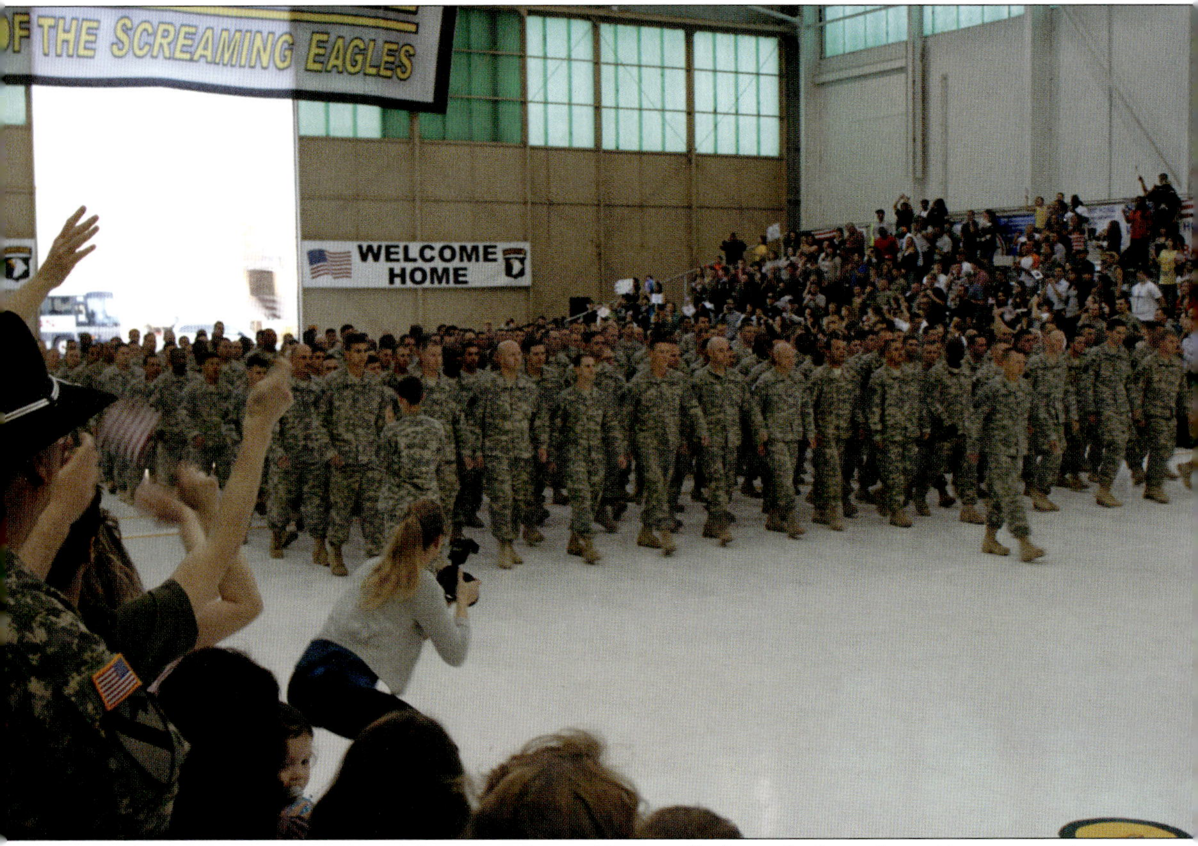

The happiest and most joyful time is when soldiers walk through these doors. During a welcome-home ceremony, family and friends gather with large smiles on their faces and tears of happiness streaming down their cheeks. Dressed in their nicest outfits and waving American flags, they hold signs saying things like, "Welcome Home Dad," "We Missed and Love You Mom," and so many more special messages from the heart. Through the years, Fort Campbell has had to activate many of its military to go into combat abroad. The families of Fort Campbell and those in the Clarksville community walk with heavy hearts during those times. Moments like the one captured here bring back the joy and smiles to so many faces. (Courtesy of Kurt Bryant.)

Four

Growth and Change

Looking at some of the buildings, businesses, and homes in the community brings to mind shepherding the past into the future. There are great examples of restoring the past when one drives through some of the local neighborhoods and sees how some families continue to put so much love and care into their homes. It is not cheap or easy to bring a home back to life when it is barely hanging on; however, it is possible thanks to organizations such as the Montgomery County Historical Society, which focuses on preserving the history of Clarksville. It continues its effort and drive to keep history alive for all to enjoy.

Individuals also take on some of these preservation jobs themselves. Dwight Eversole, for example, is a strong advocate in saving some of the most beautiful and interesting homes in Clarksville, and his last 10-year project on the Solomon House was a preservation of love. He is not alone in this quest. Darren and Paige King were once stationed at Fort Campbell and felt as if they have had found their new permanent home after leaving the military. Not only do they both work on preserving history and buildings, they are also very active in the community, once owning a popular downtown store, Hodgepodge. They are now working to preserve their home and save its history.

Individual homes are not the only buildings being saved and given a new life. The Roxy Theatre is probably one of the most well-recognized pieces of history still in operation. Once known as the Lillian and built in 1913, it sat empty for years until two men with a great vision, Tom Thayer and John McDonald, reopened it in 1983.

New life is not only coming to old buildings, as there is also a boom in new construction. With a current population estimated at 132,929 (up from 22,021 in 1960), the need for housing developments and schools is still on the rise. The photographs in this chapter show the life found in these buildings.

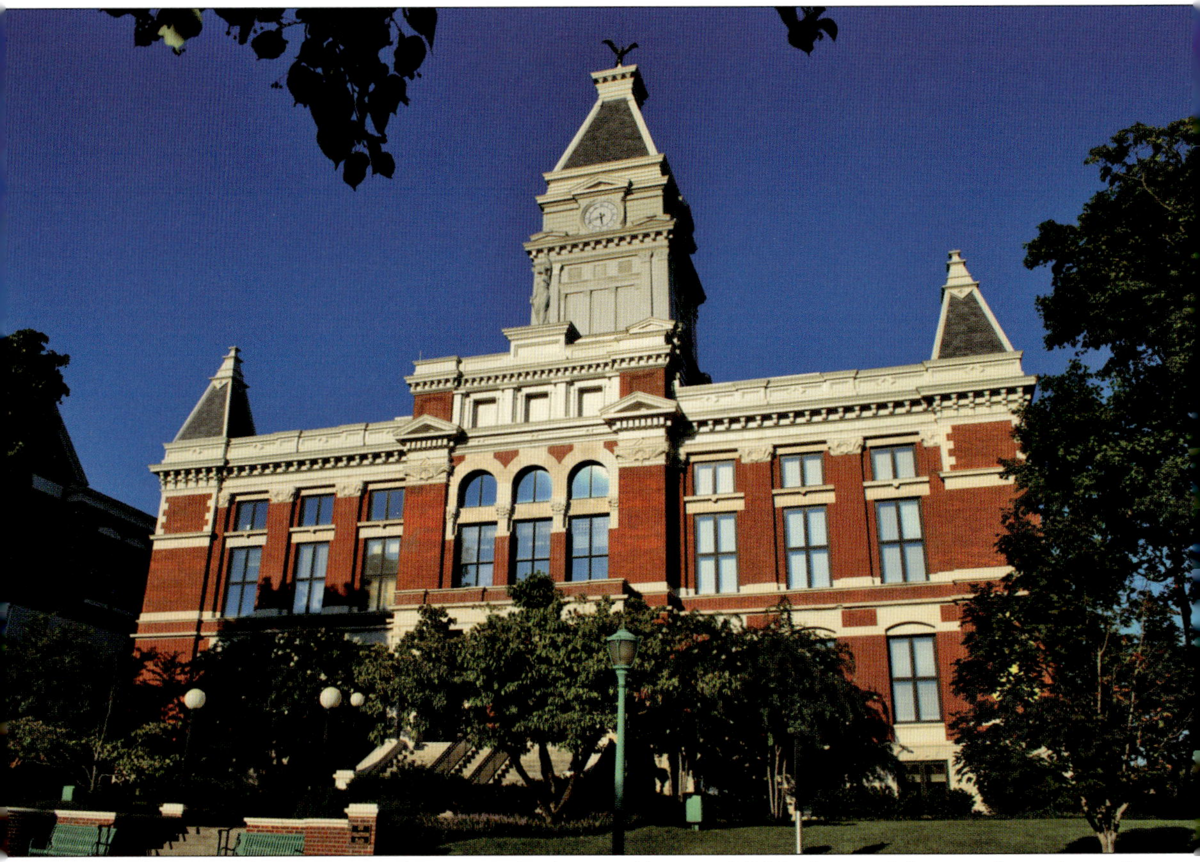

The original county courthouse was built out of logs in 1796 by James Adams and set along the riverbank. The first brick courthouse was built in 1811, the fourth county courthouse. This is the most recent photograph of the sixth and current Montgomery Courthouse after being destroyed by the 1999 tornado. (Photograph by David Smith.)

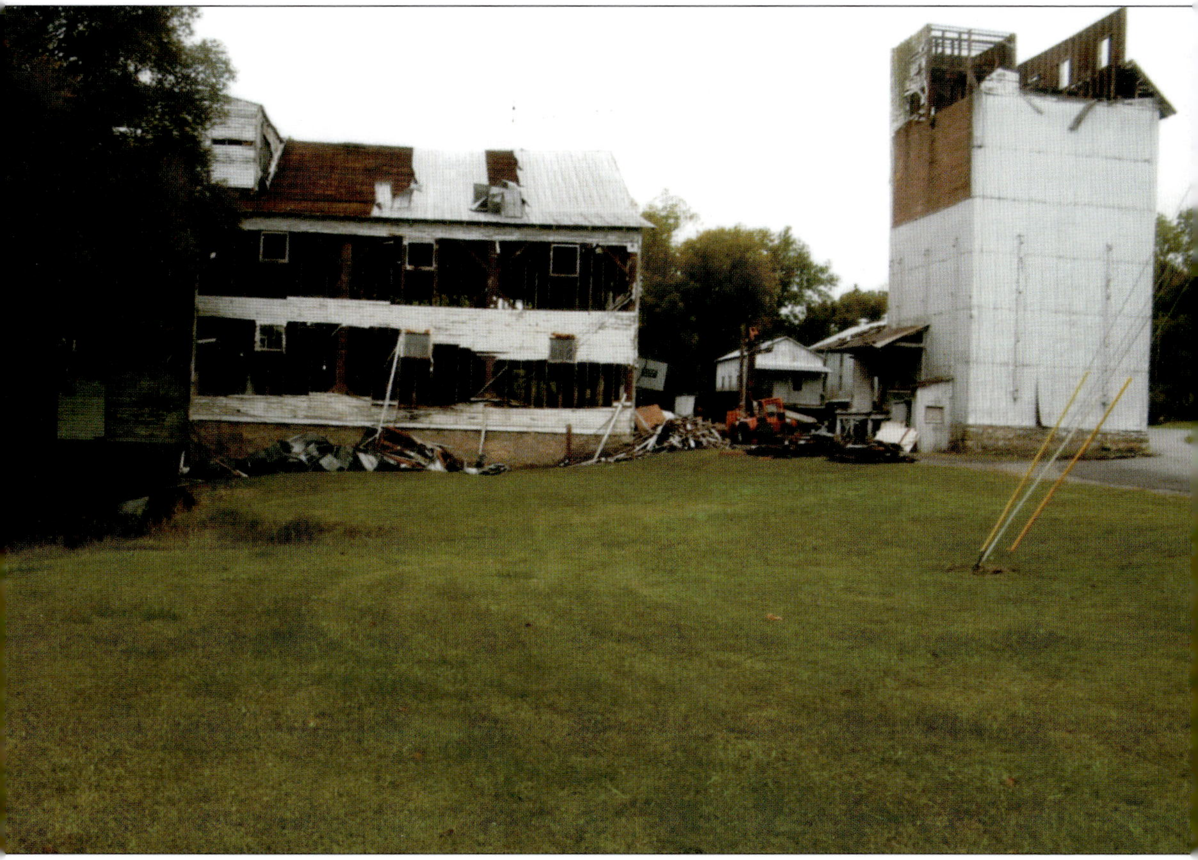

Ringgold Mill was one of the earliest commercial developments in Clarksville, located on Little West Fork Creek. It was partially destroyed in 1863 while Union troops were working to disrupt the supply line of the Confederate Army. Following its reconstruction in 1885, it was struck by lightning and then rebuilt. The mill was in use until around 1974 and is now on private property. At various times, it was used as a post office, a library, and even a voter precinct location. It was placed in the National Registry of Historic Places in 1980 for its commercial and agricultural significance. Sadly, it was removed from the registry in 2012 following the removal of the mill and grain elevator building due to safety issues. In this photograph, taken in October of 2012, the removal process is under way. (Photograph by Billyfrank Morrison.)

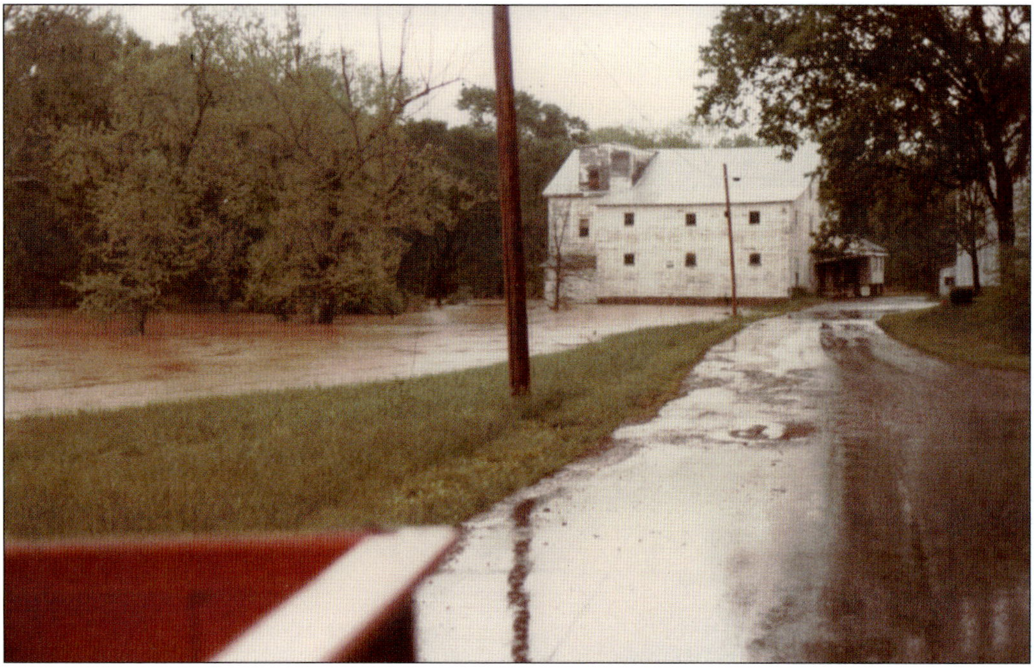

Above, the massive flood of 2010 was one that affected many families, homes, and businesses. The Ringgold Mill was visibly impacted by the event. Below is Riverside Drive during the 2010 flood that paralyzed many areas. (Both photographs by Billyfrank Morrison.)

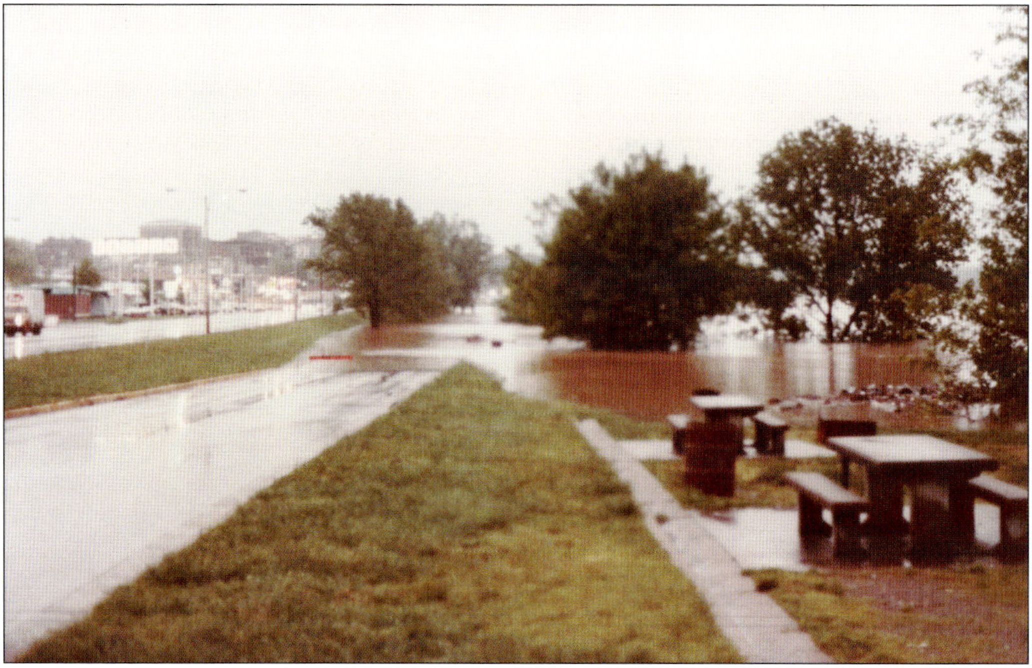

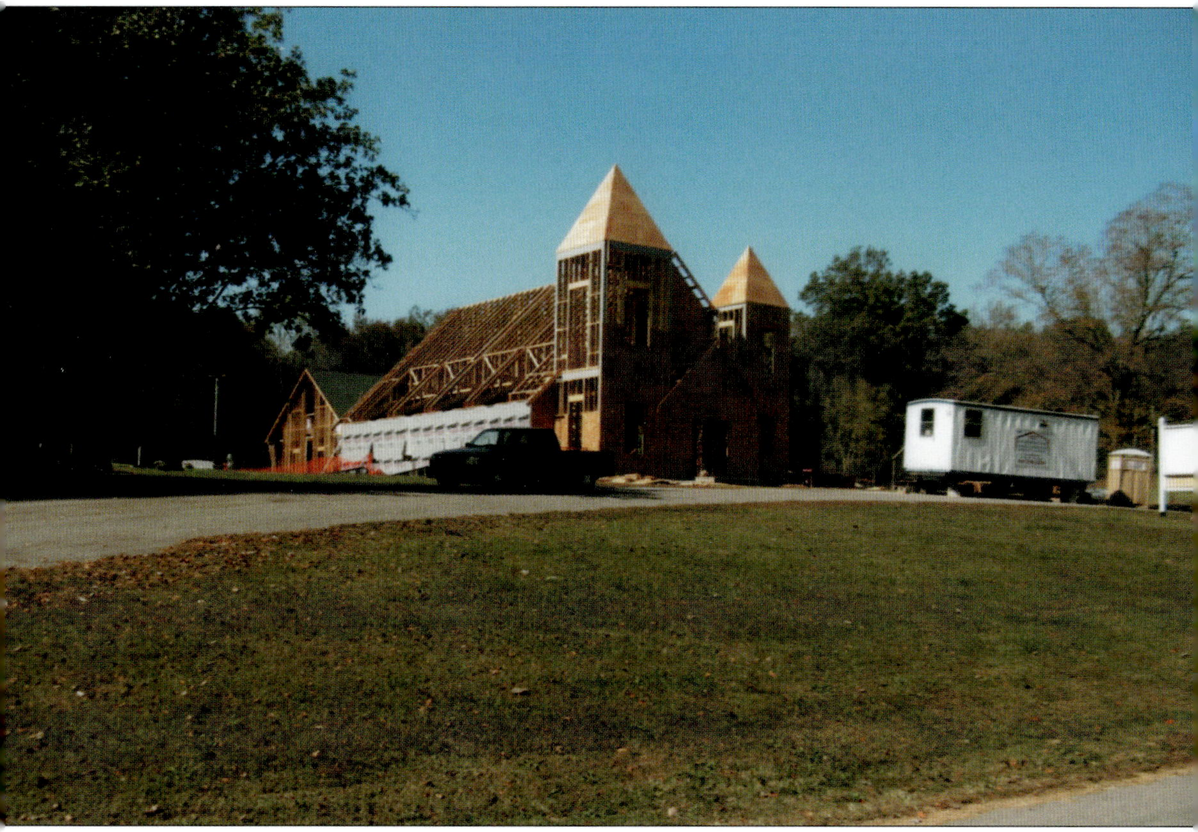

This is one of the many phases during the rebuilding of the Bethlehem United Methodist on Old Russellville Pike after the complete destruction caused by a July 2009 fire. The fire was believed to have begun with a lighting strike on the church steeple. Services were held the following Sunday on the grounds of the 110-year-old church. There was a "wailing wall" constructed from the building's original bricks, and members of church would write their prayers on pieces of paper and place them between the bricks, just like those that pray at Jerusalem's Wailing Wall. In September of the previous year, the church had served as the site of a music video filmed by county singer Trace Atkins and actor Stephen Baldwin. Built in 1836, it was placed in the National Register of Historic Places. (Photograph by Billyfrank Morrison.)

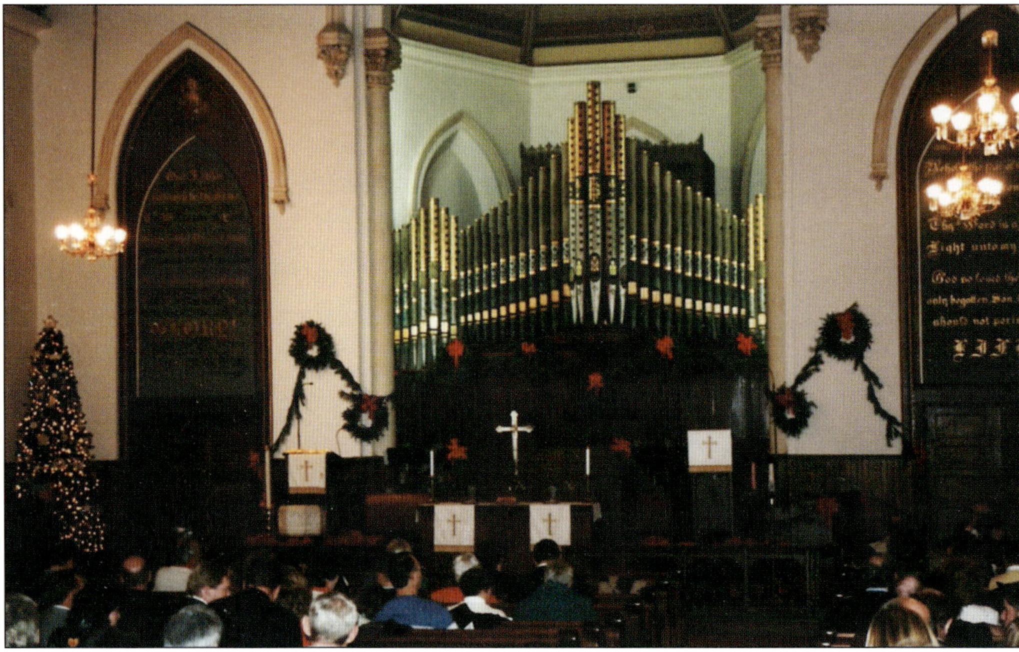

On January 22, 1999, an F3 tornado came to Clarksville with a purpose. It stayed on the ground for five minutes and traveled over four miles, its path 880 yards wide, ripping through the city. The photograph below is of the same church shown above. It is easily identifiable because of the two panels on each side of the altar—they are still standing and intact. (Both photographs by Molly Cook.)

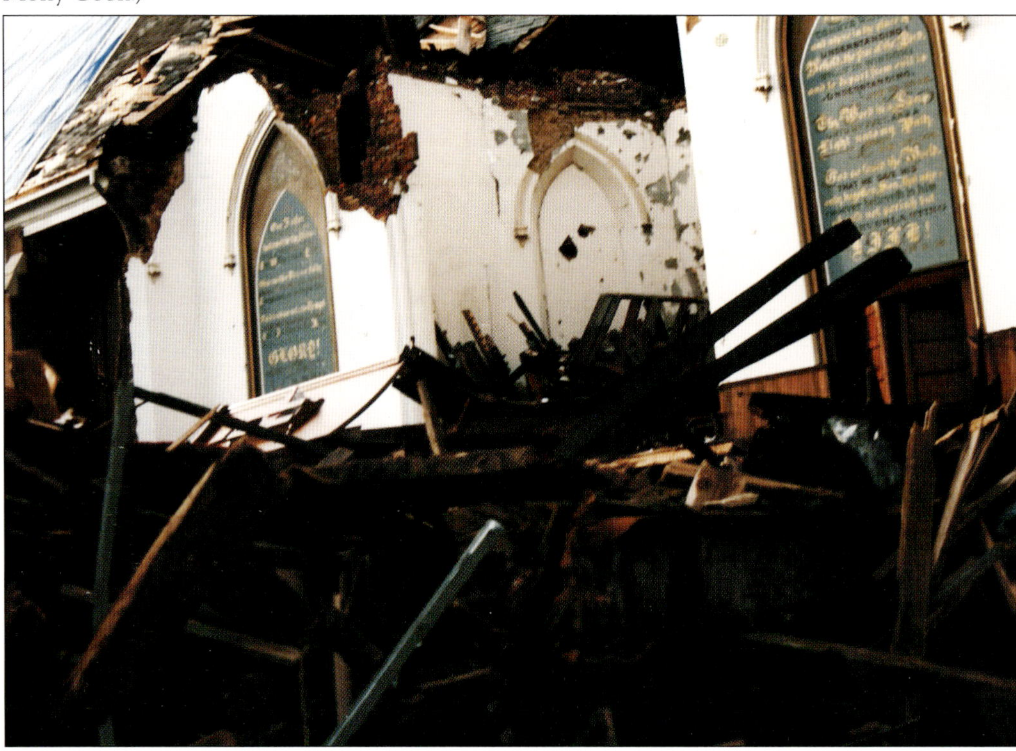

Originally completed in 1898 as the federal post office and customshouse, the Customs House Museum and Cultural Center went through a significant renovation in 1996 that made it a 35,000-square-foot building. This structure is unique in its architectural design and continues to hold its character. It is said to be the second-largest museum of interest in Tennessee. It houses art, science, and local history exhibits, as well as an interactive kid zone. (Photograph by David Smith.)

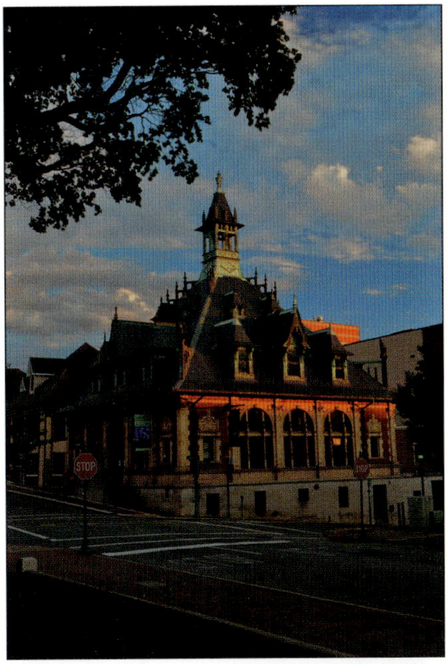

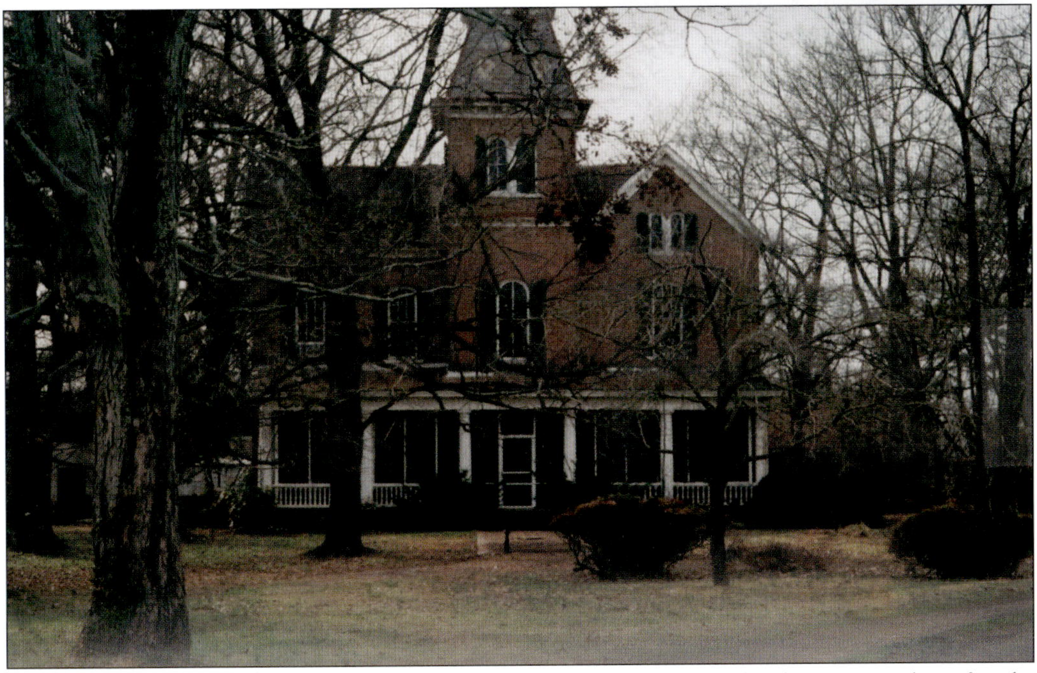

This photograph of Minglewood, which was built in 1867 and owned by the Cunningham family, was taken in March 2004. Chloe Cunningham was a loyal member of the historical society. She lived in the house with her mother, Sarah White Cunningham. After her mother's death, Chloe claimed all the family treasures, including silver, china, and furniture. After Chloe left the home, it sat empty and was the target of thieves; they even stole a Waterford chandelier. Chloe suffered a tumor but kept on fighting it until the day she passed away in August 1989. This home and all of its mysterious stories are still of interest to many in the Clarksville community. (Photograph by Billyfrank Morrison.)

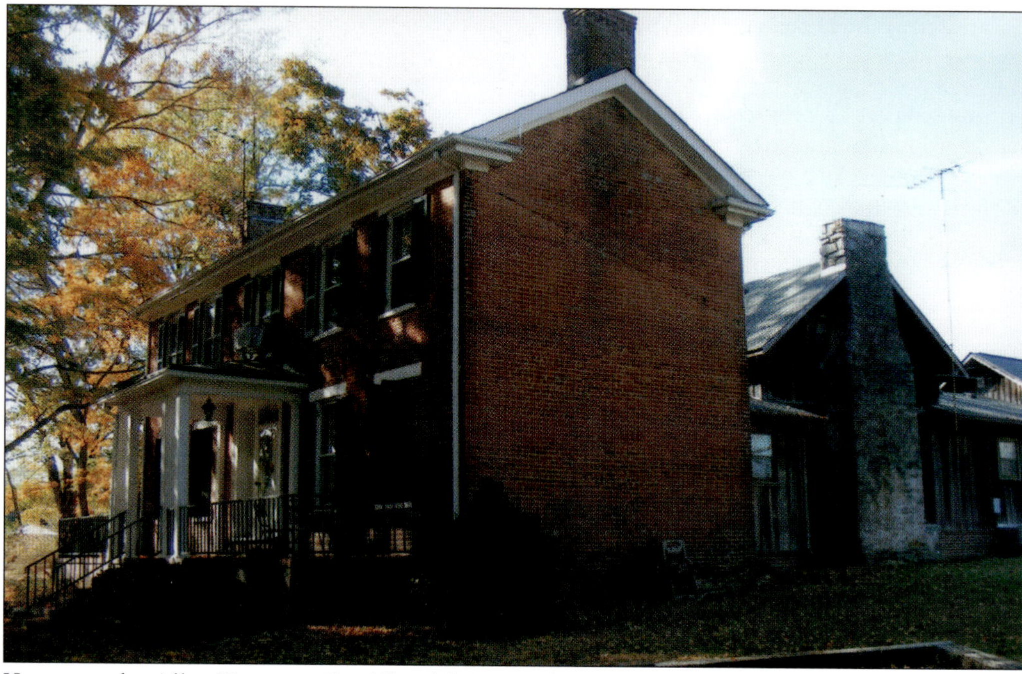

Known as the Allen House on the Allendale Farm, this structure was built in 1858 by Bailey Allen (1816–1880) and is an extension of the original log home out back. It was placed in the National Register of Historic Places in the late 1970s. (Photograph by Amelia Allen Hartz.)

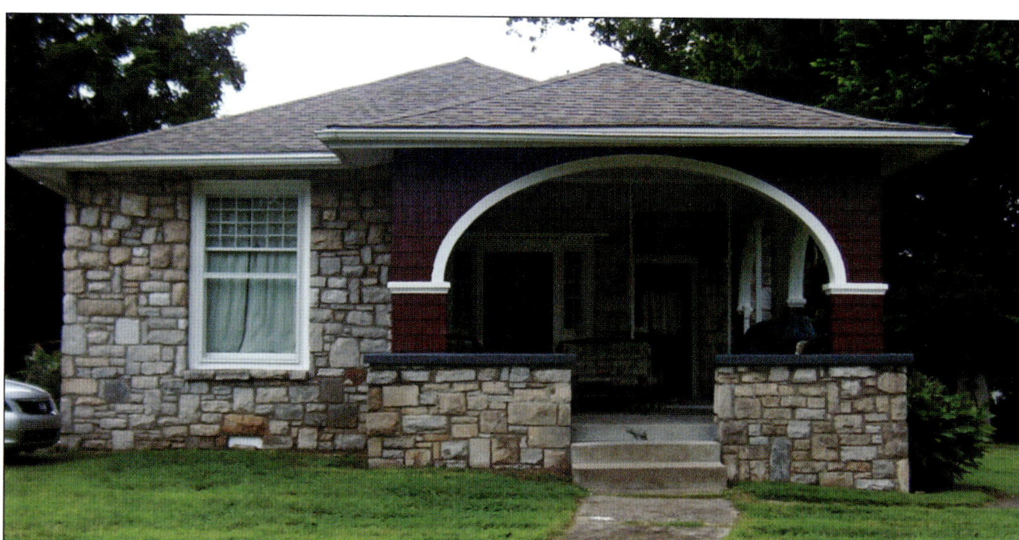

Solomon House, once owned by W. Eugene Solomon, is located at 917 Crossland Avenue. Solomon owned several businesses in Clarksville, including Columbia Produce and Exchange-Furniture. He was remembered fondly by his neighbors as being the first owner of a television set in the neighborhood. The home was built around 1910 as a craftsman/cedar shake–style house. Then, in the 1920s, the stone wall was built in front of the cedar-shake siding. The restoration of this home has been a labor of love for Dwight Eversole, who completed the 10-year project in 2012. (Photograph by Dwight Eversole.)

This towering 23-foot-circumference oak tree was hollow in the base and served as a great escape from the heat for dogs. The hollow portion also served as a place for children and their imaginary play of "house." During a storm in the 1950s, lighting snapped the top off, and the tree was eventually cut down in the late 1970s for safety reasons. (Courtesy of Elwyn and Rubye Patch.)

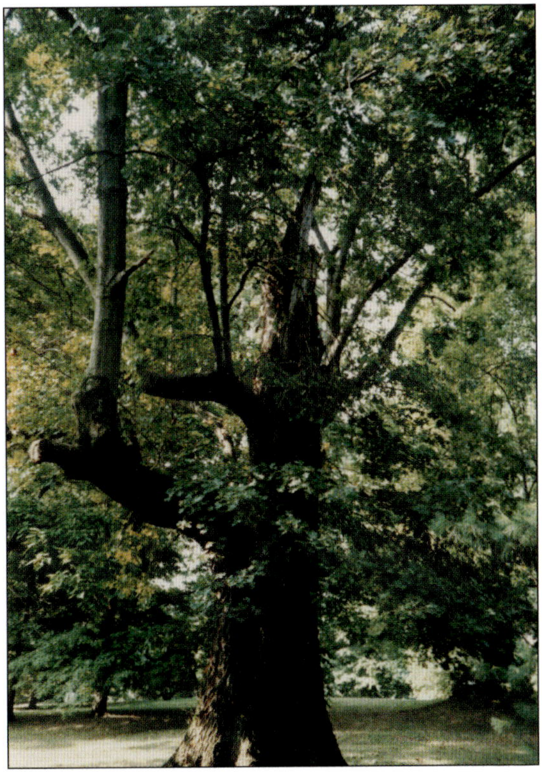

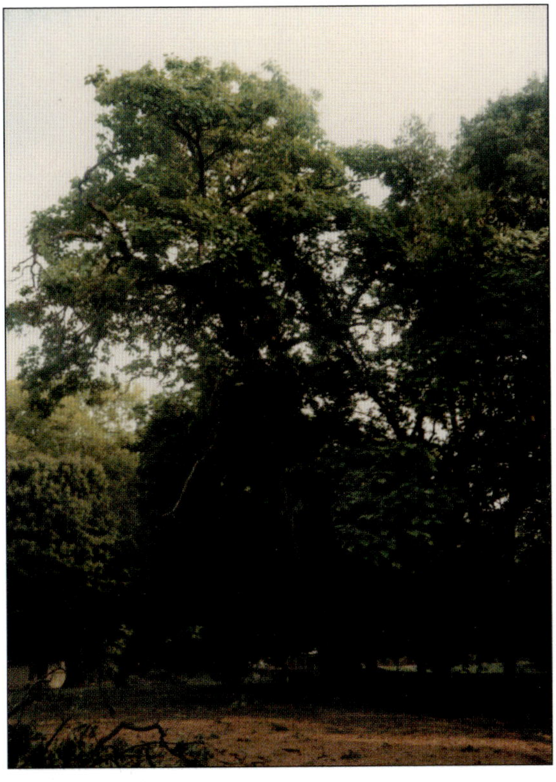

Photographed in the late 1970s, the "Leaning Tree" can be found on the Tip Top property. This particular catalpa is said to be the largest specimen in the state of Tennessee. Typically growing to 59 feet in height, it is easily recognized by its heart-shaped leaves. (Courtesy of Elwyn and Rubye Patch.)

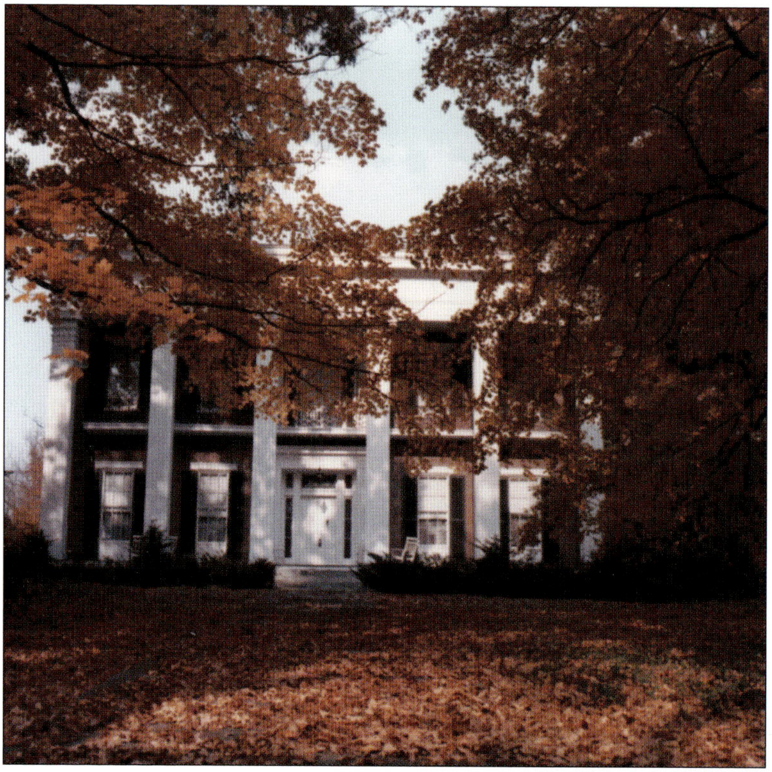

The Tip Top was placed in the National Register in July 1998. This Greek Revival building was completed in 1859 by a wealthy tobacco merchant, Joseph Philips Williams. It is believed to have been designed by Adolphus Heiman, who was born in Prussia and came to the United States in 1834. (Courtesy of Elwyn and Rubye Patch.)

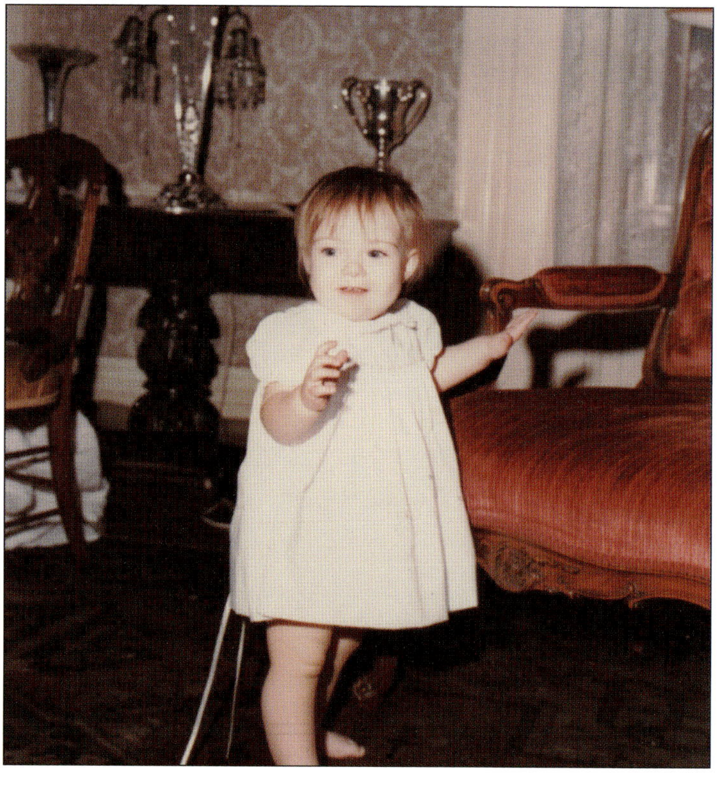

In this 1975 photograph, Elisabeth Huntington Patch is pictured in the east parlor of the Tip Top. The Tip Top once served as the temporary headquarters for Yankee officers during the Civil War and their occupation of Clarksville. (Courtesy of Elwyn and Rubye Patch.)

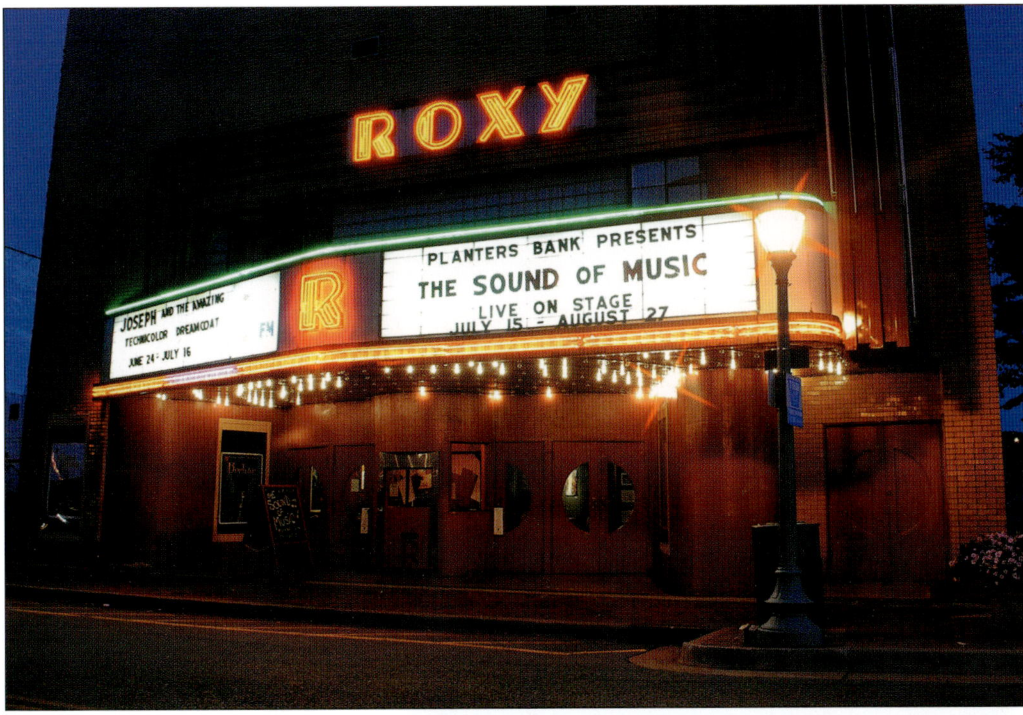

The Roxy, which sits on the corner of Franklin and First Streets, continues to offer entertainment to the community of Clarksville. It was erected in 1947 after the original Lilian Theater, built in 1913, burned down in 1945. It drew crowds of people from miles around to enjoy movies, but it closed in 1980. Sitting empty for years, it reopened in 1983 as a live theater thanks to Tom Thayer and John McDonald. Currently seating 200 visitors and boasting a 50-seat black box in the balcony, it is the home of the Roxy Regional Theatre, which has put on many amazing productions. One must remember to visit the wonderful Peg Harvill Gallery, which is located past the lobby and displays some wonderful pieces of artwork from local and national artists. (Above, photograph by David Smith; at right, author's collection.)

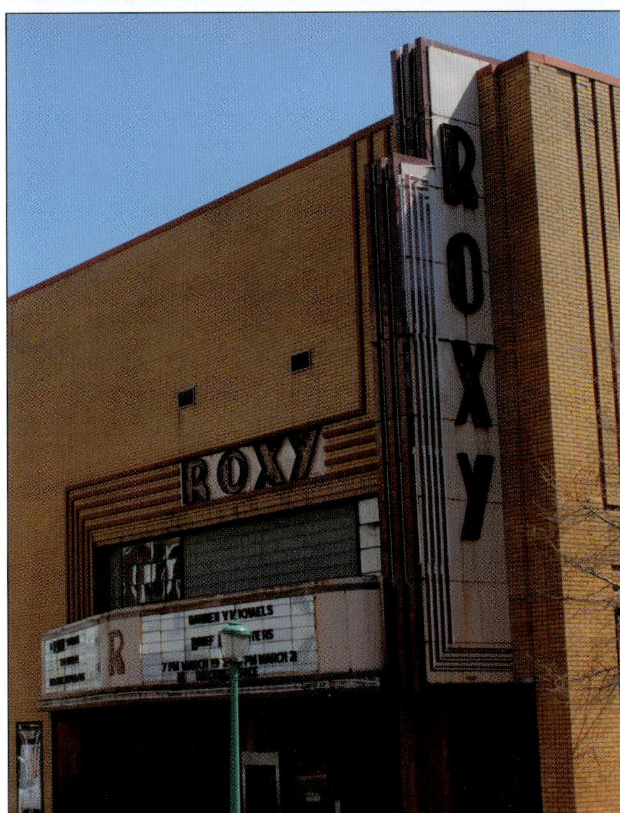

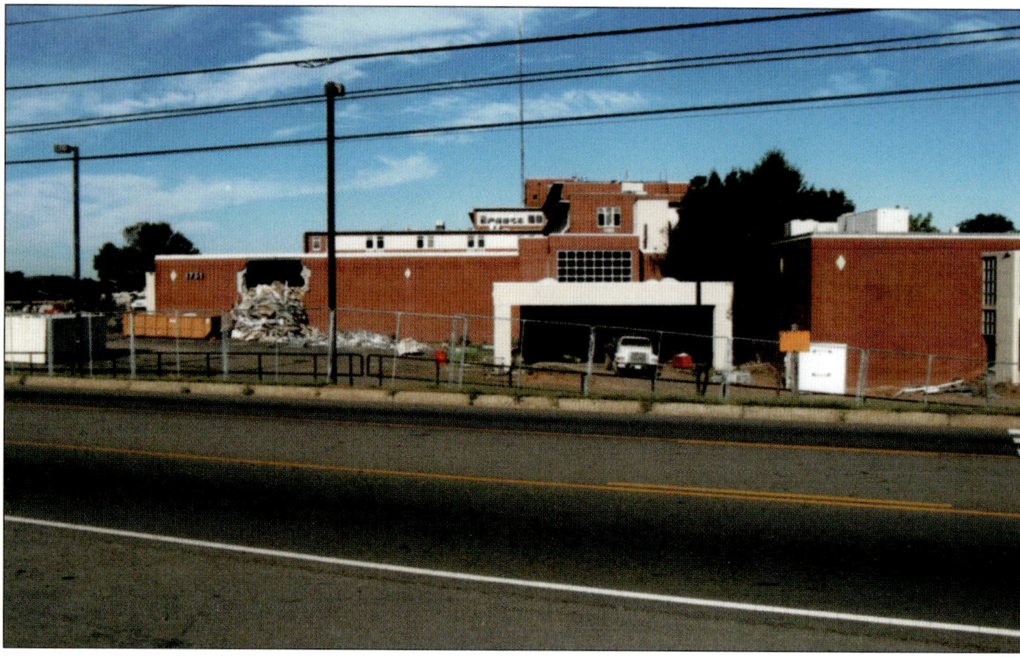

In 1954, Memorial Hospital opened after the Clarksville Hospital could barely meet the demand of health-care needs. Following World War II, the medical field grew, and with that growth Memorial Hospital was built. With more than 105 beds, the hospital offered much of what was desired at the time: updated equipment, a large, medically trained staff, a blood bank, and air-conditioning. These photographs, both taken in 2009, show the breakdown of a wonderful hospital whose great staff took care of men, women, children, and even some soldiers. (Both photographs by Billyfrank Morrison.)

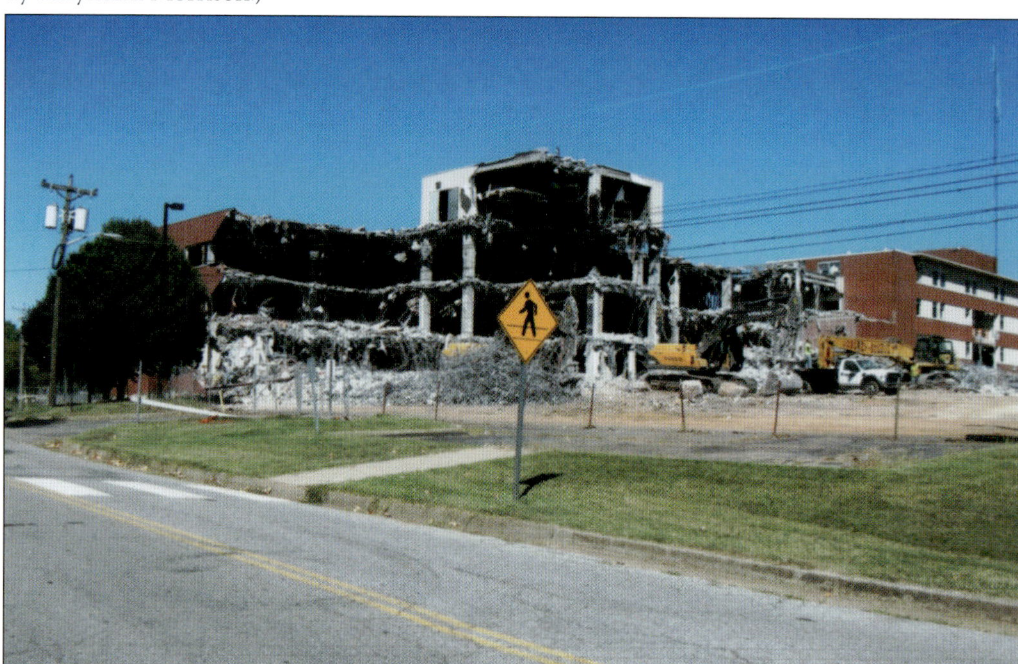

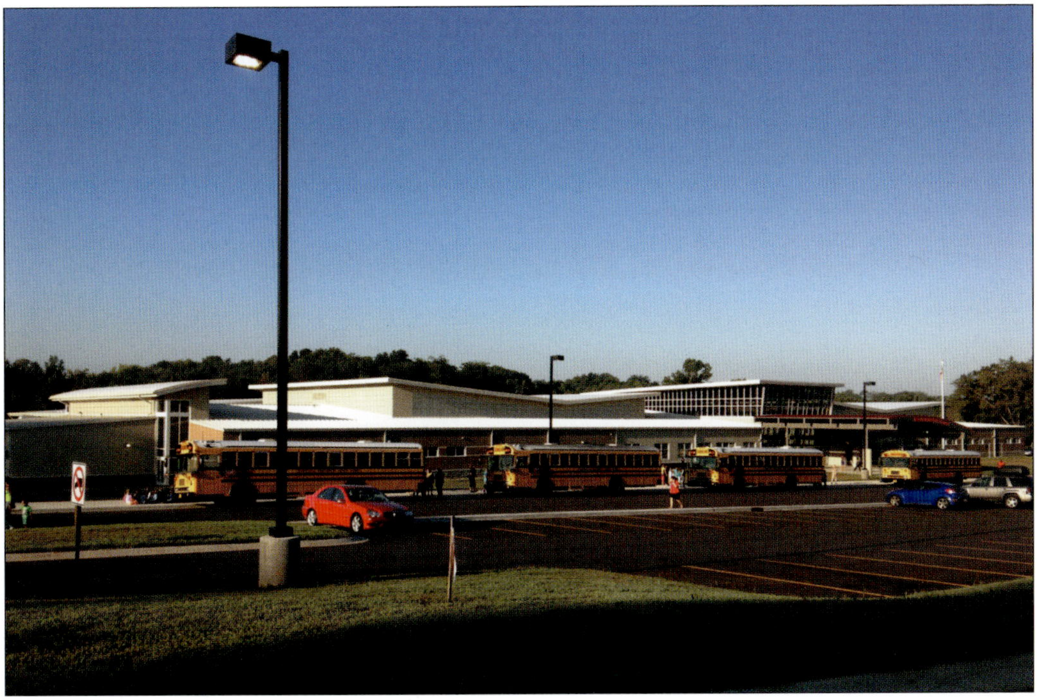

The growth of a community creates demand for more schools. Pisgah Elementary, the newest addition to the Montgomery County School District, was added to help meet the needs of the district's more than 30,400 students. It was named in honor of the Pisgah School on Martin Luther King Boulevard, a school that served African Americans from 1923 to 1962. Construction started on the new school in June 2013, and once completed, the square footage was measured at 102,000, and the facility served kindergarten through fifth grade. Typical classrooms—music, art, media, and computer—and a gymnasium were all designed in a pod layout, with large skylights to bring in the natural light and provide that open, fun feeling as students walk from classroom to classroom. (Both courtesy of Elizabeth Black.)

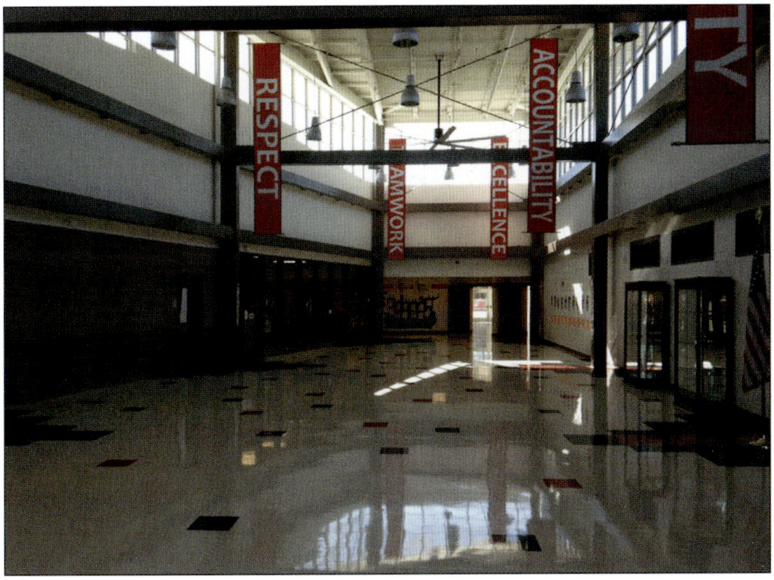

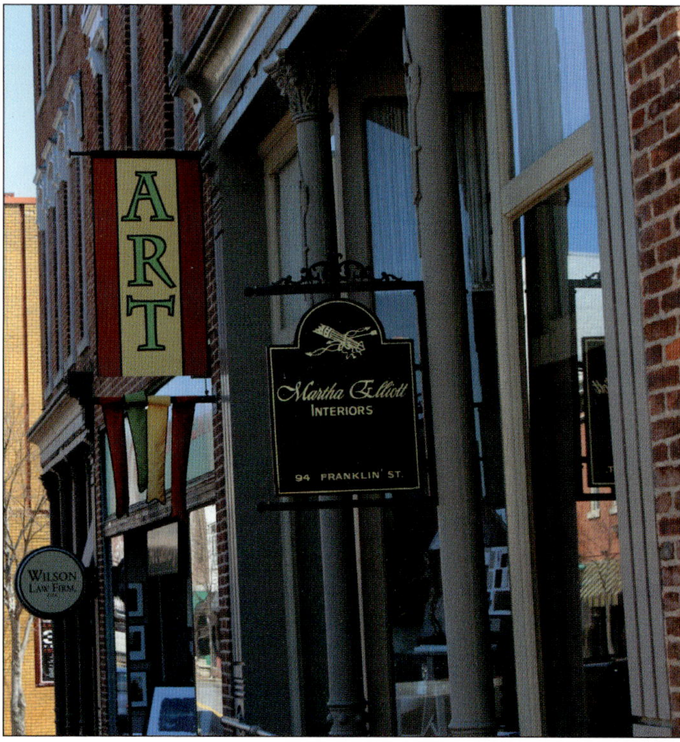

The restoration of Franklin Street welcomed the addition of many businesses. Among them were Martha Elliott's Interiors, Wilson Law Firm, and the Downtown Artists Co-op, which displays many unique and memorable pieces of artwork. (Author's collection.)

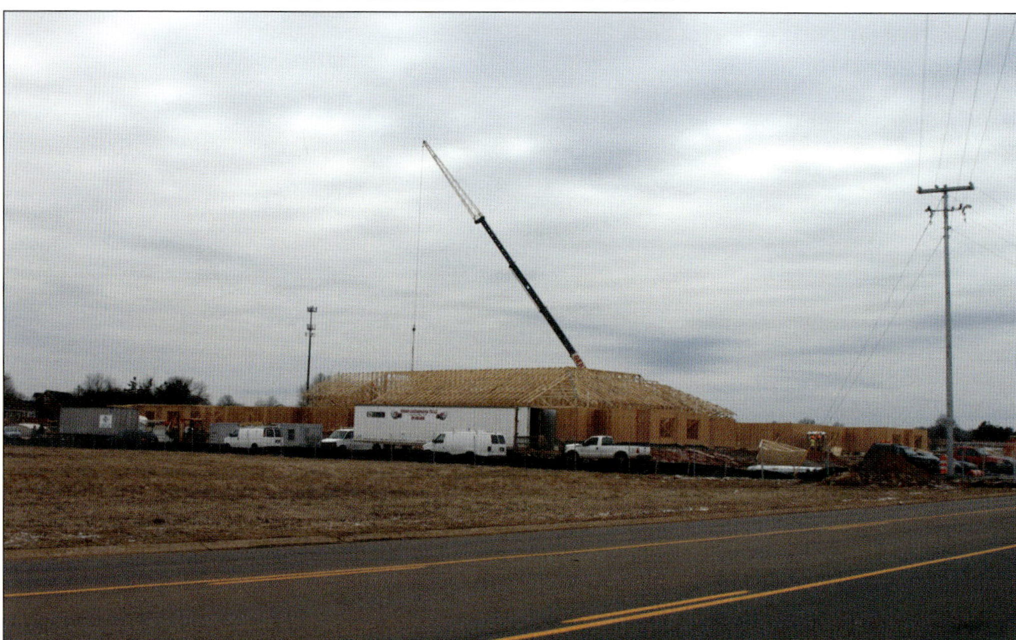

The state's new veterans home will be at 250 Arrowood Drive in Clarksville; construction began in August 2013. The location of this home is much desired by many of those retired military family members in the community. The official opening date is projected to occur in the first half of 2015. Work is still under way, as seen in this February 2014 photograph. (Courtesy of Elizabeth Black.)

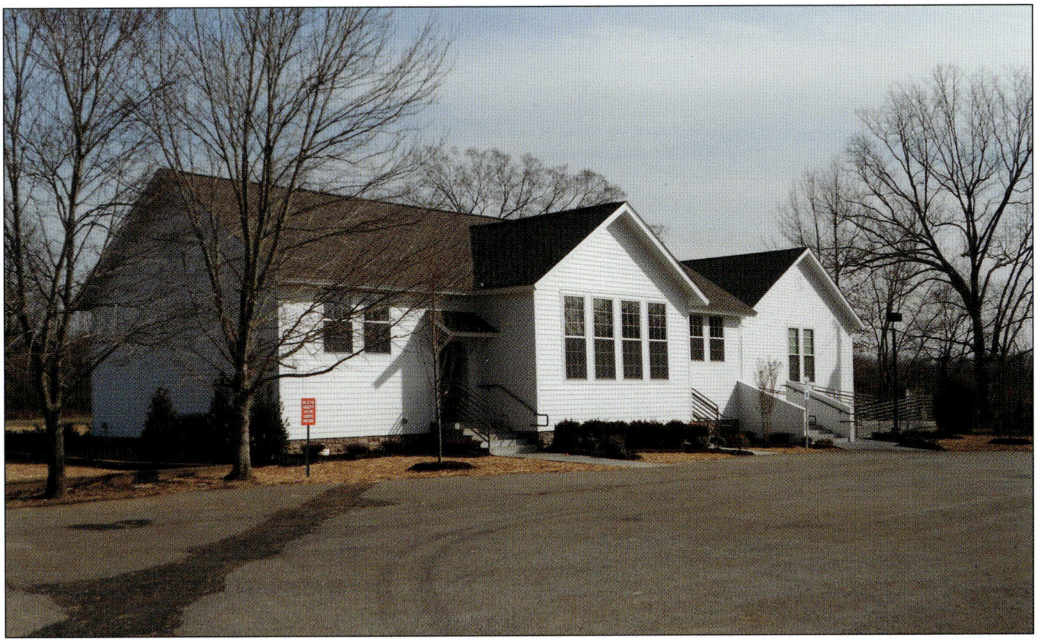

The ground-breaking for the South Guthrie Community Center took place in May 2012 at 5025 Guthrie Road. This building was formerly known as the Warfield School, constructed in 1922. Because of its history, there was concern about the memories associated with this structure, as it served as a segregated school for African American students. This photograph was taken in February 2013. (Courtesy of Elizabeth Black.)

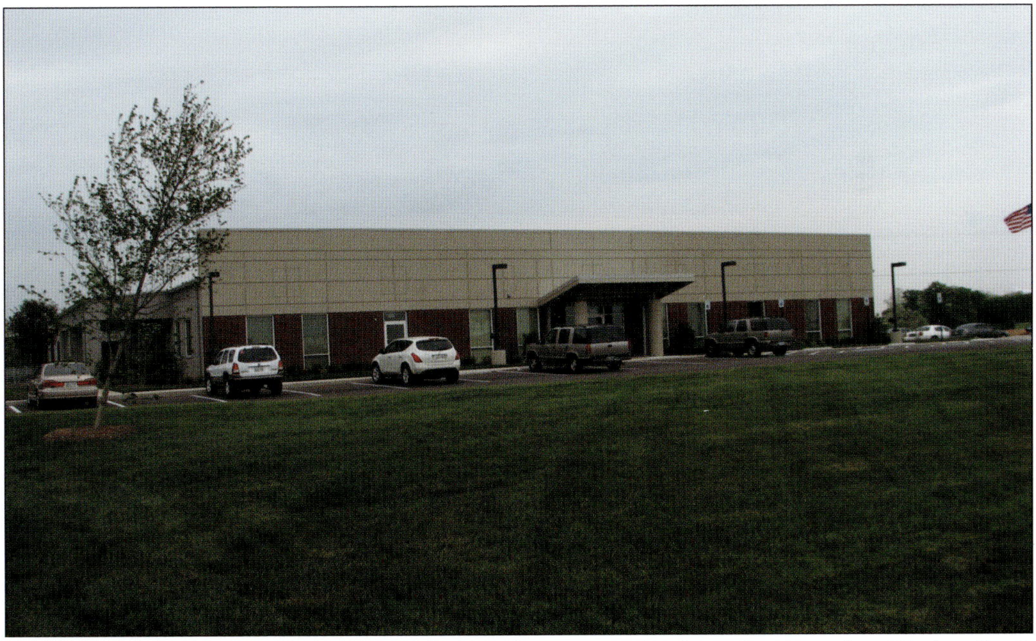

The Tennessee Rehab Center is located at 1575 Corporate Parkway Boulevard in Clarksville. It provides services for adults with disabilities and serves not only Clarksville–Montgomery County but also four surrounding counties. This photograph was taken April 29, 2009. (Courtesy of Elizabeth Black.)

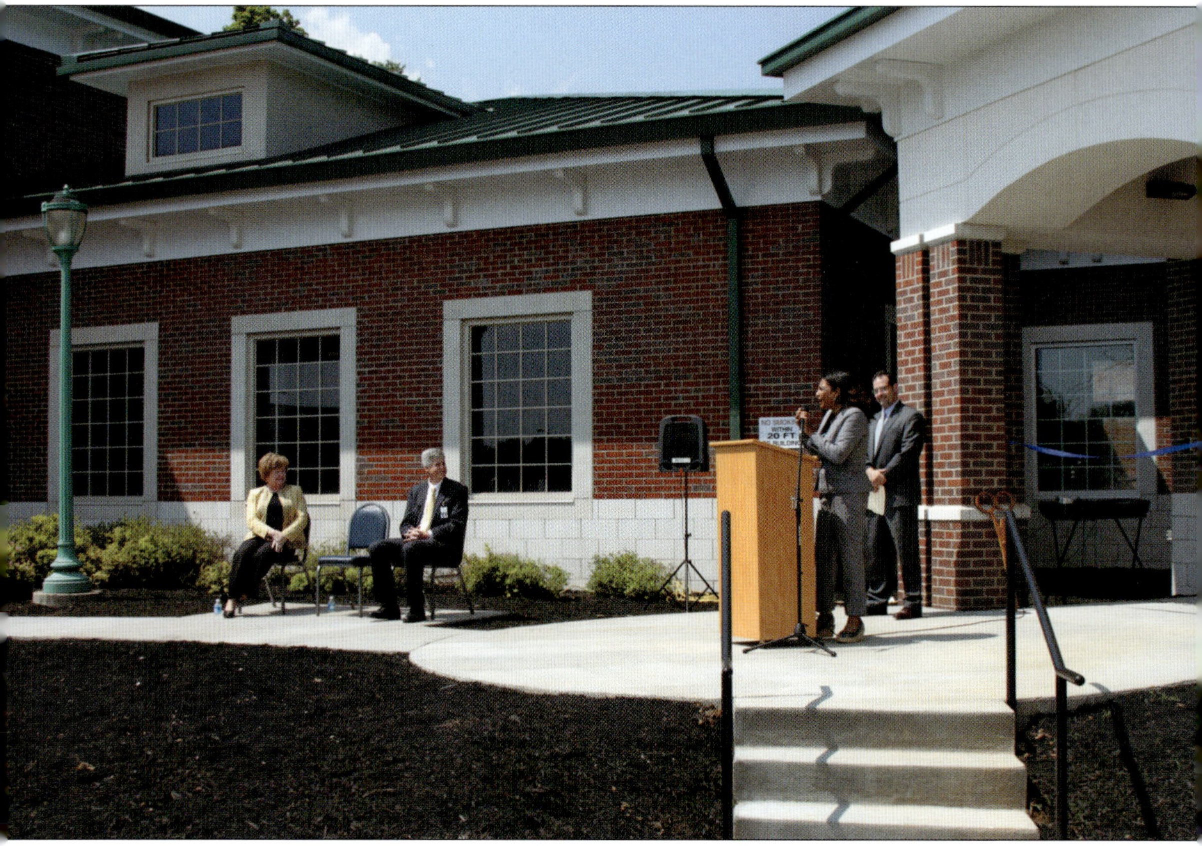

The Women, Infants, and Children (WIC) Clinic is the largest rural clinic in Tennessee, serving more than 10,600 clients both in the civilian and military sectors. It was decided in 2010 that more space was needed to help improve services. The grand opening took place in 2012 at 350 Pageant Lane. (Courtesy of Elizabeth Black.)

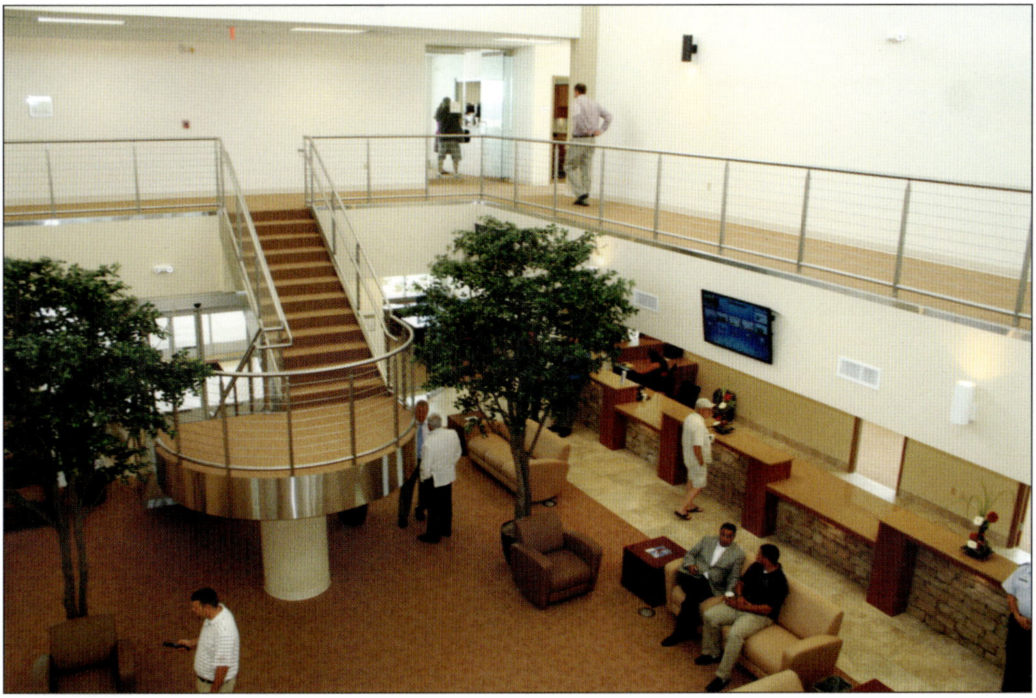

Clarksville Regional Airport, also known as Outlaw Field, has gone through some major changes. Originally opening in 1930 as the Clarksville Airport, it did not receive the name Outlaw Field until 1943. When 1940 rolled around, the facility had a new task added, serving as a military pilot-training and flight school. With the newly renovated and technically updated airport, it is hard to imagine what the original structure looked like. Opening with a new look in 2012, it now offers event spaces and large meeting rooms, including a pilot's lounge. While walking through the building, one notices some amazing original pieces of artwork. The artist is Ray Woddy, and there is a permanent collection of his work available for all to view and enjoy. (Both courtesy of Elizabeth Black.)

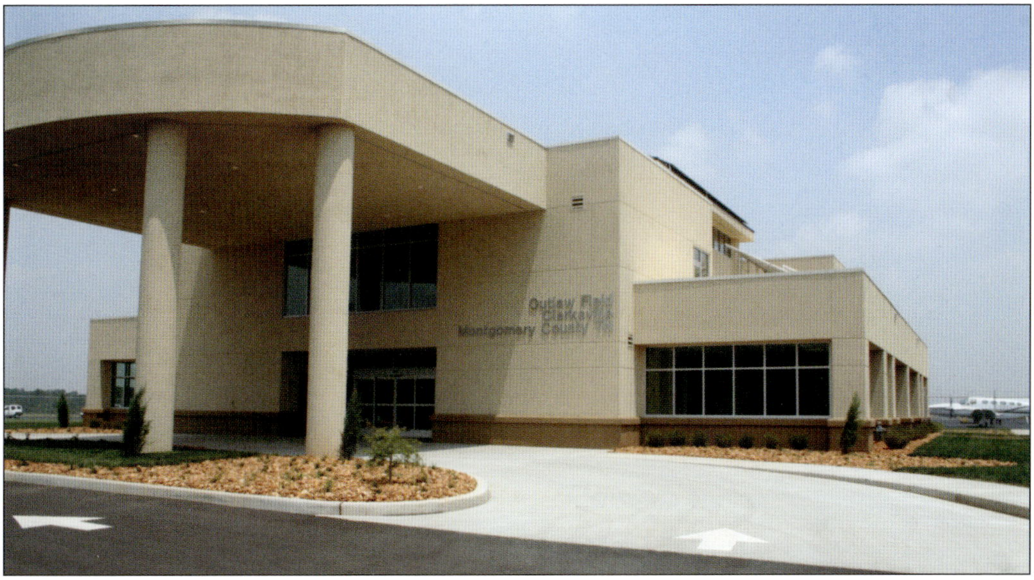

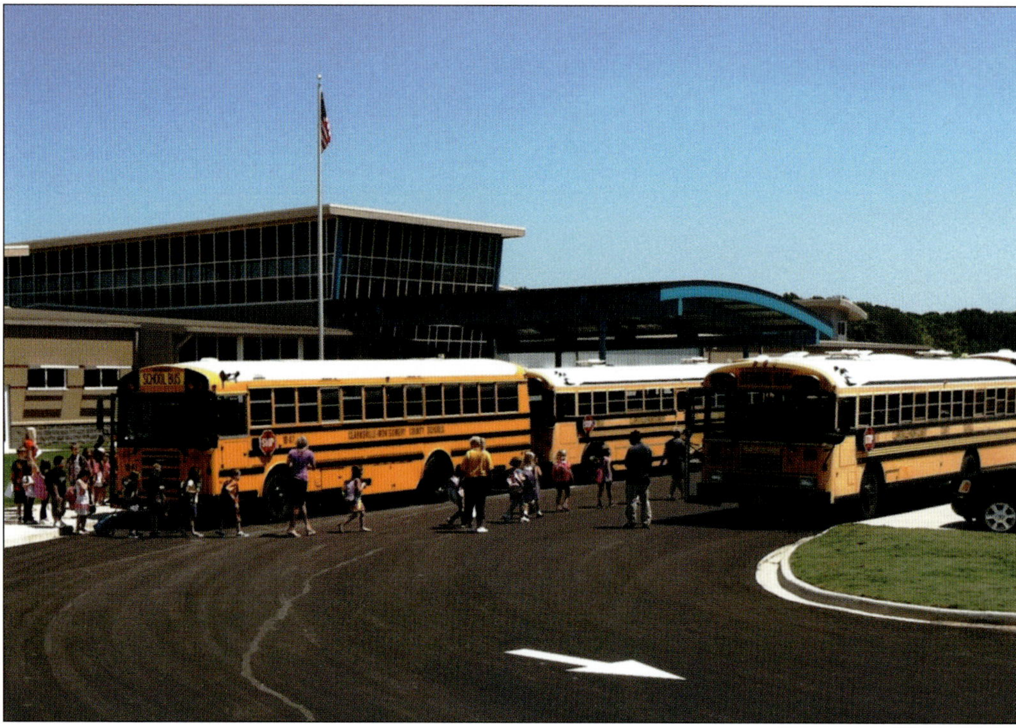

Above, buses have pulled in to pick students up after their first day at the newly built Carmel Elementary School in Clarksville. With the rising population numbers in Clarksville–Montgomery County, the need for new schools is something that is always on the minds of parents. Below is a front view of Carmel Elementary School after it had been open for 23 days. Both images were taken on August 8, 2012. (Both courtesy of Elizabeth Black.)

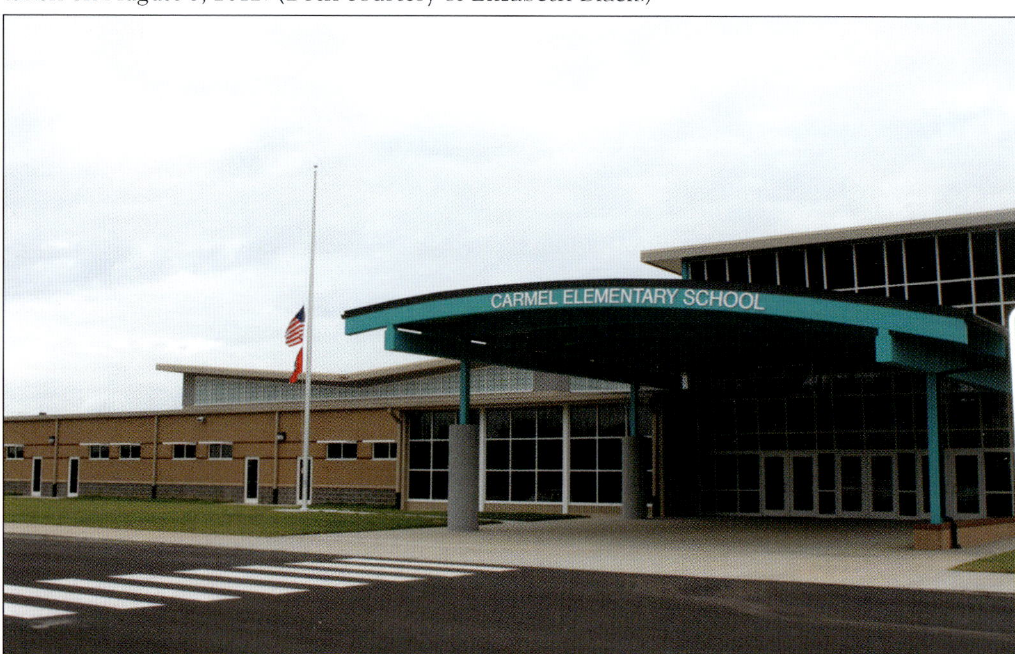

The Poston Building was constructed in 1842 by a wealthy merchant and community leader, John Poston. The side of the building was ideal for advertisements to be seen by all of the river traffic below. Some of the advertisements are still visible today. (Photograph by David Smith.)

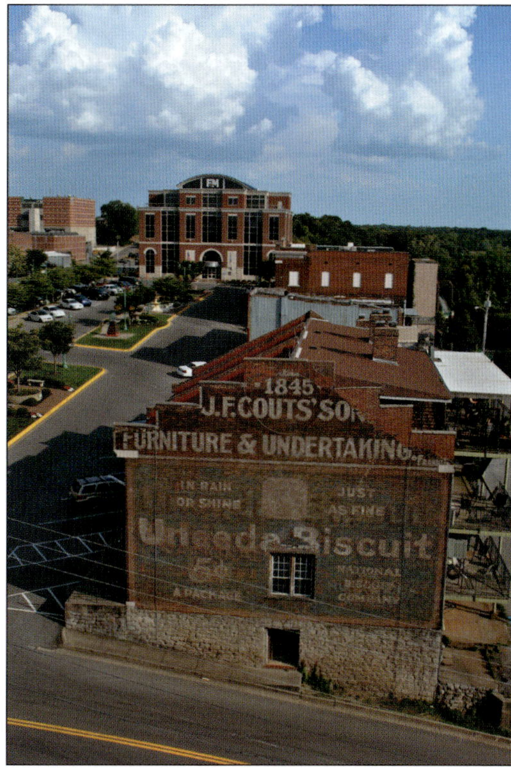

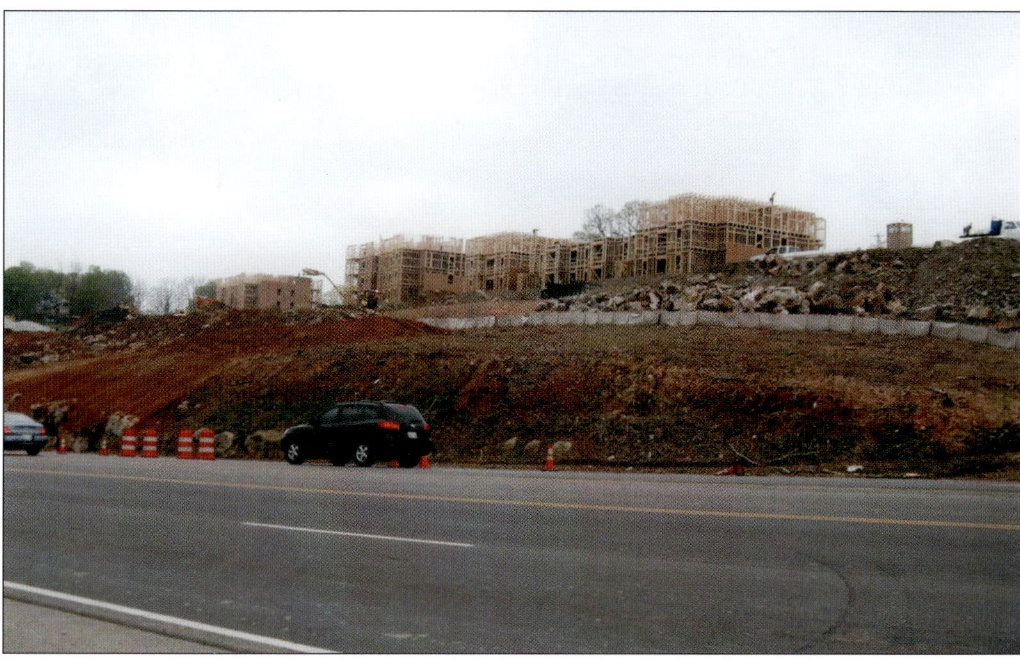

With the community still on the rise, the building of a new apartment complex should be of no surprise to most people. Construction of this housing started in 2011 on the right side of Wilma Rudolph Boulevard while approaching the Red River and heading to downtown Clarksville. (Photograph by Billyfrank Morrison.)

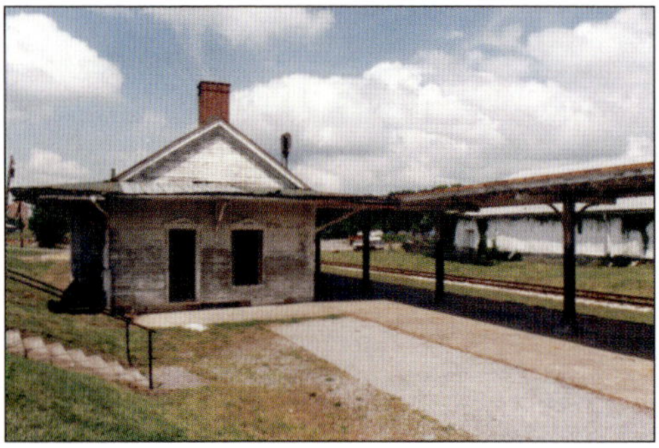

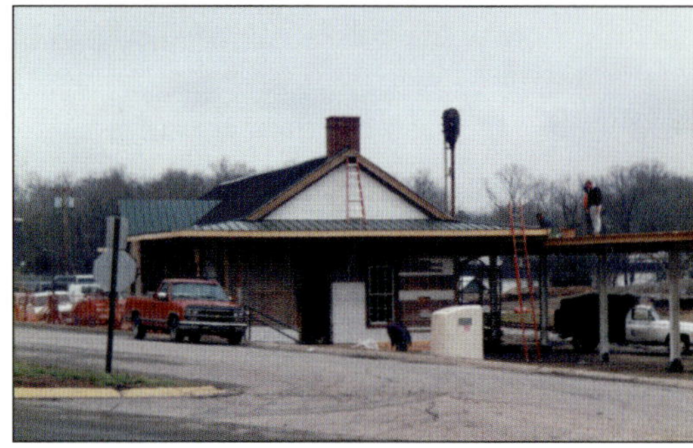

This series of images shows three various stages of the restoration process of the L&N Train Station, which began in 1995 and was completed in 1996. Over time, with use and age, the downtown station on Tenth Street was in desperate need of some TLC. The renovation has created a great location with a historic backdrop to host many events. (Both photographs by Benita Martin, courtesy of MCHS.)

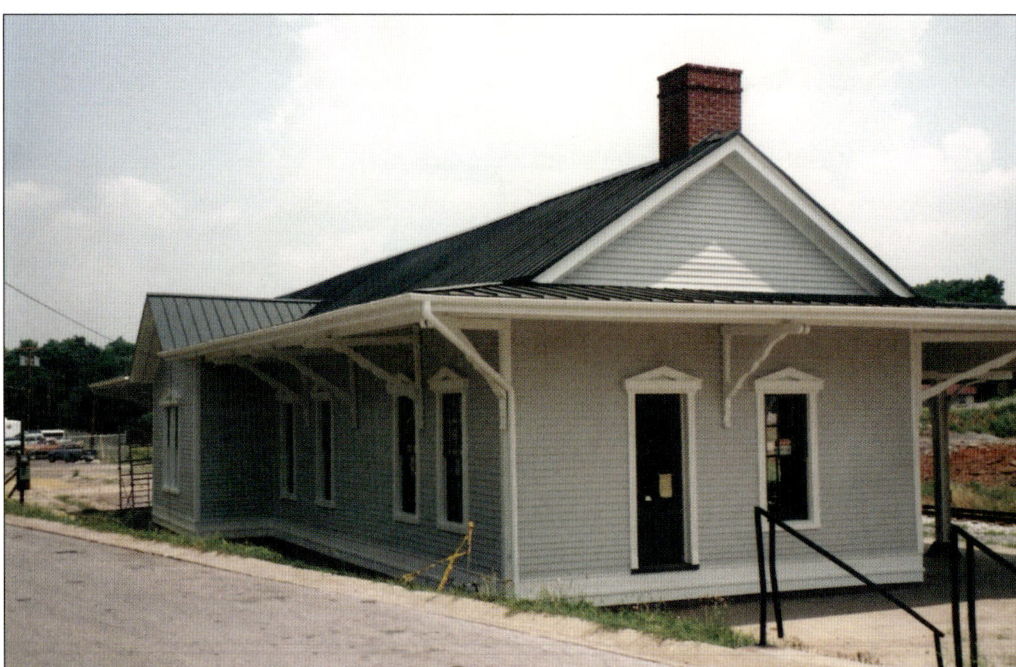

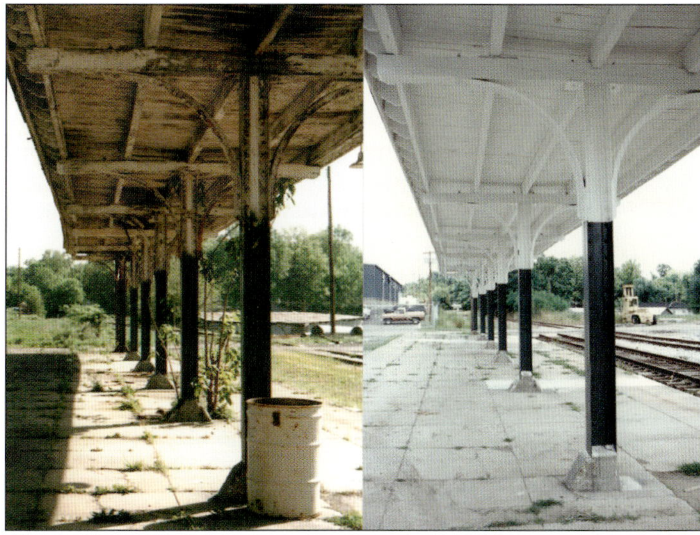

This composite image shows before and after shots of the old structure and the cleaned-up, repaired butterfly awning outside of the L&N Train Station. The restoration made a huge difference, adding a clean, welcoming feel while still maintaining the integrity of the historical structure. This awning during earlier years offered cover from the outdoor elements. (Photograph by Benita Martin, courtesy of MCHS.)

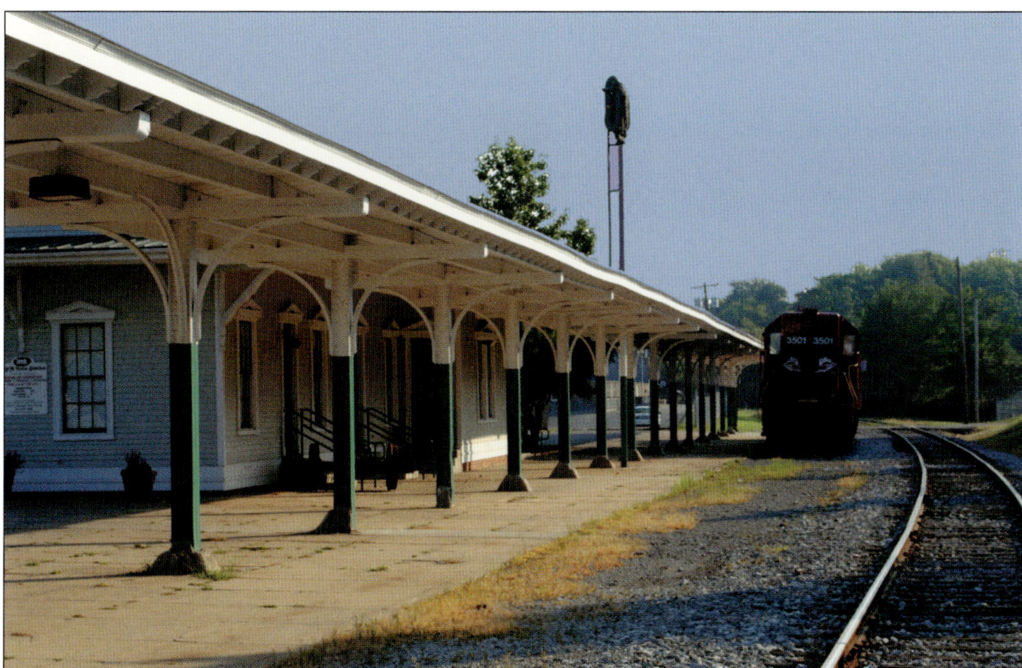

The L&N Train Station once served many travelers coming and going from Clarksville. Even after restoration, it still does not have the same hustle and bustle of yesteryear. But, the station keeps busy with the activities of the Montgomery County Historical Society and those who rent rooms for various celebration and meetings. During a few months throughout the year, a farmers' market is held under the butterfly awning. (Photograph by David Smith.)

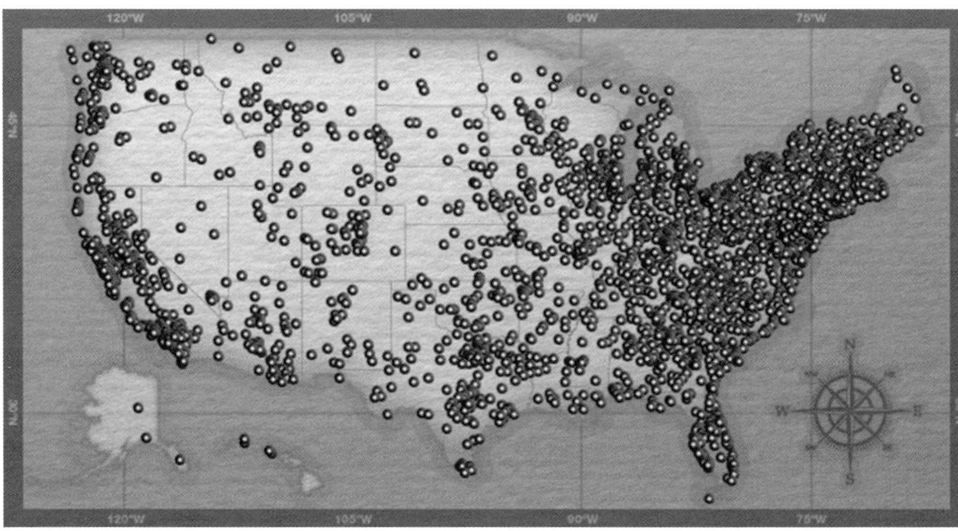